Jean-Jacques Rousseau

Twayne's World Authors Series
French Literature

David O'Connell, Editor

Georgia State University

TWAS 873

JEAN-JACQUES ROUSSEAU
Courtesy of the Bibliothèque Nationale de France, Paris

Jean-Jacques Rousseau

Peter V. Conroy Jr.

University of Illinois, Chicago

Twayne Publishers

New York

Twayne's World Authors Series No. 873

Jean-Jacques Rousseau
Peter V. Conroy Jr.

Twayne Publishers

1633 Broadway
New York, NY 10019

Library of Congress Cataloging-in-Publication Data

Conroy, Peter V.
  Jean-Jacques Rousseau / Peter V. Conroy.
    p.   cm.   —   (Twayne's world authors series ; TWAS 873)
  Includes bibliographical references and index.
  ISBN 0-8057-1616-5 (alk. paper)
  1. Rousseau, Jean-Jacques, 1712 – 1778—Criticism and
interpretation. I. Title. II. Series.
PQ2053.C66 1998
848'.509—dc21   98-23266
                                                                                      CIP

This paper meets the requirements of ANSI/NISO Z3948-1992 (Permanence of Paper).

10 9 8 7 6 5 4 3

Printed in the United States of America

Contents

Preface

To write a book on a writer as diverse and contradictory as Jean-Jacques Rousseau is a daunting task. His controversial ideas are difficult to explain, even though that has not prevented innumerable scholars from attempting to do so over the years. The passionate reactions he continues to inspire make him a contemporary presence that is as provocative as it is palpable.

In this book I have chosen to focus on the organization and structure of the works I discuss, on how they articulate the flow of ideas they put into play. My approach is linear and expository. Although such a method has its shortcomings, my purpose is to map the territory, to indicate where readers should return later to investigate details on their own. I have endeavored to articulate Rousseau's arguments accurately yet sympathetically. Presenting Rousseau's ideas as positively as possible is, I think, an important corrective to critics who are ideologically or temperamentally hostile to him as well as to readings that isolate single details and thus distort them. Because Jean-Jacques is so protean a writer, his ideas can appear contradictory when they are separated from their context. His meanings have a tendency to stabilize, however, once we understand how those parts fit into the whole.

Given the complexity of my topic, I have made a number of difficult choices. Since the body of scholarship on Rousseau is immense and growing at a rapid rate, my bibliography is necessarily very selective. It is limited to the last 20 to 25 years, and even for that period it does not pretend to be complete. Nevertheless, I have tried to strike a balance across the works of Rousseau that I discuss.

I have quoted liberally from Rousseau throughout, hoping to give my readers maximum contact with his words—even if they are translated! All translations are my own. Even as I attempted to find a contemporary American idiom and sought tonally correct words, I have respected the structure of Rousseau's phrasing. Above all I have attempted to render what I see as the immediacy of his style.

My book is intended as a beginning, an inspiration, and a springboard to further reading. I want to encourage my readers to continue along the paths of interpretation sketched out here. Nothing I say is meant to be definitive. The frustrating yet challenging fact is that Rousseau must be read, interpreted, and lived by each reader individually. If I am able to assist in that process, I will count this book a success.

Chronology

28 June 1712	Birth of Jean-Jacques in Geneva
14 March 1728	Leaves Geneva after being locked out of city
21 March 1728	Meets Mme. de Warens in Annecy
1731–1742	Liaison with Mme. de Warens
Summer 1735 or 1736	The idyll at Les Charmettes begins
August 1742	Arrives in Paris; makes a presentation at the Academy of Science on music; meets Diderot and through him makes contact with other philosophes
July 1743 – August 1744	Enters into French diplomatic service in Venice
March 1745	Meets Thérèse Levasseur
October 1749	The "Illumination of Vincennes" experience on the road to visit Diderot in prison
9 July 1750	*Discours sur les Sciences et les arts* wins a major prize and national celebrity
18 October 1752	*Le Devin du village* staged at Fontainebleau
18 December 1752	*Narcisse* premieres in Paris
November 1753	Controversy over *Lettre sur la musique française*
August 1754	Renounces Catholicism and reclaims his status as "citizen of Geneva"
April 1755	*Discours sur l'origine de l'inégalité*
9 April 1756	Moves into a cottage of Mme. d'Epinay's called the Hermitage
18 August 1756	*Lettre sur la Providence,* replies to Voltaire
Spring 1757	Sudden passion for Sophie d'Houdetot
15 December 1757	Leaves the Hermitage, breaks with Mme. d'Epinay. This quarrel, which continues through 1758, includes almost all his old friends, such as Diderot, Grimm, and Sophie.

Chapter One

Biographical Sketch

Jean-Jacques Rousseau was born 28 June 1712 into a middle-class family in Geneva, a city known then for its republican government as well as for its somber and severe Calvinism. Rousseau's mother died in childbirth, and he was raised by his impractical and sentimental father. Isaac Rousseau also had a temper, which led him into several serious disputes and eventually exile. At age 10 Jean-Jacques was sent to live in the countryside at Bossey because his father had to leave the city; in 1724 he moved back to Geneva and boarded with his mother's relatives.

A child deprived of maternal affection, Jean-Jacques had no stable family life, an absence that scholars would later judge critical in his subsequent psychological development. He had few playmates and was regularly beaten by his father, his uncle, and, while an apprentice, his master.[1] All in all Rousseau's childhood seems to have been unhappy, despite his later efforts to idealize that period of his life. What strikes us now is how powerfully Jean-Jacques evokes the happy moments he knew as a child, regardless of their frequency. Years later, for example, he nostalgically recalled spending entire nights reading with his father. Just as day was breaking, Isaac, with tears in his eyes, would send his son to bed.

Jean-Jacques did not receive much formal education; according to the custom of the time, he was apprenticed out to a manual trade. Returning a bit too late from a walk in the countryside one Sunday evening in March 1728, he found the city gates closed and locked. Instead of waiting until morning and certain punishment for not returning on time, Rousseau turned his back on Geneva and set out on foot toward Savoy, which was an independent kingdom and not yet part of France.

A week later he arrived in Annecy and met Mme. de Warens, the woman he would idealize as "Maman" and love for the rest of his life. A recent convert to Catholicism who had left her husband in the Vaud region of Switzerland and who was supported by pensions provided by the Duke of Savoy (who was also the King of Sardinia) and the local bishop, Mme. de Warens was widely known for helping young male refugees from Geneva reject Protestantism and accept Catholicism.

1

Along both sides of this borderline, the struggle to convert those of the other religion was ongoing. Jean-Jacques fell in love with Mme. de Warens on the spot. Departing a few days later, he walked over the Alps to Turin, the capital of Savoy, where he received religious instruction and was formally admitted into the Roman Catholic Church.

When he returned to Annecy about a year later, Jean-Jacques took up residence in Maman's house. Her pietistic religious upbringing emphasized her naturally intense emotions, while lack of practical business sense caused her to live always beyond her financial means. For a period of about 10 years, interrupted by Jean-Jacques's wanderings on foot, brief encounters with other women, sporadic and unpromising employment, they lived together, first in Chambéry and later in a picturesque country house at Les Charmettes. A sensual and attractive woman, Mme. de Warens was young Jean-Jacques's sexual partner from 1733 until 1738. The cloud of incest that is easily recognized in Rousseau's infantile dependency and the revealing names they gave each other, "Maman" and "Petit" (meaning "little" or "child") complicated his conflicting emotions about their sexual relationship. Even when physical consummation ceased, Jean-Jacques continued to love this surrogate mother who played so important a role in his intellectual and emotional maturation.

Largely self-taught, Rousseau completed his education under Maman's eyes. He read extensively, especially the classics. He also developed his musical talents: he learned to read music, play a few instruments, and sing. He progressed enough (despite one lamentable performance he later recounted) to give music lessons. He even aspired to being a composer. According to his *Confessions,* the idyll at Les Charmettes marked the emotional high point of his life, a time when he felt perfectly happy and fulfilled. The reality, however, was a bit different. Mme. de Warens had other lovers, and Jean-Jacques was not always the preferred or the most privileged member of several *ménages à trois.* These triangular love affairs seem to have left a deep, subconscious impression, since that pattern reappeared later in Rousseau's personal life and in his writings.

In the summer of 1742 Jean-Jacques set out on foot for Paris, determined to make a reputation for himself with a new system of musical notation he had invented. In the capital he met other young men equally eager to leave their mark on the world. Denis Diderot, who would become a major figure in eighteenth-century literature, was the most important of Jean-Jacques's new friends. Diderot introduced Jean-Jacques to the whole group of philosophes who were then on the margins of society, awaiting their chance for success and glory. Through

Diderot he became friends with Melchior Grimm, whose mistress Mme. d'Epinay would lodge Jean-Jacques gratis for almost two years (1756–1757) in a cottage called the Hermitage at La Chevrette, her country estate not far from Paris.

Rousseau had a rather incredible knack for finding wealthy patrons and protectors, the most significant of whom were female. Despite his well-known timidity, Jean-Jacques was a handsome, exciting young man who knew how to talk to and charm women. From Savoy he brought letters of introduction that opened several doors for him. Thus he entered the circle of Mme. Dupin, an extremely wealthy woman of bourgeois origin who had a salon at the Hôtel Lambert in Paris and owned the chateau Chenonceaux in the Loire valley. Her stepson Charles Louis Dupin de Francueil shared Rousseau's enthusiasm for music. The visit and compliments he paid to another wealthy woman, Mme. de Broglie, led to a position in the service of the French ambassador to Venice. This job lasted a bit more than a year and, like almost all the others Rousseau held, ended in fiasco.

Such rich and aristocratic friends contrast starkly with Thérèse Levasseur, an uneducated, illiterate servant girl who became Rousseau's companion without benefit of clergy shortly after they met in 1745. The disparity between Rousseau's wife and his friends is more than just another of his eccentricities. This common-law marriage bears evidence of Rousseau's marginality, his status as an outsider, his penchant for contradictions, and even the masochism that often inspired him to thwart his own best interests. Most of Rousseau's friends detested Thérèse, considering her a hag, a gossip, a liar, and a troublemaker. It is indisputable that she deceived Jean-Jacques, on occasion sexually, most frequently financially. Her defenders point out, on the other hand, that she protected him and nursed him through his many illnesses. Unthreatening to Rousseau's fragile sense of self-worth, she managed to live with this most cantankerous individual for 33 years, a feat no one else came close to matching. Whatever our verdict, they were a mismatched pair: Thérèse could never provide intellectual companionship for Jean-Jacques and probably never read a word he wrote. It was not until August 1768, after returning from exile in England, that Jean-Jacques finally married her in a civil ceremony.

Almost all of Rousseau's friendships eventually turned sour. Incredibly sensitive to any behavior that might hide the slightest offense, Jean-Jacques was forever seeing insult where others with thicker skin or more experience did not. For that brief time in the 1740s, however, Jean-

Jacques's possibilities looked bright. He had not yet developed the extreme paranoia that after 1762 would blacken his moods, nor had he demonstrated the insensitive and offensive behavior that would eventually alienate all his friends.

Jean-Jacques began his career as a writer by collaborating on Diderot and d'Alembert's *Encyclopedia*. Although he did write an important article, "Political Economy" (published in August 1755), which explored a topic he would return to later in *Du contrat social* (*The Social Contract*), he usually wrote articles on music. When he first arrived in Paris, he read a paper on a new system of musical notation he had invented to the Academy of Sciences, but that particular project went nowhere.

During these early years in Paris, Jean-Jacques had several promising literary successes even as he kept busy developing friendships and making contacts with potential patrons and other supporters in aristocratic circles. King Louis XV attended the debut of his opera *Le Devin du village* (*The Village Soothsayer*), for which he wrote both the words and music, at Fontainebleau on 18 October 1752; the production moved shortly thereafter to the Paris Opera. The ultrasophisticated Parisian and court audiences found its simplicity and naivete refreshing. His play *Narcisse* (*Narcissus*) opened in Paris two months later. Theater (including opera) being the most prestigious genre of this period, both socially and artistically, these productions brought Rousseau a good deal of attention and left him poised on the brink of worldly success.

Jean-Jacques followed another, diametrically opposed path, however. In October 1749, while on the road to visit Diderot, who was imprisoned in the Vincennes chateau, Rousseau read about an essay competition sponsored by the Academy of Dijon. The topic was whether the arts and sciences had contributed to purifying mores. Later he recounted how he was overcome by an "illumination" that gave him a spectacular and paradoxical answer to the question, an answer that would change his life dramatically. The answer was no. His polemical essay *Le Discours sur les sciences et les arts* (*The Discourse on Arts and Sciences*) won the competition and established Jean-Jacques as the enemy of civilization and the apologist of rude primitivism in opposition to the sophistication of Parisian society.

Rousseau's subsequent writings suggest that this first *Discourse* was not just a clever paradox but rather his sincere belief. He entered another competition a few years later. This *Discours sur l'origine de l'iné-galité* (*Discourse on Inequality*) was even more controversial, more brilliant, and more persuasive than the first essay. Though it did not win, the second *Discourse* firmly established Rousseau as a thinker to be reckoned with. It also began to separate him from his philosophe friends who were committed to progress, reason, and the perfectibility of man and who were adamant partisans of modern, enlightened society.

Rousseau repeated the positions marked out in the two *Discourses* in other writings. The *Lettre sur la musique française* (*Letter on French Music*) created quite a controversy late in 1753, even though on this issue Jean-Jacques agreed with his philosophe friends. Here Rousseau made an impassioned case for emotional and melodic Italian music while condemning the more cerebral and contrapuntal French style. The *Letter* was poorly received in traditional musical circles: Rousseau's pass for free admission to the opera was revoked.

A few historical details explain the real importance behind this seemingly insignificant event. In 1752 a troupe of Italian singers had arrived in Paris and stirred up an unbelievable ruckus with their productions of Italian operas and especially of Pergolesi's comic masterpiece *La Serva padrona* (*The Servant Mistress*). Their freewheeling style and unpretentious subject matter contrasted sharply with the reigning Parisian taste, which was formed by classical notions of the unities, *bienséance* (appropriateness), and decorum. The widely divergent reactions to the Italian *buffoni* (buffoons), which came to be called the "War of the *Bouffons,*" divided Paris into two hostile camps. The queen's side favored the Italians, whereas the more patriotic but chauvinistic king's "corner" championed such French composers as Philippe Rameau. A bit like the controversies surrounding rock and roll or rap in our own time, disagreements about music in the eighteenth century combined artistic questions with major philosophical and social issues.

Never reticent to voice an unpopular opinion or hesitant to appear in the public spotlight despite his nearly incapacitating timidity, Jean-Jacques was becoming more and more immersed in public controversy. In the summer of 1754 he returned to Geneva, a city he constantly idealized and evoked as exemplary. Having left it as a youth, Jean-Jacques had little firsthand knowledge of its political and religious reality; perhaps he simply chose to ignore its serious shortcomings. In the city of his birth he reconverted to Calvinism. This second change of religion opened him to charges that he was an opportunist who, lacking any real beliefs, embraced whichever faith was most expedient. Once again a Protestant, he could now use without fear of contradiction the title "Citizen of Geneva," which he had already begun to affix proudly to his name.

In 1756 Jean-Jacques locked horns with Voltaire in his *Lettre sur la Providence* (*The Letter on Providence*). Upset by a recent earthquake, Voltaire asked in his pessimistic *Poem on the Lisbon Disaster* why God permitted evil to happen. Rousseau rose to defend religion, a personal God, and man's need for faith and confidence in him. The *Letter* indicates that Rousseau's recent return to the faith of his youth did indeed spring from a real religious feeling. It was not the kind of reaction Voltaire appreciated, however. He never answered Rousseau's letter, and Jean-Jacques believed that Voltaire's *Candide* (1759) was a delayed response. In the course of their lives Rousseau and Voltaire exchanged a number of letters but never actually met. Although their early correspondence bears signs of mutual esteem, they eventually came to despise each other. The attitudes that these two great figures represent often serve to define two polar extremes in eighteenth-century thinking.

In April 1756 Jean-Jacques accepted an invitation to live on the country estate of Mme. d'Epinay in the forest of Montmorency, about 20 kilometers north of Paris. Mme. d'Epinay, who became the mistress of Rousseau's friend Grimm at this same time, was another of the rich and socially prominent female benefactors who were attracted to Jean-Jacques and who protected him. The cottage where he lived, called the Hermitage, was far enough from Paris to be rustic and solitary but still close enough for day trips. It seemed an ideal situation. A year and a half later Jean-Jacques left, embittered and quarreling with his protectress and her circle of friends. He accused them of trying to dominate him and dictate his actions even as he refused to see the part his own tactless and insensitive behavior played in their accusations and recriminations. His indiscreet passion for Sophie d'Houdetot, the mistress of his friend Saint-Lambert, also contributed to this crisis. In the ninth book of his *Confessions* Jean-Jacques described in minute detail this tremendous emotional upheaval that separated him from his closest friends. At the Hermitage were sown the seeds of distrust and deceit that would blossom in the bitter fruit of conspiracy. Six years later Jean-Jacques was convinced that this was the moment when the "plot" against him began.

Toward the end of 1758 Jean-Jacques finished alienating his philosophe friends with his *Lettre à d'Alembert sur les spectacles* (*Letter to d'Alembert on the Theater*) for both personal and ideological reasons. A footnote contained a personal attack against Diderot, thus climaxing the quarrel that had begun in March of the previous year. Ideologically, Jean-Jacques was less and less the rationalist contributor to the *Encyclopedia* and more and more the emotive critic of the *Discourses,* denouncing society, progress, and modernism. In an *Encyclopedia* article on Geneva d'Alembert had insinuated that the Protestant ministers there were not strictly orthodox in their religious beliefs and that the city should have a theater. Jean-Jacques rose to the defense of his birthplace. His *Letter* continued the attack against modern society he had launched in the two *Discourses.* Rousseau claimed that sophistication, most easily evidenced in the theater, inevitably led to moral corruption. Geneva, according to Jean-Jacques, had to ban the theater or risk becoming as corrupt and as sinful as Paris.

The end of Rousseau's friendship with Diderot, publicly announced in his rebuttal of d'Alembert, came at a particularly bad time. During 1758 and 1759 the philosophes were on the defensive, reeling from attacks by reactionaries in the church and in the government: the *Encyclopedia* was condemned by the Paris Parlement in January 1759, Diderot was in danger of being incarcerated again as its editor, and two of his recent publications were publicly burned. By breaking with his friends when they were so vulnerable, Jean-Jacques seemed to take a political stand against them even though his motivations were entirely personal. As he parted intellectual company with the philosophes, they felt betrayed and therefore labeled him a traitor. These public and private factors complicated an already muddy exchange of accusations and only exacerbated the hard feelings on both sides. We have to keep this turbulence in mind if we are to understand the virulent emotions, fears, and suspicions that racked Rousseau for the rest of his life and colored his subsequent recollections about all his former friends.

The early years of the next decade were extremely productive. In a short two-year span Jean-Jacques completed three major texts. Although they are all very different, critics have seen them as closely related: each seems to ponder the same issues from another perspective. Predictably, these works were even more incendiary than previous ones, both literally and figuratively.

In 1761 Jean-Jacques published his only novel, *Julie ou la Nouvelle Héloise* (*Julie or the New Heloise*). Here he celebrated passionate love in terms that moved his readers in a new way. The novel, an unbelievably successful best-seller, transformed the public mind-set from one shaped by the force of reason into one dominated by feeling. Autobiographical and intensely emotional, *Julie* bears the traces of Rousseau's unsatisfactory and ultimately frustrating relationships with women. He finished writing it in the exalted state produced by his infatuation with Sophie d'Houdetot, Mme. d'Epinay's sister-in-law. Their brief love affair, probably never consummated, lasted only for the final six months of his stay at the Hermitage. Its intensity, however, can still be felt in Rousseau's moving prose. *Julie* marks the beginnings of the tremendous emotional outburst that would swell into the romanticism of the following century.

Two other major texts were published the following year. In *Du contrat social* (*The Social Contract*) Rousseau offered a very abstract discussion of government and its relationship to its citizens. Rousseau was a radical democrat (with a small *d:* he believed that sovereignty belonged solely to the individual citizen and that it should not be diluted through representation, for example) in an age that accepted absolute monarchy, the divine right of kings, and aristocratic privilege as the norm. His purpose was to explain how any government acquired legitimacy and how a republic might actually function. The *Contract* not only ran counter to the current political ideology but also presented a number of ambiguities for later readers, many of whom continue to read it as a blueprint for totalitarianism.

Rousseau's other scandalous publication of 1762 was *Emile,* ostensibly a treatise on the education of children but a work that also contained elements of a novel and an essay on religion. Many of Rousseau's pedagogical insights were ahead of their time, predating such reformers as Montessori. What most shocked his contemporaries, however, was a long chapter called "La Profession de foi du Vicaire savoyard" (The Profession of Faith of the Savoyard Priest), in which Rousseau praised natural religion, free of any liturgy or institutional affiliation to a recognized church. The reaction of both Catholics and Protestants was swift and extreme despite the fact that Rousseau's friend and the government's director of publications, Malesherbes, had helped to publish it.

Let us not forget that the reactions to *Emile* were part of the backlash then buffeting liberal and enlightened thought. Dominated by reactionary Jansenists and their sympathizers, the Paris Parlement finally won its long struggle with the Jesuits, the liberal wing of the Catholic Church, when it succeeded in having the Society of Jesus disbanded and its members expelled from France. At the same time, the Parlement in Toulouse was persecuting Protestants in the southwest, as evidenced in the trial and execution of Jean Calas.

Despite the help of Malesherbes and such other highly placed friends as the Luxembourgs and the Prince de Conti, *Emile* was declared both religiously and politically subversive. On 7 June the book was condemned by the Sorbonne, the official authority of the Catholic Church in France. It was burned in front of the Palais de Justice in Paris by order of Parlement four days later. On 19 June it was banned and burned in Geneva. The Archbishop of Paris, Christophe de Beaumont, wrote a public letter denouncing it. An arrest order was issued for Jean-Jacques on 9 June. That very afternoon he left the comfortable existence he had been enjoying at Montlouis as the neighbor of the Duc and the Duchesse de Luxembourg and fled toward Switzerland. Once again on the road, as he had been in his youth, Rousseau the exile was denounced by a suspicious government and a hostile church. Both considered him a dangerous foe.

Now real persecution began, which only augmented Rousseau's morbidly sensitive nature and fueled his growing paranoia. His chronic illness (a deformity of the urinary tract and its embarrassing social and sexual complications) had flared up in June 1761 and continued through the rest of that year.[2] Sometime in the following spring he began to wear an Armenian caftan. This distinctive garb was unconventional but practical. Blurring the sharp distinction between male and female as well as the class indications garments usually had at this time, his exotic dress allowed him to hide the catheter he wore for his urinary problem. During this same period he was terrified that the manuscript of *Emile* might be stolen from his publisher. Feeling extreme physical and mental stress, he increasingly saw himself as the victim of an extensive plot, as besieged by former friends turned enemies. This was a reprise of the anxiety he experienced during 1757 and 1758, when he broke with Diderot, Grimm, and Mme. d'Epinay.

This road of exile eventually led Jean-Jacques, in July 1762, to Môtiers, a small town in the province of Neuchâtel, present-day Switzerland. Môtiers was then Prussian territory under the governorship of Lord George Keith, a tolerant Scotsman also in exile, who granted Rousseau asylum. The following month Jean-Jacques asked a local pastor to allow him to take communion. This apparent "conversion" startled his enemies, who considered it outright hypocrisy from the man who had just denounced organized religion. In March 1763, Rousseau's *Lettre à Christophe de Beaumont* (*Letter to Christophe de Beaumont,* dated November 1762) delivered a crushing rebuttal to the archbishop who had condemned *Emile* in August. Angered by hostile reactions in Geneva to both this *Letter* and *Emile,* Jean-Jacques renounced his cherished citizenship in May. This gesture produced another uproar. The Rousseau who had always been so proud of his status as a Geneva citizen and who had always idealized the city in his writings now seemed to repudiate those views. In October the attorney general of Geneva, Jean-Robert Tronchin, published another attack, entitled *Lettres écrites de la campagne* (*Letters Written from the Countryside*). Rousseau replied late in 1764 with his *Lettres écrites de la montagne* (*Letters Written from the Mountain*), which included sharp criticisms about the absence of political freedom in Geneva. Like *Emile* it was burned promptly, in Holland and in Paris. Seeing himself denounced on all sides, Jean-Jacques began to contemplate writing a vindication and defense of himself that would become the *Confessions*.

Although he was enmeshed in controversy and provoked powerful, often negative reactions from his readers, Jean-Jacques was also a celebrity whom many people wanted to see. Hounded by numerous friends, admirers, and curiosity seekers, including the famous Scotsman James Boswell, Jean-Jacques was unable to find any peace or quiet. To the political and religious issues swirling about him was added a vicious personal attack. An unsigned pamphlet published in December 1764 revealed a secret that only a few of Rousseau's closest friends knew: he had given up for adoption all five children that Thérèse bore him. This information provoked a scandal, since in *Emile* Rousseau had set himself up as the ideal teacher of children. Voltaire was the author of this venomous denunciation. What is particularly disheartening in this generally sordid incident is that Voltaire (once again! and unlike Rousseau) did not have the courage to sign his own work. Voltaire accused Jean-Jacques anonymously to the fanatics that he himself detested.

As if this were not enough, the controversy about Rousseau's repudiation of organized religion in *Emile* continued unabated. He was required to convince the religious leaders in Neuchâtel that he was indeed a Christian. Popular resentment, which was kept simmering by certain ministers who continued preaching against him, reached its boiling point in the fall. A crowd attacked his house at Môtiers on the night of 6 September 1765 and threw rocks through the windows. The next morning Rousseau fled the city.

Not far from Môtiers is the Ile Saint-Pierre, a minuscule island in the Lac de Bienne. There, in July, Rousseau had enjoyed a brief but happy stay. Immediately upon leaving Môtiers, he returned for six weeks of calm before his definitive exile. He recorded this bit of peaceful repose beautifully in the fifth "Promenade" of his *Rêveries*. Rousseau then took to wandering, looking desperately for a safe refuge, entertaining the prospect of going to Berlin, where Lord Keith was then residing and where, he hoped, Frederick the Great would receive him favorably.

Rousseau went to England, however, on the invitation of the Scotch philosopher David Hume, who accompanied him on the trip from Paris to London in January 1766. Jean-Jacques was inordinately sensitive and close to neurotic under even the best conditions. Now, as he saw his world collapsing about him, the attacks on *Emile* and the stress they produced took their toll. Enervated by exile and travel, living in England and not understanding a single word of English, Rousseau was soon convinced that "le bon David" had become an enemy too. His unbalanced imagination transmuted a series of minor and bizarre incidents into irrefutable proof that Hume was part of the sinister plot against him. Six months after arriving in London, he wrote a hysterical letter denouncing Hume. Jean-Jacques believed that everyone was persecuting him even as his own offensive behavior provoked those who wanted to help him.[3] Somehow, even in the throes of such emotional upheaval, he found the time and the energy to continue writing his *Confessions.*

He left England in May 1767. In June he went to Trye-le-Chateau, one of the Prince de Conti's residences, where he spent a year. He then left for the area around Lyons and Grenoble near the Savoy border, which was outside the jurisdiction of the Paris Parlement and where he remained for two years. In July 1768 he made a pilgrimage to Chambéry and the grave of Mme. de Warens. In August he finally married Thérèse in a civil ceremony in the small town of Bourgoin. Throughout this period he remained emotionally and psychologically distraught, convinced he was the victim of an ever-expanding conspiracy. The extent of Rousseau's alienation can be judged by his conviction that the plot was being masterminded by the Duc de Choiseul, the prime minister. Declaring his innocence to all and sundry, he dreamed of returning to Paris and proving his innocence to the Parlement that had condemned him in 1762.

By June 1770 Jean-Jacques was back in Paris. Although the warrant for his arrest was still in effect, it was not enforced. Rousseau lived modestly and quietly but was not in hiding. The police did not bother him even as curious visitors flocked to his door. He was earning his living once again by copying music, a manual trade he had practiced at Montmorency. His *Confessions* were now completed. Not thinking his enemies would allow him to publish them, he gave public readings to aristocratic circles starting in December. Their impact was electric. Both friends and enemies trembled. The former feared that their behind-the-scenes and sometimes illegal protection of Rousseau might be revealed and compromise them, while the latter dreaded his eloquent depiction of their quarrels with him. Mme. d'Epinay, former friend and protector, used her influence with the police to have these readings banned the following May.

Again thwarted in his efforts to reveal his true nature and to correct the fabrications being circulated by his enemies, he began composing *Rousseau Juge de Jean-Jacques, Dialogues,* in 1772. Ronald Grimsley states that in this work Jean-Jacques "returns with obsessive persistence to the notion of the universal plot" directed against him by just about everyone and that "the work for the most part reads like a paranoid nightmare."[4] In one of the more bizarre incidents of his unusual existence, Jean-Jacques took the manuscript of the *Dialogues* to Notre-Dame Cathedral on 24 February 1776, intending to place it on the main altar. He was once again convinced his enemies were trying to steal his manuscript and to alter it. The gates to the sanctuary were locked, however, so Rousseau could not approach the altar. He left the church overwhelmed with fear and despair, thinking that once again his enemies had prevailed and that God too was against him.[5]

This incident was the low point in Rousseau's emotional crisis, the paroxysm of his paranoia. Having touched bottom, he could now slowly rise. In the autumn he started writing the *Rêveries d'un promeneur solitaire* (*The Reveries of a Solitary Walker*). A series of 10 "promenades," this confessional and autobiographical work, more balanced psychologically than the *Dialogues,* shows Jean-Jacques recovering from his emotional turmoil. He still considered himself a victim, but the plot weighed less heavily on him, and his despair was less pervasive. Indeed, in these last two years Jean-Jacques finally achieved some peace of mind and at last succeeded in becoming indifferent to the animosity surrounding him. These reveries evoke some truly happy memories (e.g., drifting in a boat on the Lac de Bienne in the fifth promenade) and even re-create those lost moments with undeniable expressive power.

Rousseau never finished his *Rêveries.* The *Confessions* were not published during his lifetime. In the spring of 1778 the Marquis de Girardin, a longtime admirer, invited Jean-Jacques to live at his estate in Ermenonville, a short distance north of Paris. There, after a brief walk on the morning of 2 July, Jean-Jacques died. He was buried on the Isle of Poplars in the middle of a small pond on the estate. Almost immediately, his tomb became a site of pilgrimage for those admirers who had been profoundly touched by his writings. Within a few years, the same Jean-Jacques who had been so reviled during his life was acclaimed as a model and an inspiration by a new generation. His political ideas were admired by many of the leaders of the French Revolution, and his exaltation of emotion and of the individual inspired an entire generation of romantics. The controversy that always surrounded him continues unabated right down to the present.

Chapter Two
The *Discourses*

Shortly after he arrived in Paris in 1742, Rousseau made friends with a group of liberal thinkers known today as the philosophes. Stimulated in part by their radical views on government and society, Rousseau wrote two texts that catapulted him into the public eye and set his ideological agenda for years to come. His famous *Discourses* articulated a radical, antiprogressive polemic whose impact on political thinking is not limited to the eighteenth century.

The Discourse on the Arts and Sciences (1750)

The *Discours sur les sciences et les arts* (*Discourse on the Arts and Sciences*) marks the turning point in Rousseau's life. For its annual essay competition in 1749, the Academy of Dijon asked "whether the re-establishment of arts and sciences contributed to the refining of mores." On a hot summer day as he was walking out to visit his friend Diderot, who was incarcerated in the prison of Vincennes, on the eastern outskirts of Paris, Rousseau read that question and immediately experienced an "illumination" which he later described in his second *Letter to Malesherbes*. Rousseau's answer, which revealed how poorly adapted man was to life in society, won the prize. That essay, thanks especially to its rhetorically brilliant negative response, launched him as a thinker and writer, but it also determined the ideology that he would elaborate for the rest of his life. Henceforth Rousseau would argue against society and in favor of freedom from its constraints and obligations.

Although less radical than the second, the first *Discourse* shocked many eighteenth-century intellectuals. The whiff of sulfur and paradox that caught the judges' attention was soon understood as a serious indictment of the very society that could complacently reward such a diatribe against itself. Jean-Jacques dared to criticize seriously what most of his contemporaries understood to be the climax of historical progress and human culture. In subsequent defenses of his position, Rousseau claimed to have censured not the arts and sciences themselves but only their abuses. His apologies were as aggressive as his attack, however:

"[S]cience, whose origin is so pure and whose end is so praiseworthy, engenders so many impieties, heresies, errors, absurd systems, contradictions, incompetencies; so many bitter satires, miserable novels, licentious verses, obscene books; it engenders in those who cultivate science so much pride, avarice, meanness, cabaling, jealousy, lies, ugliness, calumny, shameful and cowardly flattery."[1] Despite Jean-Jacques's attempts to deflect its pointed attack, the danger the *Discourse* represented to social values cannot be doubted. Although he himself practiced the very arts and sciences he so vehemently criticized, Jean-Jacques seriously argued that they should nonetheless be regarded as corrupting and immoral.

Rousseau begins his *Discourse* by evoking the Renaissance and its reestablishment of enlightened thinking. The worm is already in the fruit, however: "[T]he Sciences, Letters, and the Arts, less despotic yet perhaps more powerful, stretch garlands of flowers over the iron chains they carry, stifle in [men] the sentiment of that original liberty for which they were born, make them love their slavery, and make them what are called civilized peoples" (7). Taking this premise as his basis, Rousseau offers a number of historical examples that show how the arts (he groups all the arts and sciences into one category and refers to them by either term) have led to weakness and corruption. Virtue is manly and military, the arts are soft and effeminate. Egypt, Greece, Rome, and Constantinople allowed the arts to develop and then they collapsed. Persians, Scythians, Germans, and especially Spartans retained their warlike character and therefore remained unpolished and triumphant. Rousseau conveniently ignores that the latter eventually fell too, just as the former enjoyed long periods as victors.

After the list of nations and empires, Jean-Jacques turns to individuals. Plato, in the voice of Socrates, condemns artists and poets. Cato, the great Roman censor, does the same. Climaxing the first part of the discourse is the prosopopoeia of Fabricius.[2] This rhetorical set piece puts modern words into the mouth of a famous figure from the past; it allows Rousseau to resurrect an example of virile Roman virtue who condemns the corrupt and sophisticated lifestyle that was so opposed to the frugal existence associated with the Roman republic. Such a simple life is of course Rousseau's ideal too.

What has become of those thatched roofs and those rustic hearths where moderation and virtue used to dwell? What deadly splendor has replaced Roman simplicity? . . . What effeminate mores are these? What do these statues, paintings, and buildings signify? Senseless men, what have you done? You, the masters of nations, have made yourselves the slaves of those frivolous peoples you have conquered. Do sophists and rhetoricians govern you? Is it to enrich architects, painters, sculptors, and actors that you have shed your blood in Greece and Asia? (14)

In the name of Roman virtue hardened by war and discipline, Fabricius and Rousseau condemn *la dolce vita,* which characterizes sophisticated societies that live more by their brain than by their brawn. Here Rousseau is picking up on a century-long debate about the interconnection of vigorous citizens and a healthy state. His rustic ideal, which foreshadows the Jeffersonian republic of yeoman farmers, for example, contrasts with the overly sophisticated and therefore decadent society that he condemns. The first part of the essay concludes majestically, as if this problematic argument from historical examples had been proven beyond the shadow of a doubt: "That is how luxury, dissolution, and slavery have forever been the punishment of those proud efforts we have made to quit the happy ignorance where eternal wisdom had placed us" (15).

The essay's second part amplifies the deviation that Rousseau's argument has taken. He is talking less about the arts and sciences as disciplines or mental activities than about the climate of laxness they produce. It is this climate that he perceives as soft and decadent. In a sense Rousseau is attacking the culture, or the lifestyle, or the social attitudes that attend the arts and sciences. His confusion is not unlike that in many current discussions of these same issues.

The arts and sciences originated in "our vices" (17): astronomy in superstition, rhetoric in "ambition, hatred, flattery, and lying" (17). While the sciences seek truth, they actually multiply errors because they reveal our past mistakes even as they provide new interpretations that may one day prove fallacious (18). More than simply useless, wasting time and effort, the sciences are dangerous, "undermining the foundations of faith and destroying virtue" (19).

Arts and sciences engender luxe; the term is difficult to translate because it connotes a combination of luxury, luxuriance, and concupiscence. This semantic network leads quite easily to the notion of moral degeneration that underlies Rousseau's entire attack on the arts. By also signifying the fine living denoted by our own term *deluxe, luxe* contrasts sharply with Rousseau's preference for simplicity over sophistication, for frankness over cleverness, for what is rustic over what is polished. The same duality divides money-grubbers from those with ideals, degenerate urbanites from honest country folk. Invoking this economic morality, Jean-Jacques condemns eighteenth-century leaders in terms that could be applied to other times: "Ancient politicians spoke ceaselessly of conduct and virtue; ours only speak of business and money" (19). As luxury increases (the arts depend on excess wealth and thus are assimilated to luxury), virtue decreases: "[S]tudying the sciences is more suited to softening and feminizing our mettle rather than hardening and animating it" (22). The examples of military success Rousseau cites depended not on wealth but rather on the power of frugality and virtuous poverty. Education is similarly corrupted. Youth learns everything except its civic duty (24). Consequently, society appreciates what is frivolous and not real talent. "Rewards are lavished on wit while virtue remains unhonored. There are a thousand prizes for fine writing, but none for fine actions" (25).

All these arguments point to the paradoxical nature of Rousseau's entire discourse. But paradox is a dangerous weapon that cuts both ways and can turn against the hand that wields it. All the examples I have cited contain a hint of condemnation that might be directed at organizations like the Dijon Academy, which sponsored the competition that inspired Rousseau's essay. Rousseau is clever enough to mix his attack on the arts and sciences with a few paragraphs of praise for "famous societies" that support them. Whether these references to the cultural establishment are ironic or not,[3] Rousseau succeeds in making his point about how artistry drives out virtue: "That's what in the long run must give the advantage to agreeable talents over useful ones" (26).

The conclusion of the *First Discourse* begins with a strange point for Jean-Jacques, who was surely the most democratic and egalitarian of all the eighteenth-century thinkers. He wants to limit the arts and sciences to the few who will excel. He prefers good artisans to mediocre scholars: "He who will be all his life a bad rhymer or an inferior mathematician might become a fine weaver" (29). In his defense, however, I would say that Rousseau, the quintessential outsider, is arguing against elitism in favor of the common man, against overly specialized disciplines in favor of practical employment. Only a few should study art and science, and they should be geniuses and original thinkers. "For us common men to whom Heaven has not given such great talents and whom it did not design for such glory, we should remain in obscurity" (30). The real study of most men should be civic virtue and good citizenship: "O virtue! Sublime science of simple hearts, does it really require so much difficulty and artifice to know you?" (32). While men of letters become famous and immortal, common men are also called to a "glorious distinction": the former are able to speak well, but the latter know how to behave well.

With this rhetorical climax Rousseau balances a deprecation of sophisticated arts with an appreciation of the more robust but less refined virtues of the common man. In his own polished artistic production (this essay being part of the evil it condemns, which constitutes yet another paradox), Jean-Jacques adumbrates that part of the romantic credo which contrasts good and rich, country and city, nature and artifice. He articulates such oppositions as the effeminate artist vs. the robust worker, the corrupt city vs. the healthy countryside, the antiknowledge of education vs. the true wisdom of experience. Despite the evident contradictions behind Rousseau's arguments and despite our modern faith in the positive aspects of science, this essay does offer a powerful critique of society that is as current today as it was in Rousseau's time. The disappointment we feel that science has not solved all our physical problems, the discomfort we experience in the face of challenging works of art, not to mention our nostalgia for what we think was a more perfect past in contrast to this disquieting present, all combine to make Rousseau's brief against society effective and convincing. Rousseau's uncanny ability to put his finger on the problems that still concern us today makes this one of the major texts in the movement of ideas in the eighteenth century.

The Discourse on Inequality (1755)

In 1753 Jean-Jacques again participated in an essay competition sponsored by the Dijon Academy. That year's topic was "What is the source of inequality among men and is it authorized by natural law?" This time Rousseau did not win the prize. He revised his original polemic, adding extensive notes, and published it in 1755. Known as the *Second Discourse,* it advances an argument even more daring than the first one.

Rousseau begins by distinguishing two types of inequality. The first is physical or natural (i.e., relating to height, weight, strength), whereas the second, which he calls moral or political, stems from "the different privileges that some enjoy to the detriment of others, for example being richer, more honored, or more powerful" (131). He is most interested in the transition from the first to the second inequality, from the state of nature to civil society, which is the moment when "Right replaced Violence, [and] Nature was made subject to the Law" (132). To better examine this critical juncture in human history, Rousseau suggests that we "begin by setting aside all the facts" and engage in an imaginative reconstruction of the past, a sort of creative anthropology. Lacking even the meager evidence available today about prehistoric man, Jean-Jacques used the historical documents he did have to reconstruct what the state of nature might have been. Since these eighteenth-century discussions were always limited by religious orthodoxy, Rousseau's call to discard the facts can be seen as an attempt to keep this discussion secular and to avoid any consideration of Adam and Eve, the garden of Eden, and the biblical version of man's origins. The speculative nature of Rousseau's reconstruction is apparent: in his preface he speaks of the state of nature "which no longer exists, which perhaps never existed, and which probably never will exist, and about which it is nonetheless essential to have some precise notions so as to judge our present state" (123). Despite its quasi-fictional aspect, Rousseau wants his theory to be accepted as scientific and philosophical.

The rest of the first part of the discourse contains a long list of arguments about how savage man in the state of nature is less unequal and more happy than man in society. In the state of nature the land produces, without cultivation, enough to feed man. Savages are robust and healthy, untouched by diseases that living in society has caused:

> Extreme inequality in life styles, excessive leisure for some, excessive work for others, the ease with which we can irritate and satisfy our appetites and our senses, the overly complicated food of the rich which feeds them spicy sauces and causes indigestion, the unhealthy food of the poor which they often don't have enough of thereby causing them to overeat whenever they can; sleepless nights, excesses of all sorts, the extreme behaviors produced by our passions, fatigue, stress, sorrows, the trials without number that we experience everywhere and that eat at our souls. These are the deadly proofs that most of our sufferings are our own work, and that we could have avoided almost all of them by keeping to the simple, solitary, and regular life style that Nature prescribed for us. (138)

Clearly, part of Rousseau's inquiry is motivated by a dislike and distrust of society, as this catalog of its failings shows. Just as domestic animals are weaker than their wild relations, so too is man "bastardized" by society: "By becoming social and a slave, he becomes feeble, fearful, grovelling, and this soft and effeminate style of living enervates both his strength and his soul" (139). In nature, man's instinct is a better guide than his reason. Obviously, Rousseau has idealized the state of nature, just as he has confused it with actual primitive societies. He can be excused, however, since the eighteenth century knew very little about anthropology; serious thinkers of that time, for example, entertained the possibility that the rarely seen orangutan was human, a status they did not always confer on primitive peoples that had been discovered.[4] Nonetheless, Rousseau's antithesis of natural vs. societal strikes a modern chord. We appreciate the simpler life in a way that his contemporaries did not; we know the advantage of active over sedentary lifestyles, of organic over processed foods.

In a long digression Jean-Jacques investigates the origins of human speech. How did man first learn to speak? he asks. How are the origins of language connected with those of society? "If men needed words to learn how to think [and thus to speak], they had an even greater need to know how to think in order to find the art of speaking" (147). Which came first? Can we ever know? Rousseau's questions remain pertinent today, especially for literary critics and theorists. Linguists have not advanced much beyond Rousseau's thinking.[5]

Returning to his argument about the superiority of nature over society, Rousseau distinguishes between the sexual drive in nature, which is nonconflictual and easily satisfied, and love, which, instituted by society and codified by human laws, has created only dissensions: "duels, murders, and even worse. . . . the Laws of continence and honor themselves infallibly spread debauchery and multiply abortions" (159). The first part of the essay ends with a picture of the savage "wandering in the forests without industry, without speech, without a home, without war, and without connections, without any need for his fellows . . . subject to few passions and sufficient unto himself" (159–60). He is free and happy, whereas societal man is oppressed by needs he cannot satisfy and desires that have been created only by society. For Rousseau, it is society that magnifies the original, physical, and natural inequality among men and transforms those barely noticeable differences into a chasm that separates men into social classes and makes some subservient to others.

The second part of the discourse begins with a rhetorical canon shot that still reverberates with a profound sense of moral outrage and class conflict:

> The first man who staked out a claim, declared "This is mine," and found others foolish enough to believe him was the true founder of civil society. How many crimes, wars, murders, and misery would the human race

have avoided if someone had pulled up those stakes and cried out to his fellow men, "Don't listen to this impostor. You are lost if you forget that the fruits belong to everyone and the land belongs to no one." (164)

To justify that polemical statement, Rousseau proposes to follow the path that has led man from his initial, natural equality to the "final term of the state of Nature" (164), when private property created inequality and thus gave rise to modern society. At first solitary and independent, savages gradually grouped together, discovered their shared interests (166), and instituted families. With the family began the division of labor that separated the sexes and introduced differences between male and female (168). Savages began to acquire commodities unknown to their ancestors, this being "the first yoke that they placed on their own neck without realizing it." For Rousseau, things possess people rather than the other way around: "[T]hese commodities having lost by overuse all their attractiveness and having degenerated at the same time into real needs, being deprived of them was more painful than enjoying them was pleasant. People were unhappy to lose them although they had never been happy to have them." Inspired by his own experience, this paradox informs Rousseau's entire critique of modern life and society. As these protosocial men formed larger and larger groups, speech developed. As men began to look at women, love appeared, only to be immediately disfigured by jealousy. In public men compared themselves to each other, thus initiating feelings of rivalry and hostility: "[F]rom these original preferences were born, on one hand, vanity and loathing; on the other, shame and envy. The fermentation caused by these new yeasts eventually produced a brew that was fatal to happiness and innocence" (170).

Rousseau imagines that his noble savage was "placed by nature at an equal remove from the stupidity of animals and the deadly intelligence of civil man" (170). This "savage" (I refuse to impose the political correctness of our time on the vocabulary of the eighteenth century and so continue to use Rousseau's term) cannot be identified as the primitive peoples who were then being discovered by travelers and discussed by philosophers. Those primitives had already strayed too far from nature and advanced too close to society. Although critical, this distinction is never formalized, since Jean-Jacques uses these primitive societies as examples for his conjectures about the state of nature.

Although Rousseau does not clearly identify his noble savage, he does articulate precisely how social living eliminated individual freedom. The fatal step toward civil society was taken when the savage abandoned tasks he could perform alone and joined others so they could work together: "[O]nce man needed another's help; once people noticed that it was useful for one man to have the provisions of two, equality disappeared, property was instituted, work became necessary, and the vast forests were transformed into smiling fields that had to be irrigated with the sweat of men and in which slavery and misery shortly took root and grew with the harvest" (171). Metallurgy and especially agriculture demanded mutual cooperation. From farming grew other deleterious phenomena: the use of money, laws to protect property, and an increasing inequality among laborers (174). The next inevitable step was the split between being and appearing, between truth and the appearances of truth. Here Jean-Jacques denounces social hypocrisy, posturing, "imposing pompousness, deceitful ruse, and all those vices which follow behind"; in short, the myriad ways of showing off that he so detested. Caught up in this confusion of reciprocal obligations, men from all sections of society lose their independence: "[T]he rich man needs their services; the poor man needs their help, and being in-between does not mean you can do without them either" (175). Constant contact strengthens the dependency that deprives men of their original freedom and creates inequality.

His depiction of pervasive and mutual social dependencies prompts a stunning conclusion: "This incipient society gave way to the most horrible state of war" (176). Rousseau refutes the traditional view that society ended the war, chaos, or struggle for life that was identified with the state of nature. Other theorists, such as Hobbes, Locke, and Montesquieu, claimed that society imposed peace on the unregulated conflicts of savages who had no laws to settle their disputes. Rousseau's originality is to locate this war of each man against everyone else inside society and not outside it.

At this dangerous moment when interdependency was undermining man's original freedom, Rousseau argues, the rich man decided to institute society to protect himself and to take advantage of his fellow man. One of the rare democrats of his time,[6] Rousseau denounces the rich property owners who confiscated land that had previously belonged to everyone. In a provocative attack that prepares the conclusion of the essay, he apostrophizes the rich: "Do you not know that the multitude of your brothers is perishing or is suffering from want of what you have in excess, and that the specific and unanimous agreement of the human race is required for you to appropriate from general provisions anything beyond what you need for subsistence?" (176–77). The rich were able to fool the poor into believing that society was designed to protect them, the poor, while in fact it was intended only to solidify this original theft by the rich. Society, according to Jean-Jacques, is built upon this original fraud, this first loss of man's equality:

> Such was, or must have been the origin of Society and of Laws, which imposed new restrictions on the poor and gave new strength to the rich, which destroyed natural freedom without hope of change, which fixed forever the Law of property and inequality, which made an irrevocable right out of a clever usurpation, and which for the profit of a few ambitious individuals subjected from then on the entire human race to work, servitude, and misery. (178)

After this rhetorical high point, the essay slows down a bit. Rousseau refutes other theories about the origins of society (i.e., conquest, choice of leader, patriarchal model, tyranny). He touches only briefly on the point that all legitimate government is "a true contract between the People and the Leaders that they choose for themselves" (184). He will return to this embryonically democratic ideal so at odds with the political reality of the monarchical eighteenth century in his *Social Contract.*

In his conclusion Jean-Jacques underlines those aggressive and polemical arguments that refute the legitimacy and advantages of modern society. He bemoans the fact that the original savage man is gone, replaced by a civil man who is artificial and, in modern terms, stressed out (192). Naturally the comparison between the two is all to the former's advantage: "[The savage] breathes only repose and liberty, he wants only to live and relax. . . . The ever-active citizen sweats, is constantly in motion, and torments himself with looking for even more laborious things to do. . . . He pays his respects to the big shots he hates and to the rich he despises" (192). This face-off between the good savage and the bad citizen echoes the tension between truth and appearances: "The Savage [better translated perhaps as the Natural Man] lives within himself; social man, always outside himself, only knows how to live through others' opinions, and it is so to speak from their judgment that he draws his awareness of his own existence" (193). The climax of the essay is just as ringing as the paragraph that opened the second part. Rousseau's examination of social origins leads him to condemn a society so foolish as to have child-kings (Louis XV became king at age five in 1715) and so unjust as to tolerate widespread and blatant inequality in the distribution of wealth:

it is manifestly contrary to the Law of Nature, no matter how you define that law, that a child rule over an elder, that an imbecile guide a wise man, and that a handful of men be glutted with extras while the hungry multitudes lack what is necessary. (194)

The Essay on the Origins of Language

I have included the *Essai sur l'origine des langues* (*Essay on the Origins of Language*) in this chapter because it is closely related to the *Discourses*. According to Rousseau himself this essay began as a digression that became too long to fit into the second *Discourse*. But it also reaches out in other directions, covering much of the same ground as the *Letter on French Music* (1753), namely the relationship between language and music. Several passages were also transcribed verbatim into *Emile*.

Not published until 1781, after Rousseau's death, this essay was probably completed by 1761, when Jean-Jacques sent a manuscript copy to Malesherbes, the Director of Publications. It had been largely ignored until Jacques Derrida brought it to the critics' attention.[7] Its main interest lies in the extent to which it adumbrates a number of ideas dear to contemporary literary theorists.

The *Essay*'s weak construction is testimony to its unfinished status. There are a number of closely related ideas here, but they do not interconnect smoothly. On the contrary, they remain unassimilated in four separate blocks. The first section, consisting of four chapters, explores the theoretical question of language's origins: what was the original language? what were its characteristics? The next three chapters jump ahead in time and deal with modern languages, especially their decline in comparison to the perfect first tongue. The following block, also three chapters long, rehearses the distinction between the climate, races, and languages of the North vs. those of the South. The last eight chapters turn to the question of music, which is closely related to the nature of language for Jean-Jacques. I see a chiasmus (a:b::b':a') as the rhetorical figure structuring this essay. More abstract or philosophical, the first and last sections deal with the nature of language and its close connection with music, while the two middle sections address more polemical issues, especially the decline of modern music and speech.

The opening section is the most interesting for modern literary theory. A product of local conditions, language defines nations and holds the key to individual identity. Language is human, not divine, because it produces communication through "perceptible signs":[8] language that shows is superior, in Rousseau's opinion, to one that tells. Belonging ambiguously to the realms of both nature and convention (i.e., speech is a human invention, as are social or political institutions), language is the basic reality upon which all the rest is built. In the beginning there was both gesture and voice. Gestures were better for practical and physical needs (378), being more direct and yet symbolic. "Thus we speak to eyes better than to ears" (377). We need our voice, however, to express our passions. Emotions are the source and true nature of all spoken language. The most primitive languages "have nothing rational or methodic about them; they are alive and figurative. We have been told that early man had a mathematician's language, but we see that it was a language of poets" (380). Jean-Jacques further claims that "it was neither hunger nor thirst, but love, hate, pity, anger that loosened the first tongues. . . . that is why the first languages were singing and passionate" (380–81). That language originates in emotion and music (these metaphorical suggestions will become more explicit later) forms the bedrock of Jean-Jacques's theory.

Being poetic and emotive, the first language was based on tropes or metaphors (381). This mythic *Ur*-language is vocalic. Vowels allow the voice to speak, whereas consonants "articulate" speech; that is, they stop the vocalic/voiced flow and interrupt the natural, internal accent that best expresses emotion. Since Rousseau uses the same vocabulary in different contexts, his precise meaning in any specific case can be unclear. Such ambiguity, he will later remark, perhaps mindful of his own situation, characterizes the perfect natural language. The term *voix* means both the human voice, speech or language, and voiced sounds like vowels; *sons* means sounds, including musical notes, as in a musical scale. The frequently used adjective *sonorous* always combines the physical production of sound with this notion of intrinsic musicality: "thus the *voix, sons,* accent, and number, which are natural, leave little for the articulations to do, which are conventional" (383). Vowels are emotional and natural, while consonants are social constructs that break up that natural emotional flow. Here Jean-Jacques is planting the seeds of later connections not just with music but also with the social implications of language. This first theoretical section closes with a long description of what a perfect, Edenic language would be:

> This language would have many synonyms to express the same being in
> its different contexts; it would have few adverbs and abstract words. . . .
> It would have many diminutives, composed words . . . to give cadence to

its periods and a fullness to its phrases. It would have a lot of irregularities and anomalies, it would avoid grammatical analogy to embrace euphony, number, harmony, and the beauty of sounds [*sons*]. . . . it would persuade without convincing, and depict without reasoning. (383)

Rousseau is quite technical here. The accent, poetry, and passion that characterize his Edenic language are intrinsic to the very substance of language and its physical production. They do not yet apply to the subject matter or intellectual content of that wonderfully (self-) expressive tongue.

Turning from the ideal to the decadent, from the past to the present, the second section considers language in Rousseau's day. Just like the arts and sciences, which, as recounted in the first *Discourse,* were in steady decline, modern languages have evolved, but badly: "[T]he more vowels [*voix*] become monotone, the more consonants multiply; new articulations and grammatical combinations replace accents which disappear and quantities [i.e., length: short or long vowels] which all become the same" (384). Thus modern language, in stark contrast to its primitive model, "becomes more exact and less passionate; it substitutes ideas for feelings, it speaks no longer to the heart but to the head."

Some of Jean-Jacques's most interesting ideas touch on the relationship between writing and speaking. He recalls the evolution of writing, from hieroglyphs, which represent objects; through abstract characters like Chinese calligraphy, which represent sounds; to the modern alphabet, which does not represent at all but disarticulates. Modern language "decomposes the speaking voice into a certain number of elementary parts" (385), such as syllables and letters, which have no direct connection to nature. Each of these stages of language corresponds to a certain type of society, savage, barbarian, and modern government respectively. Invented for commercial reasons, the alphabet remains tainted by its practical, economic, and emotionless origin as well as by its distance from primitive speech. Consequently, "the art of writing has nothing to do with the art of speaking" (386). More than that, "writing, which ought to solidify language, is precisely what alters it; it doesn't change words but their genius; it substitutes precision for expressivity" (388). Modern European languages, especially in their written forms, have lost all the qualities Jean-Jacques appreciated in his primitive, spoken language. Emotion has been sacrificed to reason, expressivity replaced by precision, and the once intrinsically sonorous, musical accent broken by grammar, harsh articulations, and consonants. "We have no idea of a harmonious and sonorous language that speaks as much by musical accent [*sons*] as by vowels [*voix*]" (390). I could also translate that final phrase as "by vowels and the human voice."

This screed against modern written languages takes another turn in the third section of the *Essay,* which is "a long digression . . . to find the origin of human institutions" (394). The longest in the essay, chapter 9 makes explicit the connection between language and society. "The three states of man considered in relation to society are connected to this last [historical] division: savage man is a hunter, the barbarian is a herdsman, and civil man is a farmer" (400). Each social and political stage corresponds to a linguistic one. Language (or more accurately, its corruption) played a critical role in the creation of society and therefore in the enslavement of modern man. "I cannot imagine how [natural men] would ever have renounced their primitive freedom and left an isolated and pastoral life so suitable to their natural indolence, in order to inflict upon themselves unnecessarily the slavery, the hard work, and the consequent miseries of the social state" (400–401).

Next Jean-Jacques exploits an antithesis that had been made famous by Montesquieu several years previously in his *Spirit of the Laws* (1748). He compares the nations, the races, and the languages of the North with those of the South. In the dry South, water was an absolute necessity so men congregated around it. "Such must have been the origin of societies and languages in hot countries. There the first family connections were formed; there the first meetings between the two sexes took place" (405). Just as these southern societies most resemble the lost golden age of freedom in the state of nature, so too do their languages recall the original human tongue. "There the first festivals took place, feet jumped with joy; a hurried gesture was no longer enough, the voice accompanied it with passionate accents; mixed together, pleasure and desire were felt simultaneously. There was the real cradle of humanity, and from the pure crystal of fountains flowed the first fire of love" (406). Similarly, local factors like climate and physiology caused the northern languages to be harsh and less passionate. The languages "of the South must have been alive, sonorous, accentuated, eloquent, and often obscure because they were so energetic; those of the North must have been dull [unvoiced], rude, articulated, shrill, monotone, and precise because of their forceful words rather than good construction" (409).

These ideas set the stage for the essay's last and longest part, which comprises 8 of the essay's 20 chapters. Finally Jean-Jacques reaches his real topic, the relationship between language and music, a connection

alluded to in his subtitle, "In Which Mention Is Made of Melody and
Musical Imitation."

Picking up where he left off in chapter 4, Jean-Jacques identifies his
Ur-language with music: "Around the fountains I already mentioned,
the first discourses were the first songs; the periodic and measured repetition of rhythms, the melodious inflection of accents gave birth to
poetry and music along with language, or rather all of that was language itself for those happy times and places when the only pressing
needs that required the help of others were those of the heart" (410).
Just as poetry predated prose, the passions spoke before reason. Melody
was the only kind of music: "[T]here was at first no other music than
melody, and no melody other than the varied sound [*son:* musicality] of
the word; accent constituted song. . . . singing and speaking used to be
the same thing" (411).

Plunging into another controversial issue of the times, Rousseau
compares painting and music. Just as for him line is more important
than color (echoing the debate between the supporters of Poussin and
those of Rubens), melody is more important than harmony. For Jean-
Jacques, imitation is the key to art. Line imitates or represents reality
better than color does. So too melody: "By imitating the inflections of
the [human] voice, melody expresses complaints, cries of pain or joy,
menaces, groans: all the vocal signs of passion belong to its domain. . . .
[Melody] does not only imitate, it speaks and its language, inarticulate
but alive, ardent, passionate, has a hundred times more energy than the
word itself. Hence the strength of musical imitations; hence the empire
of song upon sensitive hearts" (416).

Harmony, which is to say counterpoint in Rousseau's antithesis, is
opposed to melody just as consonants are contrasted to vowels. Jean-
Jacques does not hesitate to refute the ideas of Philippe Rameau (chapter 13), the famous composer and theorist who was arguing at this time
that contrapuntal harmony was the basis of music.[9] In Rousseau's
scheme, the opposition is clear although he never spells it out. I would
reformulate Rousseau's more delicate distinctions in this blunt way:
poetry, melody, primitive language, accent, emotion, and *voix* stand in
stark contrast to intellectual discourse, counterpoint, written language,
articulation, reason, and consonants.

Jean-Jacques then moves on to a question dear to literary theorists.
The sounds of melody are not just sounds; they are also "signs of our
affections, of our sentiments" (417). Music is not just a physical phenomenon; it is also symbolic and moral. The reaction of the listener is critical

to the meaning of a sound (i.e., a word) or a musical note: "[I]n order to charm and move me, a series of sounds must offer something that is not just sound or harmony, but which moves me despite myself" (419). Listening is not passive, it is active. By participating actively in what we hear, we help create what we are hearing: "It is not so much the ear which gives pleasure to the heart, as the heart which gives it to the ear."

Chapter 16 develops that brief, earlier comparison between music and painting into an extensive analysis. Music is superior because it develops in time, successively, whereas a painting presents everything all at once. The domain of music is time, that of painting, space (420). Furthermore, music does not depict an object literally, as painting does. More sophisticated, music "will not represent these objects directly, but will excite in the soul the same sentiments that we experience while seeing them" (422). Here again Rousseau adumbrates an aesthetics of reception in which the reader or listener cooperates with the text or the music and thereby generates meaning through his own active participation. This notion is much more modern and provocative than the traditional concept of mimesis (direct imitation), which dominated eighteenth-century thinking about art.

The penultimate chapter explains (and complains) that music has degenerated just as language has. In both cases, the original expressivity and accent were lost to the advance of reason. The asperity of the northern barbarians won out over the melodic South: "All their articulations being as harsh as their vowels were nasal and unvoiced, they could only give a kind of peal to their song whose effect was to reinforce the sound of vowels in order to cover the numerous hard consonants" (426). Guttural tones ruined melody: "Soon song was nothing but a slow and boring sequence of drawn out shouts, without sweetness, measure, or grace."

Although unsatisfying because it starts off in a new direction, the last chapter does indicate what is really at stake in Rousseau's essay. Music and language are not minor matters; on the contrary, they have enormous political repercussions. "There are languages that are favorable to liberty; they are the sonorous, harmonious, metrical tongues whose words can be heard at a distance" (428). Primitive societies were healthy in terms of both their language and their politics; in contrast, modern society is corrupt linguistically and socially. To be suitable for freemen and thus to a free state, language must be easy to speak. It must carry the voice audibly so political affairs can be discussed in the open air, in public assemblies, in a kind of town meeting reminiscent of the Greek agora. "So I say that any language in which you cannot make yourself heard before an assembly of the people is a servile language; it is impossible that a people speaking such a language remain free" (429). These are dangerous and provocative words, especially in the absolute monarchy that was eighteenth-century France. Rousseau does not elaborate here the political implications of his stirring alliance of free speech and free government, but he will in other works.

Despite its shortcomings this *Essay* is intriguing. Because it was both unfinished and unpublished, its position in Rousseau's evolving thought is problematic. Although it contains provocative insights, it lacks an overarching coherence and thus is ultimately unsatisfying. Nonetheless, its ideas do possess a curious retrospective power. Precisely because they are unstable chronologically, they produce an unexpected impact when they appear elsewhere. Reworked and reexpressed in Rousseau's other writings, this essay's ideas acquire a supplementary meaning from their reformulations and additional contexts.

Chapter Three

Letters

This chapter groups several works that at first glance do not have much in common. What does connect them is simply that they all have "Letter" in their title.

Letters were a more effective and prevalent form of communication in the eighteenth century than they are today. Even if they were originally intended to be private and intimate, letters could easily become public and social. When read out loud in public gatherings, as they often were, they entertained, presented novel opinions, or contained noteworthy news. Widely accepted conventions governed this public writing and reading of letters. In an age without mass media or modern communications, circulating a letter produced a kind of open forum that reached a large audience. Published as pamphlets or brochures and sold relatively cheaply, the genre of "public" letters functioned as the equivalent of today's op-ed page or current-events discussions on television and radio.

Rousseau published a number of important works in the form of letters. An originally private letter sent to Voltaire in August 1756 took on a large and very public subject, the role of Providence in human life. Jean-Jacques wanted to refute the pessimism that Voltaire had expressed in his *Poem on the Lisbon Disaster.* In a very intimate and personal series of letters sent in 1762 to Malesherbes, a high-ranking government official, Rousseau offered an autobiographical sketch of himself. These three letters are close to the *Confessions* in tone and content. Although the *Letter to d'Alembert on the Theater* was not intended as private correspondence, it did name its addressee and interlocutor. Both personal and public, this letter refuted the views on Geneva that d'Alembert had just published in the *Encyclopedia.* Its subject matter, then, was a very public and philosophical one: should there be a theater in Geneva? and what was the connection between morality and the arts? Similarly, Rousseau entered an ongoing controversy on musical matters with his *Letter on French Music,* which generated a polemic of its own. These last examples illustrate how flexible and protean the letter as a genre could be. Responsive to the latest events, unafraid of controversy, willing to address adversaries as well as issues in the news, the "public" letter presented its arguments directly to the public and asked for its approval. For Rousseau, a master of rhetoric, yearning for transparency, afraid that he was misunderstood or misrepresented and yet determined to speak his mind even when his views were not popular, the public letter had a strong appeal. And he used it quite effectively.

Letter on French Music (November 1753)

In 1752 a troupe of Italian singers brought their repertory of comic operas to Paris. Their performance style and music were a revelation, especially Pergolesi's comic masterpiece, *La Serva Padrona* (*The Servant Mistress*), because they were so different from the heretofore unquestioned French manner, which had become staid and stuffy. They were also a direct challenge to the French certitude about their artistic supremacy. The cantabile and emotional Italian music divided the city into two warring camps: the chauvinistic "King's Corner," which favored French music and tradition, and the liberal, modish "Queen's Corner," in which the philosophes argued that Italian music was better. This "War of the *Bouffons*" had just about died down when Jean-Jacques published his *Lettre sur la musique française* (*Letter on French Music*) in November 1753 and rekindled the whole debate. Music was merely a pretext in this polemic that surreptitiously dealt with larger ideological issues.

Rousseau opened his letter by asking somewhat indirectly but nonetheless provocatively whether French music really existed. The entire letter answered his question with a resounding "No!" Obviously, Rousseau was playing with hyperbole; after all, French opera was a major artistic enterprise that boasted such internationally famous composers as Lully and Rameau. Nonetheless, in this *Letter* Rousseau is playing the self-appointed role of iconoclast as he connects this apparently minor musical topic with some major philosophical preoccupations.

The basic ideas underlying Rousseau's thinking demonstrate the close connection between this *Letter* and the *Essay on Language*. First, he posits an intimate link between language and music. Characteristics of one determine the other. He claims, for example, that "rhythm is to melody approximately what syntax is to writing: it is what links the words, distinguishes phrases, and gives meaning and connection to the whole."[1] Second, he holds that melody constitutes the essence of music, not harmonic counterpoint. Italian music is melodic, whereas French music is contrapuntal. Finally, he criticizes French music in the same terms he used in both his *Discourses* (1750 and 1755) to castigate French society. An overly sophisticated society along with its overly intellectualized music has lost contact with its emotions. Lacking expressivity, the French can only rationalize what they should feel. Reason, sophistication, and the French stand opposed to emotion, naturalness, and the Italians. This clear-cut dichotomy between antagonistic extremes underlies Rousseau's argument.

After sowing that initial doubt that a French national music exists, the essay then identifies the three components of music: melody, harmony, and rhythm (*mesure*). Like most theorists of his time, Rousseau thought words were more important than music in opera, a point that most opera lovers today would dispute. The eighteenth-century view can be explained in part by the predominance of religious music in which the content, the prayer, was more important than the musical embellishment. National music depends on the national tongue, and from this claim about different national styles Jean-Jacques slips into his argument about the French not having any music whatsoever. In these opening pages Rousseau disguises his real target, French society, which was then generally perceived to be the acme of civilization. Hence he indicts an unspecified language (but he is talking about French) that would be unsuitable to music: such a language is "composed of mixed sounds, of mute, unvoiced, or nasal syllables, with few sonorous vowels, many consonants and articulations" (292). To make music in such an inhospitable tongue one would have to employ "fallacious and unnatural beauties . . . frequent and regular modulations [that, however, would be] cold, without grace or expression." All ornamentation would be "languishing and expressionless" (293). Such a language would of course not possess a natural melody, forcing composers to emphasize harmony: "lacking real beauties, they would introduce conventional beauties, whose only merit would be a difficulty vanquished; instead of good music, they would imagine an intellectual music. . . . they would think they were making music but they would only be making noise." Flaws in language lead to flaws in music. An unnatural and deformed language needs the inferior beauties of harmony because it is unable to sustain a melody.

In contrast to this unidentified language, Italian is perfect for music because it is "sweet, sonorous, harmonious, and accented" (297). With the help of a few examples from Tasso, the great Italian epic poet and source for the plots of numerous contemporary operas, Jean-Jacques shows how Italian can handle inversions of word order that are impossible in other languages. Flexible syntax enhances a language's expressivity in both poetry and music.

The main development of the essay compares French and Italian music. Jean-Jacques is no longer talking about national styles but rather about the essential elements that constitute musicality for him. In Italian (and here Jean-Jacques is referring to music, language, and society simultaneously), melody predominates. Speaking directly to the soul and emphasizing expressivity and emotions, only melody can produce the "divine singing [that] tears or ravishes the soul, puts the listener beside himself, and draws from these emotional transports cries that never honored our tranquil operas" (304). Counterpoint and chordal harmonics never produce such emotions: "All that commotion, which is only a last resort for those lacking genius, would stifle singing rather than animating it and would destroy our interest by dividing our attention" (304–5).

The antithesis of melody vs. harmony, of the single horizontal singing line vs. the vertical chordal structure, lies at the heart of Rousseau's concept of music and deserves some amplification. Melody is single and undivided. When there are different voices or vocal lines, they sing the same notes in unison, at full octave intervals, each in its own range, and thus preserve melodic unity. By avoiding distractions, melody concentrates our attention on the expressive words in its single line while counterpoint offers in its complex chordal structure several competing aural lines. Counterpoint interweaves mutually dependent voices and subordinates emotion to the more cerebral play of those multiple voices and their intricate infrastructure based on the complex rules that govern the acceptable intervals. Directly and immediately perceived, melody is emotional and personal, warm and expressive; governed by mathematical calculations, counterpoint is cold and intellectual, unemotional and unintuitive. Rousseau's main adversary in this dispute about the nature of music was Philippe Rameau, the great French theorist of counterpoint and the uncle of Diderot's nephew. Rameau criticized most of what Rousseau wrote on music, especially his articles for the *Encyclopedia*. This *Letter* continued the hostilities and the disagreement between them.

Always extolling its superiority over harmony, Jean-Jacques claims that melody is "an indispensable rule and no less important in music than the unity of action in a tragedy" (305). With this reference to the literary code for the French classical tragedies of Racine and Corneille,

Rousseau is beating the French with their own stick, their own master-pieces, and their own artistic criteria.

Such large-scale generalizations as the preceding are balanced by close attention to specific operatic features. Before discussing Italian duos, which unlike their French counterparts move the audience to tears (thus proving their exquisite expressiveness), Rousseau criticizes the fugue, one of the quintessential examples of counterpoint, as the "remains of barbarism and bad taste, which subsist, like the portals of our gothic churches, only to shame those who had the patience to construct them" (308). Unfortunately this blanket condemnation dismisses such masterpieces as J. S. Bach's *Art of the Fugue* and the elaborate, sculpted facades of such cathedrals as Amiens and Notre Dame de Paris! But I would rather insist on the real target of Rousseau's polemic. Counterpoint and fugues constitute "methodological music, stiff and studied, but without genius, which is called in Paris *written music* par excellence and which in fact is only worth being written and never worth being performed" (309). Performance demands expression and emotion, whereas "written music" smells of the scholarly dustbin.

Having sung the praises of Italian melody, Rousseau continues his attack on French harmony. Vocabulary is critical here: Jean-Jacques uses *harmony* as a noun to mean "counterpoint," although the adjective *harmonic* may mean "musical" and even "melodic." Rousseau notices more expression and "simplicity in Italian harmony, while I found ours [i.e., the French] so composed, so cold, and so languishing" (312). Part of the Italians' secret is not overwriting their counterpoint, and leaving out the complex chords the French would put in. An Italian child prodigy impressed Rousseau with his improvisations. "What! I said to myself, a completely scored harmony produces less effect than a mutilated harmony, and our accompanists, by filling in all the chords, only produce confused sounds, while this fellow makes more harmony with fewer sounds or at least makes his accompaniment more agreeable and more striking?" I wish that Jean-Jacques had further developed this insight about suggestive minimalism. Unfortunately he gives us only a tantalizing hint: "[T]he great art of the composer is not less in knowing which sounds should be eliminated as those which should be used" (314). Rousseau's own aesthetic of suggestion is not much more than a suggestion itself. Nonetheless, it is a powerful theory and one that Jean-Jacques himself practiced. What is purposefully unfinished can inspire the listener more than what is complete because the listener can imagine and participate in the former. This notion of trying to evoke a response rather than providing the complete sensation echoes the kind of reverie and imaginative fantasy that a single detail could evoke for Rousseau himself and that inspired some of his most memorable pages.

Comments on technical matters are precise and pointed, but they all tend to fall into the same pattern. The Italians are superior because they are expressive and give voice to their emotions, whereas the French are too intellectual, using complicated techniques and lacking any real feeling. He discusses recitatives, which should be a strong French point since here words and their meaning are primary. But even Lully, regarded as the best French composer of recitative, fares badly in Rousseau's eyes.

The final fifth of the letter parses a famous monologue in *Armide,* one of Lully's operas. In an extended, line-by-line analysis, Rousseau enumerates all of Lully's mistakes, all his failures to seize upon the poetic text and give expression to its changing emotions. For example, he asks, "[C]an you conceive of anything worse than this scholastic regularity in a scene where haste, tenderness, and the contrast of opposing passions provoke the sharpest agitation in the actress and the spectators?" (322). His exhaustive critique of one of the high points of French art culminates in a thundering dismissal of all French music and terminates the entire *Letter:*

> I think I have shown that there is neither rhythm nor melody in French music because the language does not lend itself to them; that French singing is a continual barking which no ear can stand without a warning; that its harmony is brutal, expressionless, and shows itself to be mere schoolboy's filler; that French arias are not arias; French recitatives are not recitatives. From all this I conclude that the French do not have any music and that they are incapable of having one; or, if they ever do acquire one, it will be so much the worse for them. (328)

The War of the *Bouffons* might be remembered only as a minor cultural imbroglio had not Jean-Jacques poured these combustible remarks upon its smoldering embers. The Paris Opera immediately withdrew the pass for free admission given to him for his own opera, *Le Devin du Village* (*The Village Soothsayer*).

Clearly Rousseau did not fear controversy; on the contrary, he sought it out. It was perhaps this *Letter* that earned Rousseau the most enmity from Frenchmen. His criticisms hit them in their pride, their language. Yet it was difficult to refute him. Indeed, many people today would agree wholeheartedly with Jean-Jacques that some languages are unmusical or at least unsingable. Americans would probably choose German despite all those lieder and Wagner's operas. We have to recognize that great vocal music, whether harmonic or melodic, has been written for and sung in all languages. Even if we can no longer accept Rousseau's ideas at face value, we nonetheless have to recognize that they have a tenaciously long life.

The Letter to d'Alembert (1758)

The *Lettre à d'Almbert sur les spectacles* (known as either the *Letter to d'Alembert* or the *Letter on Theater*), finished in the spring of 1758 and on sale in October, came at a critical juncture in Rousseau's life. Living a solitary existence at Montmorency, he was experiencing a severe personal crisis, the devastating breakup with his protectress Mme. d'Epinay and his close friends Diderot and Grimm. Traces of this rupture are found in the text. Jean-Jacques was also distancing himself from the ideological positions of his friends, the philosophes. The *Letter* was written to refute d'Alembert's article "Geneva," which had appeared in the seventh volume of the *Encyclopedia* in December 1757 and had presented a number of liberal philosophic positions.

Although the letter was clearly addressed to d'Alembert, Rousseau had several other addressees in mind: "But I am already forgetting that I am not writing [only] for d'Alemberts" (92). Behind d'Alembert was Voltaire, that preeminent man of the theater who produced plays privately (and somewhat illegally) on his estate just outside Geneva. D'Alembert had spent several weeks in Voltaire's home at Les Délices while researching and writing his article. Just about everyone recognized Voltaire behind this proposal to introduce a permanent theater and acting company into that austere Calvinistic city. Rousseau was also directing his remarks to those Genevans who opposed the theater. As a highly visible public figure, even something of a celebrity, Jean-Jacques could become the champion they needed, lending his weight and his voice—as well as his arguments—to their cause. Finally, over the heads of these interlocutors, Rousseau was also addressing the larger French public, which had reacted favorably to the social and moral critique in his *Discourses* and which was following the debate between conservative, bourgeois, and religious values and the more liberal views of the philosophes.

Despite the word *letter* in its title, this text's length, its rhetorical strategies, and its extensive use of classical history all indicate that it is a formal essay. Elaborate digressions on side issues, for example the tribunal of the Marechals of France (62–67) as well as several disquisitions on women, belong more to the essay than to personal correspondence. After a short preamble in which he criticizes d'Alembert for having suggested that the Protestant ministers in Geneva were more deists ("socinians") than traditional Christians because they did not really believe in the Trinity or the immortality of the soul, Rousseau addresses the main issue, whether Geneva should have a permanent theater and a resident troupe of actors. His resolutely negative answer falls into two roughly equal parts. The first half criticizes theater's subject matter while the second analyzes its social impact.

The discussion of how a play's content corrupts society is itself divided into three sections based on the major theatrical genres: tragedy, comedy, and love stories. Despite its partisans' claim about its positive moral value, theater fails to make "virtue amiable and vice odious" (21). It does just the opposite. Jean-Jacques denies that Aristotle's catharsis purges our passions. On the contrary, tragedy foments emotions and leads its spectators only to "a sterile pity, fed by a few tears, and which never produced the least act of humanity" (23). Comfortably depicted on the stage, tragic emotions assuage our conscience and encourage us to avoid our social obligations. Enjoying the thrill of tragedy's fiction makes us insensitive to real life: "[W]hen a man has admired fine actions in fables, and cried over imaginary sorrows, what more can be asked of him?" Rousseau questions ironically.

In discussing comedy, Jean-Jacques penned an analysis of Molière and his *Misanthrope* which has become famous.[2] Rousseau earnestly condemns Molière for mistreating Alceste, the hero of his play. "Who can disagree that the theater of this same Molière, whose talents I admire more than anyone, is a school of vice and evil conduct, more dangerous even than books which profess to teach that?" (31–32). In his attempts to make his audience laugh, Molière "troubles the entire social order; how scandalously he topples the most sacred relationships on which society is founded" (32). Remember all those valets who are more clever than their masters, all those young lovers who marry despite parental opposition. In Rousseau's eyes Alceste "is a straightforward, sincere, and estimable man, a really worthy man. . . . the author makes him a ridiculous personage. This is enough, in my opinion, to make Molière inexcusable" (34). Molière does this just to make "the crowd laugh" (38, 39) because that is what succeeds. Obviously there is no moral advantage in a theater that plays to the pit and speaks to the lowest instincts of its audience. Employing an anacoluth whose awkwardness emphasizes the radical content of his phrase, Jean-Jacques concludes "that the author, wishing to please these corrupt souls, either his moral leads us to evil or the false good it preaches is more dangerous than the evil itself" (42). Other playwrights are even worse because they depict dubious behavior and outright crimes as funny: "Who does not become for a moment dishonest himself by identifying with a thief?" (43). On this point Jean-Jacques is not far from those who argue today that depicting violence on television and in the movies inspires that very same conduct: spectators "leave the theater with this edifying thought, that in their heart of hearts, they were accomplices to the crimes they observed" (42).

Now autobiography sneaks into the polemic. The Alceste who cannot abide the backbiting of the Parisian salons is Jean-Jacques himself in self-imposed exile at Montmorency. Rousseau condemns Molière's polite, politic, and nonconfrontational Philinte for the same reasons that he detested his onetime friend Grimm, whose social aplomb and tact he saw as deceit and treachery. In the very public forum of his preface, Jean-Jacques had already burned his bridges with Diderot: "I used to have a severe and judicious Aristarus [the classical exemplum of friend and adviser]; I no longer do, I no longer want him; but I will regret him unceasingly and my heart will miss him more than my writings" (7).

Rousseau's third complaint is the prevalence of love in stage intrigues. He decries those authors who give "a new energy and a new coloration to this dangerous passion" (43). Here he places one of those digressions that punctuate this essay. Love is dangerous because it confirms the "reign of women." It would seem that Jean-Jacques, after defending the misanthrope, becomes a misogynist. He denounces as debilitating the social and moral influence of women over men: "There might be some worthy women an honest man can listen to; but is it from them, in general, that he should seek advice? can't there be any other way to honor their sex without debasing our own?" (44). In this same digression Rousseau laments that youth has lost respect for its elders, a situation often depicted in comedies.

Love is dangerous because it undermines more serious and important emotions. When we sympathize with Titus's love for Bérénice in Racine's tragedy we forget our original disdain for this emperor who so easily forgot his duty in favor of love (48–49). "Let them depict love as they will: it seduces us, or it is not love. If badly depicted, the play is bad; if it is depicted well, it offends everything that goes along with it" (51). Rousseau ends his brief against love in the theater and the first half of his essay with a truculent conclusion: "[T]he theater, which cannot

correct our mores, can alter them. By favoring all our inclinations, it
gives new strength to those that dominate us. The continuous emotions
we experience [in the theater] eviscerate us, weaken us, and make us
more incapable of resisting our passions" (52–53). Theater saps the
moral fiber of its spectators. The examples it presents so powerfully
work against the best interests of the state and of its citizens.

After this internal critique of the theater, that is to say of its content
or subject, Rousseau turns in his second part to external matters: how
the mere presence of actors and their theater can adversely affect a community. He begins with a typically Rousseauian antithesis: big city vs.
small town (53–54). To illustrate the latter he describes Neuchâtel, a
small Swiss town he knew from his youth, as an ideal community where
there are no specialists and everyone does everything for himself (55).
This type of equality would be frustrated by the professionalization that
a theater requires.

Then comes the paradox of corruption. For city dwellers who are
already corrupt, having a theater is acceptable, whereas it would be a
positive evil in a smaller, rural community where the people are still
good and innocent. Actors always provide a "bad example" for others
(69). Actors corrupt others because their profession is in itself corrupt.
Actors are intrinsically meretricious: the player "gives himself over to
representation for money, submits to the ignominy and the insults that
the buyer has the right to inflict, and publicly puts his person on sale"
(73). There is something so "servile and low" in this profession that it
has no moral status: the comedian's state is "a mixture of lowness, of fal-
sification, of ridiculous pride and worthless abasement, all of which
makes him apt to play all sorts of personages except the noblest one of
all, that of being a man, which he has forsaken." Because they are gifted
in the art of deception, actors will doubtless use that talent to seduce
innocent youth.

This question of actors who corrupt introduces another digression on
women. As a subject women weave in and out of the *Letter,* each time
adding a different facet to Rousseau's complex, but not very sympathetic, portrait of them. He praises women when they are in their place,
at home (80), inspiring their husbands, raising their families, running
their households. He attacks them as pernicious and destructive when
they appear in public. Actresses are doubly dangerous because they
exercise a corrupting profession and because they are out of their rightful place (82). Even when they are simple spectators, women put their
innocence at risk.

The following section is the climax of this second part and indeed of the whole essay. Echoing the earlier and brief discussion of Neuchâtel, Jean-Jacques now focuses explicitly on Geneva and on how a theater would affect it. After enumerating several practical difficulties a permanent theater would face (insufficient audience and financial base; possible recourse to additional taxation), Jean-Jacques declares that Geneva's culture and government would both be adversely affected. What Rousseau has been suggesting throughout the *Letter* becomes explicit here: any theater has moral *and* political consequences for the city that accepts it. A theater, with its facile entertainment and easy appeal, would ruin the traditional Genevan *cercles,* which were something like men's clubs, and would as a result produce a civic and political disaster. According to Jean-Jacques, these "circles" maintain the manly virtues that are necessary in a republic, so their loss would deprive the city of its lifeblood. "That a King rule over men or women is of no consequence . . . but in a republic, men are necessary" (92).

This interconnection of morality and politics explains some of what might be called Rousseau's "politically incorrect" thinking. Women's participation in public life robs men of their political virility. Remember that Rousseau's complaints about effeminization and emasculation are not sexual but political concepts. It would be a serious mistake, I think, to consider him homophobic because of them: he is using the contrast of masculine and feminine in a then ordinary but now outmoded antithesis. A long comparison linking notions of confinement and loss of manhood illustrates this dilemma. Rousseau's poetic style traffics in dangerous metaphors: "[E]very woman in Paris assembles in her salon a harem of men who are more women than she is. . . . look at these men constrained in their voluntary prisons" (93). True to his nostalgic bent, Jean-Jacques finds the men of his day less robust, less strong, less capable of physical effort than those of the past, especially his heroes of Rome and Sparta: "We have collapsed in everything" (94). Since the Genevan *cercles* sustain these manly virtues of yesteryear, their survival is critical to the city and its republican government.

A theater would also upset the delicate balance among the various social classes in Geneva, which would in turn have enormous political ramifications. "But let us not flatter ourselves by thinking we can preserve our liberty while renouncing the customs that won it for us" (103). Much of what Jean-Jacques says about Geneva repeats in detail the generalizations he voiced earlier. For the culmination of his critique, Rousseau finds some rhetorically effective arguments. For example, he

invokes the specter of increased taxation, claiming that the price of theater tickets is a kind of tax. Ticket prices are unfair because they are disproportionate to the wealth of the buyer: "[T]he one who has little
[money] pays a lot, while he who has a lot pays little. I do not see any
great justice in that" (104). He also reiterates his condemnation of theater's subject matter, repeating the objections he leveled at Molière. The
tragic heroes of Racine are poor role models because they are effeminate
due to the playwright's emphasis on love. Actors will spread their "taste
for conspicuous dressing and dissipation" (111), especially among the
impressionable youth. Rousseau claims that in 30 years actors will be
the uncontested "arbiters of the state": "[E]lections will be decided in
actresses' loges, and the leaders of a free people will be the playthings of
a band of actors. The pen falls from my hand at the thought of it" (112).

The playhouse as seat of government is the dystopia that menaces a
sober, Calvinistic Geneva where sumptuary laws were still in effect. It is
not necessary to consult the historians of fashion to realize how sartorial
display can mirror politics. From longhaired hippies to skinheads, from
the international youth democracy of blue jeans to the militant femi-
nism of bra burning, clothes and fashions, as Jean-Jacques so clearly saw,
can indicate the direction in which a nation's moral character and its
political institutions are heading.

As he nears his conclusion Jean-Jacques changes gears. Negative critique turns into positive proposal. Rather than a professional theater,
Rousseau suggests outdoor public festivals for both entertainment and
civic self-affirmation. "For what peoples is it more appropriate to assemble together often and to tie the sweet bonds of pleasure and joy, than
those who have so many reasons to love each other and to want to
remain forever united?" (114). Such spectacles would be active and participatory rather than passive: "[M]ake the spectators part of the spectacle; make them the actors" (115). Part of Rousseau's distrust of theater
is precisely that it divides the playhouse into actors and spectators, the
specialists and the disenfranchised. His ideal festival would abolish that
distinction and make every man the equal of all the others. The balls
and dances he describes here foreshadow similar festivities that will take
place on the utopian estate of Clarens.

The *Letter* now reaches its sentimental crescendo. In a long footnote
Jean-Jacques recounts his own emotional participation in one such
spontaneous and wholesome festival. Moved by his memories, Jean-
Jacques believes similar happenings would encourage many Genevan

emigrants to return to their native city, where they would rediscover these nostalgic reminders of their youth and of a past marked by social harmony and happiness. That such an idyllic or perfect Geneva never existed is beside the point. Jean-Jacques is operating in the imaginative mode where dreams supplant reality: "Oh, where are the games and the festivals of my youth? where the harmony of citizens? where the public fraternity? where the pure joy and true bliss? Where are peace, liberty, equity, and innocence?" (121).

In conclusion I should point out that the kind of public festivals Rousseau imagines did take place during the Revolution (e.g., the Festival of the Federation on 14 July 1790, the Festival of Reason in 1793, and the Festival of the Supreme Being on 8 June 1794) and created precisely the social and political solidarity Jean-Jacques desired. On the other hand, critics have claimed that these festivals also adumbrated the mass rallies of Nazi Germany, even though it is not entirely fair to accuse Rousseau of excesses that he could not have foreseen.

The Letters to Malesherbes (1762)

Written while he was the guest of the Duc and Duchesse de Luxembourg at Montmorency, the four *Letters to Malesherbes* offer a few short but incisive vignettes that supplement the autobiographical *Confessions* while remaining happily free of the paranoia about the plot against him that marks especially the second half of that text.

In the first letter Jean-Jacques once again declares his intention to show himself truthfully and thus to thwart those who seek to misrepresent him: "I will paint myself without make-up and without modesty, I will reveal myself to you just as I see myself, and such as I am. . . . No one in the world knows me except me alone" (I, 1133). He gives two reasons for his rejection of society and his love of solitude. First, solitude allows him to create his imaginary world: "I am better off with those chimerical beings that I gather around myself than with those I see in society, and the society created in my retreat by my imagination has soured me on all those I have left behind" (1131). Second, only solitude frees him from those social constraints that he later compares to slavery (1137) and that his "unconquerable spirit of liberty" cannot accept: "[T]he most insignificant obligations of civil life are unbearable. A word to say, a letter to write, a visit to pay, once they are obligatory, become punishments for me" (1132).

The second letter recounts at length the "illumination" Rousseau experienced as he went to visit Diderot in the Vincennes prison and that inspired his first *Discourse:*

> Suddenly I felt myself blinded by a thousand lights; a mass of ideas surged up together with a force and confusion that threw me into an inexpressible emotion; I felt my head seized by a dizziness just like drunkenness. A violent trembling crushed me and pushed on my chest; unable to breathe standing up, I fell down beneath the trees lining the avenue, and I spent half an hour there in such a fit that when I got up I noticed the front of my jacket was covered with tears although I didn't realize I had been crying. (1135)

This is obviously an earth-shattering experience but one that was entirely appropriate to the effect that the *Discourse* had on Rousseau's life.

Only late in life did Jean-Jacques come to enjoy "the true happiness of my life, without bitterness, without worries, without regrets" (1142). The third letter describes one such ideal and happy day. Avoiding visitors and escaping into the countryside, "where no importunate third party could interpose between nature and me" (1140), Rousseau reaches a pantheistic communion with the whole cosmos. "My mind wandering in this immensity, I no longer thought, no longer reasoned, no longer philosophized; with a kind of voluptuousness I felt myself burdened by the weight of the universe; amazed, I let myself go in the confusion of these grand ideas. . . . I would have wanted to throw myself into the infinite" (1141). This "dizzying ecstasy" is an overwhelming physical experience of the same intensity as the illumination on the road to Vincennes.

The tone changes in the last letter as Jean-Jacques turns from self-contemplation to an attack on the idleness and corruption of the society he had forsaken. He contrasts the useful peasants of Montmorency to the "those crowds of idlers paid with the sweat of the people to go chat six times a week in an academy" (1143). Although he is perfectly aware that he is writing to Malesherbes, an influential political figure, "born of an illustrious bloodline, son of the Chancellor of France and the First President of an independent [judicial] court" (1145), Rousseau does not hesitate to denounce aristocracy and privilege: "I hate the grandees, I hate their estate, their hardness, their prejudices, their smallness, and all their vices, and I would hate them even more if I despised them less."

Following this outburst, Rousseau admits his love for the aristocratic Luxembourgs, whose guest he then was. The letter ends on a reconciliatory note as Jean-Jacques dreams that he, the Luxembourgs, and Malesherbes are all social equals in an imaginary countryside: "[D]reaming like that, I would not want to wake up for a long time" (1146).

Although there is little material here that is not treated in more detail in the *Confessions,* these short letters contain what some critics consider Rousseau's most beautiful prose.

The Letter on Providence (1756; published 1764)

The *Lettre à Voltaire sur la Providence* (*Letter on Providence*) is a real letter with a real date line that was sent to a real correspondent. Rousseau did, however, allow some of his close friends to read his copy of the letter to their friends, and so the private text became a public one. The first of a number of unauthorized versions appeared in Germany in 1759. To prevent these pirate editions from bowdlerizing his words and ideas, Jean-Jacques published his own reworked text in 1764.

Rousseau just finished reading Voltaire's *Poem on the Lisbon Disaster* and *The Poem on Natural Law,* which the author had sent him. In Rousseau's mind, both poems asked that eternal question, why does evil exist if God is good? Convinced that Voltaire was attacking divine Providence, Jean-Jacques felt compelled to respond, particularly to the first poem.

His *Letter* is short and neatly constructed. Following the principles of classical rhetoric, the exordium opens with an attempt to win the reader's goodwill. Jean-Jacques thanks Voltaire for the gift of his two poems, praises his talent, and assures him of his admiration. In reading these poems he has "found pleasure along with instruction, and recognized the hand of a master" (IV, 1059). Such compliments of course hint that serious disagreement will follow. Rather cleverly Rousseau suggests naming Voltaire's poem "against Providence," just as Voltaire had proposed calling Rousseau's *Second Discourse* "a book against the human race" (1061). Two of the master writers of the century, each so different in style and temperament, are crossing rhetorical swords here.

Rousseau's first point engages Voltaire directly and addresses the question of why evil exists. As regards physical evil, Rousseau reiterates essentially what he said in the *Discourses:* it is man's fault. "Most of our physical sufferings are our own handiwork" (1061). The earthquake that destroyed a city where too many men were crowded together would have caused no damage in a sparsely populated rural area. In his arrogance man labels as evil those natural phenomena that affect him adversely. What egotism! "Would this then be to say that the order of the world should change according to our caprice, that nature should submit to our laws, and that, to prevent an earthquake anywhere, all we have to do is build a city there?" (1062).

On the moral plane, "the evils to which nature subjects us are much less cruel than the ones that we add on" (1062). Human beings are unhappy because of their very sophistication, especially writers who comprise "the most sedentary, the most unhealthy, the most thinking, and consequently the most unhappy" group imaginable (1063). Still, living is so positive an experience (we would all prefer living to not living) that even death and suffering cannot diminish it. Finally, we do not have sufficient intelligence to distinguish actual evil from the ordinary course of natural events. Referring to *Zadig,* a philosophical tale in which Voltaire voiced a similar skepticism, Jean-Jacques says that we simply cannot judge evil with certainty: "[T]hese apparent irregularities doubtless stem from laws we are unaware of and that nature is following just as faithfully as the ones that are known" (1065).

This section closes with an ecological vision that sounds surprisingly modern. For Jean-Jacques, humanity is only one part of a vast universe, not its sole purpose or justification. Placed in the context of the whole cosmos, man's suffering becomes a minor issue. "That a human cadaver nourishes worms, wolves, and plants is not, I admit, an excuse for the death of that man. Nevertheless, if in the system of the universe, the conservation of the human species requires a circulation of substance among animal, vegetable, and human, then the particular harm of an individual contributes to the general good" (1068). To this notion of ecological recycling Jean-Jacques adds a list of classical heroes who sacrificed their lives to keep their countries free. What is evil for an individual, suffering and death, can become good and ennobling when seen from a wider perspective.

Moving in a more general direction, the second part of the *Letter* deals with issues that have little direct connection to Voltaire's poems. Rousseau attacks those who have misinterpreted Providence to fit their own narrow ideology. Priests are first, followed immediately by philosophes. The latter are so self-centered that they see their minor inconveniences as major evils. They "cry out that all is lost when they have a toothache" (1069). Rousseau reiterates his notion of the whole ecological system having priority over its component parts: "Perhaps in the order of human things [Providence] is neither right nor wrong, because everything obeys a common law and there are no exceptions." Providence is "universal" because God "limits himself to preserve groups and species and to preside over all without worrying about how each individual spends his short life."

Logically following from all this is the question of God's existence. Although neither the atheist nor the true believer can claim certitude, Jean-Jacques favors the latter: "[F]inally a thousand preferences draw me to the more consoling side and join the weight of hope to the balance of reason" (1071).

In the third and final development, Jean-Jacques finds common ground with Voltaire. All men should enjoy freedom of conscience (1072). Governmental authority should be limited to civic matters while religion should emphasize good deeds rather than inactive faith (1073). In a passage that foreshadows both the *Social Contract* and *Emile,* Jean-Jacques sets out his "profession of civic faith." All religious beliefs should be allowed in a state except those that preach intolerance or fanaticism. Religions "that attack the foundations of society" should be eliminated "to assure peace within the state." Returning to the conciliatory tone of his opening, Rousseau suggests that such a "moral code" or "catechism of the citizen" would be a worthy subject for Voltaire's next poem (1073, 1074). It would be "a benefit to the human race" and form the capstone to "the most brilliant career that a man of letters ever knew" (1074).

A brief peroration parallels the exordium in tone and content. Tongue in cheek, Rousseau compares himself to Voltaire. "Surfeit with glory and disabused of vain titles, you live free in the lap of abundance; assured of your own immortality, you philosophize peacefully on the nature of the soul . . . ; however, you find only evil on this earth. Whereas myself, obscure, poor, tormented by an incurable illness, I meditate joyfully in my retreat, and I find that all is good" (1074). After an apology for his poor letter ("I have as much difficulty closing this boring letter as you will have reading it"), Jean-Jacques ends with a stirring affirmation of religious faith. His religion is not a traditional cult with dogmas, liturgy, and buildings. Rousseau's religion consists rather of the deep emotions within his heart and soul. "No, I have suffered too much in this life not to expect one hereafter. . . . I feel it, I believe in it, I want it to be so, I hope it is so, and I will defend it to my final breath" (1075).

Voltaire chose not to respond to this moving personal confession and so the debate on divine Providence did not continue. Rousseau later claimed that Voltaire's reply to his letter was *Candide.*

Chapter Four
Julie (1761)

Julie ou la Nouvelle Héloïse (*Julie or The New Heloise,* 1761) marks a major turning point in literary history for at least two reasons. First, as a runaway best-seller and the most popular French novel of the century, it quite simply transformed the genre. Lacking a classical pedigree, the novel had little prestige in the literary pantheon before *Julie;* after it, the now-respectable novel started along the path of success it would tread in the nineteenth and twentieth centuries. Second, *Julie* was both a shock and a revelation that permanently altered the attitudes of the reading public. Renting it by the page in lending libraries, readers snatched it from each other's hands. According to one famous anecdote, the Princesse de Talmont, after calling for her carriage, began to read the novel. Totally engrossed, she forgot her opera ball, read through the night, and only at dawn remembered to have the horses unhitched!

Such a reaction is incomprehensible now. Today's readers find this novel too long and slow moving, a slight story swelled out with philosophical digressions and constantly delayed by minute self-analyses. What seems so tedious now is precisely what the eighteenth century enjoyed so much. My task in this chapter is to explain how and why *Julie* was once a novel that could enthrall its readers.

Structure and Technique

Julie is an epistolary novel, a form that has been largely abandoned today but that was very common in the eighteenth century. The novel is told in the words of its various protagonists, who write letters to each other. There is no omniscient point of view, no narrator or other filter between the reader and these fictional interlocutors. Readers have a direct perception of the fictive personages and read the actual words that these intradiegetic characters (i.e., those who are inside the novel) write to each other. One consequence in *Julie* is that internal emotions take priority over external actions. The epistolary characters express their personal and subjective reactions to what is happening around them rather than record objectively those outside events.

An exception perhaps best illustrates this point: it is the long letter that climaxes the entire novel and that provides a factual, objective, and apparently neutral description of Julie's death. Written by Wolmar, Julie's husband, it appears unemotional because it concentrates on external events and focuses on what is happening. Such a detached perspective is clearly out of keeping with the rest of the novel. But the author is facing a dilemma here. For the climax of his drama, Jean-Jacques needs this edifying and moving death scene. But how to tell those visible incidents that are usually not the subject of intimate letters like these? What is amazing is that Wolmar's subdued account is so effective. What he describes is overwrought and pathetic: in a fit Claire chews on the furniture while servants gather in the hallways and weep convulsively (VI, 11).[1] Although these details border on the grotesque, the ultimate effect is saved by Wolmar's understated tone, which miraculously avoids being either ridiculous or pathetic. In the gap between the exaggerated content and Wolmar's laconic retelling lies the overpowering emotional impact that Jean-Jacques wanted us to feel as we witness Julie's death.

Wolmar's depiction of Julie's apotheosis, the longest letter in the book and one of the most traditionally narrative, is exceptional, however. Usually the internal life of the characters takes precedence over external reality. It is therefore logical that the first act of lovemaking between Julie and Saint-Preux is never described; literally, it is absent from the narrative because it takes place between two letters and is unrecorded *per se* (I, 28, 29). However, the reactions, thoughts, and impressions of the characters before and after that event are presented in full detail. Similarly, the famous "kiss in the grove" is elided from the text. All that remains is Saint-Preux's reaction to and memory of what happened:

> What have you done, oh! what have you done Julie? you wanted to reward me and you have damned me. I am drunk or rather crazy. My senses have been changed, all my faculties troubled by that immortal kiss. You wanted to soothe my ills? O cruel one, you have turned them bitter. It's poison that I took from your lips; it is fermenting, it is roiling my blood; it is killing me; your pity is the death of me.
>
> O immortal memory of that instant of illusion, of delirium, and of enchantment, never will you fade from my soul. As long as the charms of Julie are engraved there, as long as this upset heart will supply me with sighs and sentiments, you will be the pain and the happiness of my life! (I, 14, pp. 63–64)

By concentrating on Saint-Preux's internal emotions rather than on external events, the novel intensifies the letter writer's sentiments and encourages readers' involvement with them.

Indeed, many of Rousseau's contemporaries were convinced these were authentic letters written by real individuals. Such mistakes were relatively frequent in the eighteenth century. In the preface to the novel Rousseau plays with this confusion by debating with himself the question of the novel's fictionality vs. its veracity. Eighteenth-century readers were overwhelmed by their emotional identification with the characters, as can be seen in the letters they wrote to Rousseau.[2] Although we might marvel at such naive reactions, they stand nonetheless as incontrovertible proof of the unprecedented impact that *Julie* had upon those who first read it.

In terms of plot the story is a simple tale of thwarted love told in six books. A commoner, Saint-Preux, falls in love with Julie d'Etange, the noblewoman he was hired to tutor. Her father rejects any idea of marriage, even as the two protagonists taste the joys of mutual love (book I). Although they separate to better hide their passion, they in fact augment it by continuing to write letters. When their secret correspondence is discovered, the scandal requires Saint-Preux's immediate departure (II). Having rejected Saint-Preux out of aristocratic pride and arrogance, Julie's father selects a friend his own age, Wolmar, as son-in-law. Despite her love for Saint-Preux, Julie obeys her violent, prejudiced father and marries Wolmar (III). Six years later, having traveled to distant places, Saint-Preux returns to find Julie happily married and the mother of two small sons. Wolmar invites Saint-Preux to stay with them at Clarens. He hopes to cure Saint-Preux's passion for Julie, which he correctly suspects is not yet extinguished (IV). An idyllic period of happiness follows when all the principals are united at Clarens, which is depicted as a sort of pre-Edenic paradise (V). Before she can yield to the passion that she too has kept alive in her heart, Julie dies pure and chaste, faithful both to her husband and to her lover (VI). Her death is a saintly apotheosis that paradoxically affirms both the conventional morality of marriage and chastity as well as the primacy of sentimental passion. Julie dies because she still loves Saint-Preux. Her passion, which cannot be satisfied, consumes her.

Structurally, this plot is articulated in two equal parts of three books each. The first half climaxes with Julie's spiritual transformation upon her marriage to Wolmar (III, 18). During the ceremony she undergoes a "conversion" experience. She renounces her previous illegal and immoral passion in favor of conjugal contentment. Formerly her lover, Saint-Preux is now only her friend. Suicidal and filled with despair, he departs upon a four-year sea voyage around the world to palliate his suffering.

The entire novel terminates on another moral and physical transformation. In a letter written from her deathbed and presented only after her death, Julie confesses that she has never stopped being passionately in love with Saint-Preux, thus reversing her position at the end of the novel's first half. She dies chaste, however, physically faithful to her husband and still the model wife and mother. Her passion transcends the normal moral categories of mere earthly experience rising to a higher, celestial level. With these two balanced climaxes, Rousseau neatly establishes his paradoxical message. He proclaims simultaneously the invincible power of passionate love and the sanctity of marriage. In letters placed before and after Wolmar's lengthy description of her death, Julie first exalts her conjugal bliss and then confesses her unconquerable passion (VI 8, 12). Julie dies admitting her extramarital, sinful love while she remains an exemplar of conjugal and maternal virtue. Lover, wife, and mother, she reinforces societal conventions even as she violates them.

To provide some excitement in this slow-moving novel, Rousseau closes each book on a powerful, dramatic note. The first ends with Claire's vivid description of a discouraged and emotionally broken Saint-Preux being led away by Edouard Bomston after the Baron d'Etange has rejected any possibility of marriage with his daughter. Because the account of this violent and emotional departure is told by Claire, an observer and not a participant, it adumbrates Wolmar's report of Julie's departure/death at the end of the novel. In both instances an important action has to be told by an uninvolved observer because the participants are too confused, too much under the impact of their emotion to be able to describe what is happening. Book II climaxes with Julie's anguish when she reports to Saint-Preux that her mother has discovered their secret correspondence: "All is lost! All is discovered! I can't find your letters in the place where I hid them. . . . My whole body trembles, I'm unable to take a step" (II, 28, p. 306). A violent storm that endangers Julie and Saint-Preux both physically and morally caps book IV, while in the last letter of book V Julie proposes that Claire and Saint-Preux marry. Each of these finales gives a needed jolt to the narrative's slow pace and sagging action.

The novel opens brusquely, however, plunging the reader directly into the middle of Saint-Preux and Julie's passionate affair, which has already started. Beginning in medias res is a classical rhetorical device that challenges readers by omitting the normal exposition. The background and context needed to understand what is happening is precisely what this type of opening does not provide. Readers are caught up in this fragmentary incipit that allows them to see, or rather to hear, only certain parts that they have to arrange into a coherent whole by and for themselves.

As in many contemporary epistolary novels, these letters are not dated. There is no indication about how much time separates them; consequently, the novel's chronology is somewhat problematic. Omitting datelines might seem insignificant, but Rousseau obtains some very dramatic effects by using this blurry chronology. At the climax of book III, for example, Julie describes her wedding day and her moral transformation. Immediately following is Saint-Preux's letter contemplating suicide. Because the letters are undated, what escapes the reader is that as much as two years separate them . Giving these letters precise dates would diminish that dramatic juxtaposition between a spiritually transformed Julie who happily embraces married life and a suicidal Saint-Preux who is crushed by despair at losing her. The contrast between these letters and their very different states of mind has to be intense and immediate. Any lapse of time would negate their stark contradiction and diminish their emotional punch. Given the logic of the plot, however, this time lag is absolutely necessary to give substance to Julie's happy married life with Wolmar and to allow her the time to have a child of six when Saint-Preux returns from his four-year trip around the world at the beginning of book IV.

To provide variety for his monochromatic story, Jean-Jacques distributes the important act of writing letters among his limited cast of characters. Saint-Preux is the most prolific correspondent, writing 65 of the novel's 163 letters. Readers usually think of him (and behind this transparent autobiographical fiction, of Jean-Jacques himself) as the voice of the novel. Julie, however, writes 53 letters and Claire 26, thus giving weight to the female perspective. In addition, Claire plays a critical role as *listener:* writing cannot be separated from its companion act of reading. Since Julie and Saint-Preux write to Claire frequently, she enjoys the privilege of being confidante to both. In the end Jean-Jacques balances almost exactly his male and female voices (81–82). Passion speaks through both sexes. Neither sex dominates the exchange of letters; neither sex gives more input to the reader.

I would like to discuss this distribution of speaking roles on an even smaller scale. Saint-Preux dominates book V by penning 8 of its 14 letters, only to fall nearly silent with one single letter in the final book. The despair, the temptation of suicide, and the escape in travel that all marked Saint-Preux's reaction to losing Julie at the end of book III are very subtly echoed in his less obvious but equally real disappearance from the last book of the novel.

Counting letters, as I have done, prepares a study of rhythm and pace. The number of letters in each book decreases as the novel advances; thus the novel's pace slows as its subject matter become more dense and as it involves its readers more intensely. As befits an exposition in medias res, the opening book is rapid. Its 65 letters set a brisk tempo of exchanges and back-and-forth conversations primarily between Julie and Saint-Preux. Containing only 13 letters, the final book, in which Julie dies and Saint-Preux loses his voice, is slow and grave, a rhythm that is entirely in keeping with this somber and tragic denouement.

The overall pace of the narrative action is very slow by today's standards: very little actually happens as far as events are concerned. *Julie* moves to the rhythm of another epoch, when people had the leisure and the inclination to both read and write at length. One example will suffice to illustrate this deliberate pace and how a single scene can be spun out in time and in detail. Julie is telling Saint-Preux how she reacted to her father's announcement that Wolmar was returning to marry her. "It was then that invincible love gave me a strength that I thought I no longer possessed. For the first time in my life I dared to resist my father to his face. I told him clearly that M. de Wolmar would never be anything to me; that I was determined to die unmarried; that he was the master of my life but not of my heart, and that nothing would make me change my mind" (III, 18, p. 348). Although her words are presented as indirect discourse, they are deployed in space and time almost like real dialogue. In addition to Julie's private thoughts, the text makes quite vivid and almost audible her sharp tone and confrontational attitude. Nevertheless, her spirited resistance is overwhelmed by her father's unexpected and pathetic reaction, which is described at length and in precise detail:

> But what happened to me when all of a sudden I saw this most severe father at my feet, overcome and bursting into tears? Without allowing

me to stand up, he clutched my knees and fixing his teary eyes on mine, he said to me in a touching voice that I still hear inside me: "O daughter! respect the white hair of your unhappy father; don't send him suffering to the grave, as you did to the one who carried you in her womb. Oh! do you want to be the death of your entire family?"

Imagine my confusion! That posture, that tone of voice, that gesture, those words, that awful idea, everything upset me to the point that I collapsed half-dead into his arms. It was only after my many sobs, which were strangling me, that I could answer in an altered and feeble voice: "Oh father! I was armed against your menaces, but not against your tears. It is you who will be the death of your daughter." (III, 18, p. 349)

Here is a scene out of Greuze, that eminently successful painter of emotional family confrontations that Diderot presented so eloquently in his *Salons*. The eighteenth century reveled in this kind of emotional crisis, in which tears flow copiously, men fall to their knees, and sobbing women faint.

But even as this heartrending scene is presented in dialogue and description, Rousseau changes sentimental gears. Passing from bathos to harsh patriarchal authority, the Baron voices the prejudices of his class and totally disregards his daughter's autonomy: "I know what fantasy, unworthy of a noble woman, you nourish in your heart. Now it is time to sacrifice to duty and honesty a shameful passion that dishonors you and one that you will never satisfy except at the cost of my life. Listen for once to what your honor and the honor of a father demand of you, and then judge for yourself" (III, 18, p. 349).

Although dripping with sentimentality, this powerful scene reveals the hard social reality of aristocratic prejudice. Just beneath the surface of his sentimental plot Rousseau places a trenchant social commentary. These two weeping figures incarnate two antagonistic worldviews that frame a bitter critique of a corrupt society and its coercive behavior. The Baron's authoritarian, even dictatorial concept of parental prerogative is opposed by Julie's desire for self-fulfillment and personal happiness. Julie represents the nascent tendencies of romantic individualism, whereas her father embodies the absolutism of the ancien régime that would disappear in 1789. The Baron himself uses a metaphorical comparison that is instructive for this confrontation of values: "See if a passing adolescent flame and an attraction that shame disavows can ever be placed on a scale with the duty of a daughter and the compromised honor of a father" (350). Granted, this scene is long and advances slowly, but without that deliberate, slow-paced depiction of the participants' words and gestures, it would lose much if not all of its dramatic power. Despite or perhaps because of its length, it captures (dare I say succinctly?) the mix of contrary desires, the conflict of generations and duties, and the paroxysm of powerful emotions that all lie at the heart of Rousseau's novel.

Characters

Julie is an autobiographical novel. In it Rousseau has fictionalized events and feelings taken directly from his life, not to mention individuals who were and still are easily recognizable. Julie is modeled in part after Sophie d'Houdetot. Jean-Jacques, a plebeian, fell in love with the aristocratic Sophie, who was married and also the mistress of Saint-Lambert, a good friend of his. His passion for her was never requited. Sophie was as unattainable for Jean-Jacques as Julie is for Saint-Preux.

By imagining not one but two charming heroines in Julie and Claire, "one blond, the other brunette," Rousseau replicated the double vision of a single feminine ideal that he had experienced throughout his life. How often did Jean-Jacques find himself attracted by two women simultaneously, each appealing to a different emotional need? Georges May has pointed out how *blond* is a code word for maternal, comforting love, whereas *brunette* suggests a more aggressive and possibly dangerous lover.[3] This variation on the ménage à trois—the trio of Julie, Claire, and Saint-Preux parallels that of Sophie, Saint-Lambert, and Rousseau as well as other groups, like Mme. de Warens, Claude Anet, and Jean-Jacques—points furthermore to one of Jean-Jacques's typical attitudes: he enjoys these unresolved possibilities, that suspension between two desirable alternatives. Choosing either one deprives him of the other; rather than choose, he prefers to remain indecisive, in the middle, frustrated but still maintaining this pleasurable balance in his imagination.

Saint-Preux, impossibly in love, thoroughly in love and yet unable to satisfy his passion, is of course Jean-Jacques himself. The hero of this novel is in fact nameless; "Saint-Preux" is only a nickname invented by Claire (III, 14, p. 332; IV, 5, p. 417). With its resonances of chivalry and courtly love, and of course the medieval love story of Heloise and Abelard, which provides the novel with its subtitle as well as its narrative grounding, this name suggests the ideal and impractical side of Rousseau's passion.

Edouard Bomston is Saint-Preux's indispensable friend, companion, and adviser. This pair of male heroes is set symmetrically against the pair of female heroines. The English lord was a common figure in French literature of this time. The English were stereotyped as taciturn, phlegmatic, moody, and suicidal, characteristics that contrasted with the French self-image as sociable, witty, and sparkling conversationalist. In his own life Rousseau was indebted to foreigners who helped him in his moments of need: the governor Lord Keith during his persecutions in Neuchâtel and the philosopher David Hume when he was in exile in England, both Scotsmen. However, milord Edouard is a double for Rousseau, just as he is a dramatic foil for Saint-Preux. Bomston is the urbane, wealthy, independent, and sophisticated man of the world who is totally at ease in high society and aristocratic salons. In short he is the man Rousseau wished—in other words, depicted himself fictionally—to be.

Adored both by Jean-Jacques and Saint-Preux, Julie, the emotional center of the novel on whom every loving eye is fixed, is the incarnation of perfection. All the characters constantly praise everything about her. Even Claire, who might be excused a bit of jealousy now and then, cannot stop touting her virtues and exclaiming how everyone recognizes her preeminence: "Have you never noticed, my Angel, how everything that approaches you clings to you? That a father and a mother cherish their only daughter is not, I know, very astonishing; that an ardent young man should conceive a passion for such an amiable thing is not extraordinary either; but that in middle age a man as cold as M. de Wolmar could be moved for the first time in his life upon seeing you; that an entire family idolize you unanimously . . . ; that friends, acquaintances, servants, neighbors, and a whole town adore you . . ." (II, 5, p. 203). Saint-Preux's hyperbole also captures the tone of veneration bordering on idolatry that surrounds the incomparable Julie: "How can anyone not be eternally yours since your reign is celestial, and what good would it do to cease loving you since we would always have to adore you anyway?" (I, 43, p. 122). Everything about her is perfect. Indeed, one of the most galling features of this novel is how all the characters are so hopelessly enamored of Julie. What is worse, they repeat their admiration endlessly, ad nauseam.

Like all his characters, Rousseau himself is totally smitten with Julie. Julie can do no wrong; her every gesture and word are reported with awe. For me, this cloying sentimentality diminishes my appreciation of Julie as an authentic person. Let us remember nevertheless that this sugar coating is the creation of the other characters in the novel, who present her in that ideal mode. When I look at her own words, I find that Julie does have a few flaws. And how welcome they are! Quite capable of deception, she coquettishly entices an unsuspecting Saint-Preux into the "kiss in the grove." She has flashes of humor and bad temper: "So I chased you away, then, as you dare to claim? For whom would I have done that? Ungrateful lover lacking in finesse! . . . Tell me, what will become of you if I am covered with opprobrium? Can you hope to endure the spectacle of my dishonor?" (II, 7, p. 211). Still how much more attractive would she have been with just a hint of human failing! How much more interesting a fallible Julie would be!

Perhaps because of her goody-two-shoes character, modern readers are apt to question why Julie, the incarnation of honesty and transparency (always Rousseau's ideal), is praised for producing adulterated wine at Clarens. Despite her much-proclaimed aversion to any sort of trickery, Julie quite willingly deceives her guests with spurious wines that fraudulently imitate other vintages. This is admittedly a minor detail, but a telling one nonetheless. In *Emile,* to show that chemistry is useful knowledge, Rousseau demonstrates how wine can be altered. "There, I continued, is the pure and natural wine we can drink, and there is the faked wine that poisons."[4] The lesson Emile learns about unhealthy additives—poisons that operate both physically and morally, of course—is surely one that Julie should know and practice. This is but one of a number of disturbing details that hint at the troubling underside of Clarens. Although Rousseau intended to depict a paradise on earth, his dreamlike estate often teeters between utopia and dystopia as the workers are conditioned into believing that their boss is always right and Julie brews her deceptive and manipulative concoction.

Claire, on the other hand, is a spirited young woman and subsequently a "merry widow." No plaster saint, she jokes, cajoles, and teases Saint-Preux mercilessly. A brunette and thus according to Rousseau's typology more energetic, aggressive, and in short sexy, Claire is an authentic, down-to-earth woman, whereas the blond Julie is a porcelain doll constantly placed on a pedestal. Claire is never afraid to show her emotions or to express an opinion, either positive or negative. She is presented with both her virtues and her flaws, and she wins me over nevertheless. Indeed, I find her more attractive and more human than Julie even though she is described as "simultaneously an ardent friend and a cold lover" (V, 13, p. 629). All the terms here are loaded. Claire's passionless (loveless?) marriage with M. d'Orbe made no real impression on her affections, which she was always able to focus on Julie. The latent lesbianism in Claire and Julie's intense relationship is a possibility some critics are exploring with little regard for what Jean-Jacques intended. Be that as it may, in dividing his ideal woman into two characters, Rousseau did not endow them equally. In Rousseau's eyes, Claire is the lesser figure; to me, she is by far the more sympathetic one.

Wolmar is a problematic character who has suscitated some very extreme reactions. Identified as the "living eye" who sees and understands everything around him,[5] Wolmar resembles the Legislator of the *Social Contract,* which Rousseau was also working on at this time. Taciturn and unemotional in a novel that celebrates both verbosity and emotion, Wolmar constantly manipulates those around him. He secretly undertakes an "experiment" to cure Saint-Preux of his love for Julie. As the owner of Clarens, he has devised a number of techniques for controlling his workers and increasing their productivity without their being aware of or rewarded for it. Saint-Preux discusses and praises these devices in his glowing description of life at Clarens (V, 7). Today, however, critics question certain aspects of this utopia. Rousseau is a troubling author who lends himself (perhaps too well) to Derridean deconstructions that show him to mean something quite different from what he appears to say.

Although a short volume like this one cannot deal with all these issues in depth, I can briefly indicate what is at stake. The paternalism that surely indicated real concern and a helping attitude in the eighteenth century (i.e., separating the sexes both at work and at play; the master's absolute right to dismiss a worker; "company" recreational activities that all workers must attend) has taken on another color in light of modern concepts about individual freedom and labor rights. But even in eighteenth-century terms Wolmar casts a shadow that is upsetting. His invisible power as Julie's husband is an ominous reminder of the definitely abusive authority of Julie's father. His secret, insidious presence seems to justify suspicions that Jean-Jacques's ideal community might harbor a repressive component.

Saint-Preux, Rousseau's alter ego, incarnates some of the psychological mechanisms I have already pointed out in Rousseau. Saint-Preux is a dreamer, more content to contemplate the impossible (happiness with Julie) than to accept the practical (marriage with Claire). The emotions that torture him are in fact the emotions that allow him to exist. I suspect that, like Jean-Jacques, Saint-Preux would not have known how to enjoy the happiness he constantly seeks. The physical consummation of his love for Julie literally disappears from the novel. The first instance is mentioned only in retrospect, in the glow of the emotions it has provoked (see my earlier discussion; I, 28 and 29). The second takes place during Julie's sickness, while she is delirious. She does not know therefore if their lovemaking was real or a dream. The love Jean-Jacques celebrates, then, is a love that cannot be depicted. Love is best not when it happens but rather when it is recalled in memory or created in imagination.

Saint-Preux's attitude toward Wolmar is instructive in light of his passion, which at one level does not want to be consummated. Although Wolmar is the most obvious obstacle to Saint-Preux's happiness, Saint-Preux does not see him as a rival or as the cause of his distress. He calls Julie's husband his "father" and wants to be regarded as his "son." This is a curious desire that delights Freudians and deconstructionists, of course!

Digressions

This autobiographical and very personal novel also furnished Rousseau with the opportunity to introduce many topics that were extraneous to his love story. The eighteenth century appreciated novels that treated issues that were hot topics in the public's mind even if they were unrelated to the plot. The extremely flexible epistolary format lends itself to digressions because letters are written by multiple characters for diverse reasons. The logic behind this and indeed behind any epistolary novel is physical separation: why should Julie and Saint-Preux and all the others write if they can see and talk to each other? The same separation that inspires their emotional exchanges also motivates them to discuss any topic or event that their correspondents might not be aware of. The connective tissue binding discrete letters together can at times relax, thereby permitting any single letter to expand into an essay on a subject extraneous to the main plot. Thus Saint-Preux, having embarked on several trips and self-imposed exiles, can at times write as a reporter, bringing back information from the larger world to his friends in their isolated countryside. His trip to Paris motivates a description of its opera house and of how operas were staged there (II, 23). Additionally, the letter offers a welcome change in tone: it is a comic presentation, since all is seen through the astonished eyes of a rather unsophisticated provincial experiencing for the first time the flash of city lights.

Saint-Preux the bumpkin is not unlike Jean-Jacques himself on his first trip to the capital. When Saint-Preux gets drunk in the big city, his misbehavior prompts a moralizing sermon (another type of digression)

from Julie on the virtues of temperance (I, 50; II, 26). Book IV in particular is filled with digressions that almost become autonomous essays.
Saint-Preux's lengthy description of the domestic economy at Clarens is
a philosophical treatise illustrating Wolmar's physiocratic approach to
agriculture (IV, 7). More interesting and yet disquieting is the critical
deconstruction of this model estate mentioned earlier. Although Wolmar is for the eighteenth century an exemplar of enlightened economic
and agricultural thinking, to modern readers his progressive but paternalistic attitude might suggest a potentially totalitarian regime for his
employees.[6] One letter-essay celebrates the grape harvest at Clarens as a
biblical pastoral (IV, 12). Another digression develops ideas on rearing
and educating children (V, 5; Rousseau was working on *Emile* at this
time, too). Saint-Preux voices Rousseau's opinions about Italian music
(I, 47 and 48). Although better motivated in terms of plot and emotion,
Saint-Preux's letter in favor of suicide, followed by Bomston's rebuttal,
are further examples of digressions that pick up on philosophical issues
that were of interest to the public.

The plastic and fluid construction of the epistolary novel also gives
Jean-Jacques the latitude to include exact and extensive descriptions
that might otherwise seem extraneous in an intimate love story
recounted by the participants. I have already demonstrated how Julie's
death and the departure of Saint-Preux at the end of book I are special
instances of descriptive letters. Detailed, physical description, especially
of the countryside, was rare in eighteenth-century French fiction. One of
Rousseau's most important contributions to the novel as a genre was his
ability not just to describe natural sites like mountains but also to infuse
those descriptions with a powerful sentimental charge. "Seeing them
myself after such a long time, I felt how much the presence of objects
can rekindle powerfully the violent sentiments that moved us when we
were near them. . . . There is the rock I sat on to contemplate in the distance your lucky home; on that one was written the letter that touched
your heart." (IV, 17, p. 519). Separated from Julie, Saint-Preux invested
the mountains around him with all the intense emotions he felt for his
absent lover. Establishing a metonymic connection between the hero's
soul and nature, Rousseau pioneered the romantic technique of assign-
ing strong emotional connotations to imposing natural sites:

> Slowly I climbed on foot the rocky path. . . . I wanted to dream and I
> was constantly prevented from doing so by some unexpected spectacle.
> Sometimes immense rocks hung in ruins over my head; other times

steep and noisy cascades inundated me with their thick mist. At times an eternal torrent right next to me forged an abyss whose depths my eyes dared not measure. Some times I lost myself in a thick grove of trees. Occasionally as I left a valley, a friendly prairie suddenly refreshed my gaze. . . . Nature seemed to take pleasure in opposing herself because I would find her different under many guises in a single place. Toward the east, spring flowers, in the south, autumnal fruit, and in the north, winter ice: nature collected all the seasons in the same spot and reconciled, something unknown anywhere else, the products of the plains and the Alps. (I, 23, p. 77)

Not only did Rousseau inaugurate the description of natural phenomena, but he made nature reflect the observer's state of mind.

A sudden, unexpected storm on lake Meillerie endangers Saint-Preux and Julie while they are taking a boat trip (IV, 17). This natural phenomenon translates perfectly the emotional torment, the metaphorical storm of emotions, that Saint-Preux is suffering. The storm's violence represents the danger that passion poses for these chaste lovers, a danger they recognize only when it has passed:

Slowly the moon rose, the lake calmed down, and Julie suggested we leave. . . . The steady and rhythmic sound of the oars sent me dreaming. The happy sound of the water fowl, retracing for me the pleasures of a past time, made me sad instead of happy. Little by little I felt a growing melancholy that oppressed me. A serene sky, the soft moon beams, the silvery shimmer of the water shining around us, the accumulation of these most agreeable sensations, the very presence of that dear person: nothing could spare my heart a thousand sorrowful reflections. . . .

At that my agitation began to take another direction; a calmer feeling slowly infiltrated into my heart, sentiment overcame despair. I shed abundant tears. Compared to the one I had just left, this state was not without pleasure. I wept a lot, for a long time, and felt better. When I had quite recovered, I went back to Julie's side and I took her hand. She was holding her handkerchief which was soaking wet. Ah, I said to her softly, I see that our hearts have never stopped communicating. It's true, she said in a changed voice; but let this be the last time they speak on such a tone. (IV, 17, pp. 520–21)

Love and Obstacles

The passionate love that Jean-Jacques so eloquently evoked throughout his novel and through his three leading characters was a new phenome-

non. With only a few exceptions, for example Prévost's *Manon Lescaut,*
the eighteenth-century French novel was concerned with libertinage:
sex was routinely depicted as an expression of power, struggle, and
deception. The metaphor of the "war between the sexes" was almost
always implied and often explicitly evoked. The libertine novel, which
reached its apex with Laclos's *Dangerous Liaisons* (1782), was a disheartening but accurate reflection of those aristocratic circles in which marriage was deprecated and infidelity rampant. Every man had a mistress,
it seemed, and wives slept with everyone and anyone except their husbands. It was into this immoral and corrupt society that Rousseau's
paean to sincere, persevering, passionate love fell like a bombshell.

The notion of obstacle permeates this novel, as it did Rousseau's life.
Every character is blocked, caught in an intense emotional dilemma that
cannot be resolved. Obstacles, however, allow the emotion to endure.
The abundant tears that flow so frequently mark both the sadness of
disappointment and the pleasure of maintaining a doomed emotion.
Thus Saint-Preux refuses to marry Claire as Julie had requested: "No
Julie, I will not realize my happiness at the expense of hers. I love her
too much to marry her" (VI, 7, p. 679). He loves Claire, just as she loves
him. Had he not been Julie's lover, Claire would have snapped him up:
"If his misfortune had directed him to me first, he would have been done
for, and whether I am crazy or not, I would have driven him mad" (VI,
2, p. 640). However, their love for Julie prevents either one from finding
another outlet for their feelings: "[W]e grew accustomed to putting you
[Julie] between us, so that unless we annihilate you, we cannot reach
each other. The very familiarity that we were so sweetly accustomed to,
a familiarity which in any other situation would have been dangerous,
was my safeguard. . . . we can not take guilty kisses from the lips where
we once took innocent ones" (640–41).

Early in the novel, Claire, "the inseparable Cousin," helped to check
Julie and Saint-Preux's passion simply by her presence. Later, Julie's
husband and her two children fulfill the same function: "Julie de Wolmar is no longer your former Julie" (i.e., Julie d'Etange; III, 18, p. 363).
Like a complicated set of imbricated moving parts, each character serves
to incapacitate the others' emotional options. The perspicacious Wolmar
sees that Saint-Preux is fixed in one emotion, frozen, as it were, and
incapable of proceeding further: "It is not Julie de Wolmar he loves, it is
Julie d'Etange" (IV, 14, p. 509). This sequence of blockages fits well into
the epistolary format Rousseau has chosen. Unlike traditional narrative
that is retold retrospectively, these letters exist in a continuous present

time frame. Every letter is written in the present tense even though as a whole they all belong in the past. Each letter occupies one point in an ongoing present and remains unchanged by what the future will bring. Each letter is suspended then in the present, just as the plot is trapped in a maze of obstacles that paradoxically both frustrates the characters' desire and eternalizes their act of desiring.

Failure

Perhaps the biggest challenge this novel presents to any interpretation centers around the apparently monumental failure that informs its entire denouement.[7] As she lies dying, Julie confesses that, despite her happy marriage to Wolmar and her beloved children, she has never stopped loving Saint-Preux. Adulterous, extramarital love triumphs, then, over the legal and legitimate love that respects social conventions and religious values. Furthermore, Julie's death plunges Saint-Preux into solitude and despair, and guarantees that they will never enjoy physical happiness together. Even as their mutual love finally triumphs, the lovers are separated and thwarted in a terribly definitive manner. Can any positive message resist so bleak an ending that simultaneously frustrates both traditional morality and individual satisfaction? Is there any cause for optimism here? How can this depressing climax be reconciled with *Julie*'s immense popularity and its ability to exhilarate its readers?

There can be no doubt that this apparent failure establishes a theme dear to Rousseau. What unites Julie and Saint-Preux in the final pages of the novel is a spiritual understanding that transcends any question of carnal knowledge. For Rousseau, love is not limited to its sexual expression. For him the communion of mind and heart far outweighs any contact between bodies. Indeed, I might even go further and argue that sex precludes love. Each of those terms contradicts and excludes the other: for Jean-Jacques love cannot be true when sex is involved. The love of Julie and Saint-Preux provoked such an unprecedented emotional response from its overwhelmed and tearful readers precisely because it existed on such a refined and ethereal plane. Julie dies of love, because of love, rather than from any physical illness after rescuing her son from the freezing lake. Such a noble concept of love is of course completely at odds with the libertine behavior that was so prevalent in the eighteenth-century novel, not to mention the society that novel imitated. Love as an intensely spiritual, nonphysical experience is a major part of the fascination *Julie* exerted on its readers and explains the revolution in attitudes that it announced for both society and literature.

I would further argue that this failure becomes sublime and attractive precisely because it recognizes the possibility of its own failure. Indeed, the novel risks and even depends on failure for its ultimate emotional high, just as Rousseau's own life and psychology did. At Clarens Saint-Preux enjoys the passivity and impotency that any triangular amorous relationship implies, whether that triangle involves Julie, Wolmar, and him or Julie, Claire, and him, just as Jean-Jacques found himself blocked in similar three-sided configurations with Maman or with Sophie d'Houdetot. Such emotional relationships, whatever temporary thrill they may have, preclude any sexual congress: the spiritual aspect of love outweighs the physical. Rousseau's own life, then, displays the same failure that he depicts in his fiction. This autobiographical element explains the source of the emotional intensity that Rousseau captured in his text and that his readers felt in his depiction of tragically doomed love.

Finally, I would connect this failure to the role of imagination as it functions in so many of Rousseau's other works. For Jean-Jacques, expectations usually win out over realizations; what is potential is preferred to what is actual; the unlimited realm of the possible is more attractive than the deceptions inherent in what has already taken place. Jean-Jacques is always too much the idealist and the dreamer. Invariably he chooses the might-yet-happen he can project into the future over any real event that has already taken place because sooner or later he will discover a flaw in the latter that ruins whatever pleasure he found there. What might have been can always be embellished in the eye of his imagination; what has taken place will just as predictably reveal its sorry state.

To appreciate, then, the exalted tenor of what by all appearances should be a depressing denouement, this paradoxical relationship between imagination and failure must be kept firmly in mind. Many of Rousseau's other works end in similar failures. The educational process painstakingly detailed in *Emile* terminates in the sequel with Sophie's infidelity and the breakup of her marriage to Emile. The critique of civilization voiced in the *Discourses* and the *Essay on Language* is ultimately frustrated by the impossibility of leaving society or of finding the lost state of nature. Nonetheless Jean-Jacques succeeds in transforming these ostensible failures into triumphs, but triumphs that exist at another, higher level. In his *Confessions* Rousseau tries to explain how his passion for Sophie d'Houdetot has attained this higher level and transcended the physical: "The brilliance of every virtue embellished in my eyes the idol of my heart; to dirty that divine image would have been to destroy it. I would have been able to commit the crime, it was committed a hundred times in my heart; but debase my Sophie! oh that could never happen! . . . I would have refused to be happy at that price. I loved her too much to want to possess her sexually" (*Oeuvres Complètes,* I, 444). What is amazing is that in *Julie* Jean-Jacques is able to make such a difficult transformation credible and this ethereal passion so satisfying. It is only on second thought that readers question Saint-Preux's bliss at Clarens or even imagine that the relationship among Julie, Wolmar, and Saint-Preux is unhealthy or unstable. Few if any readers hesitate to accept the deep satisfaction that both Saint-Preux and Julie find in their unconsummated passion.

I do not, then, read *Julie*'s ending as an avowal of failure or as a negation. Rather, I find in this tragic denouement Rousseau's personal disappointments transformed into an inspiring triumph that belongs to a higher, spiritual plane and to a level of intensity and feeling that reality cannot match. Fiction literally wins out over fact. The power of Jean-Jacques's imagination redeems the bleakness of ordinary life. The pessimism one expects to find in such a failure only hides a deeper optimism and sets it off even more powerfully than any other strategy. Rousseau enthralled his readers because he depicted the failures that belong to life while simultaneously offering hope that they can be overcome in a deferred hereafter. I imagine that even in their darkest hour Saint-Preux and Julie, and behind them Jean-Jacques himself, are, like Sisyphus, happy.[8]

Chapter Five
The Social Contract (1762)

Published in 1762, *Du Contrat social* (*The Social Contract*) was, and still is, a controversial political text. In the age of monarchy it argued that the authority of the state came from the voluntary association (or contract) of individual men; in an age that disdained the notion of democracy as mob rule and chaos, it stressed the importance of the individual in deciding which laws would bind him; in an age that had little or no experience of government by the people, it offered a model of how self-government could function.[1] The *Contract* addressed many of the issues Rousseau had discussed in the two *Discourses,* which described the corruption of natural man by society and the fundamental injustice that is inherent in social groups. But it brought a new perspective to these questions because now Jean-Jacques was offering an apology of society, a vision of how social living could be superior even to the state of nature. Knowing where Rousseau started and what his previous thinking had been allows us to better appreciate the task he sets for himself, which is to imagine a government and a society that would preserve rather than deny individual freedom.

Despite its radical premises, this treatise did follow in the footsteps of the political theorists who were most influential in the eighteenth century. Rousseau addresses the principal theories but largely to refute them. His book combines a dialogue with the past and a provocative vision of what is possible for the future. One of the most disturbing aspects of the *Contract* is that many modern commentators have seen in it a blueprint for totalitarianism. I do not think this is an accurate interpretation of Rousseau's intentions. Jean-Jacques is, however, a confusing writer who did not always clarify his complex ideas. Without sidestepping this critical issue, I will endeavor to show how Rousseau's political ideas are in fact libertarian, although they, like any other political system, can be perverted into something their author did not intend.

The First Book

Despite his claim to talk practical politics ("taking men as they are and laws as they can be," I, p. 351),[2] Rousseau produces an abstract and theoretical construct to explain how men can live in society without losing the liberty they had before society existed. His conception is elusive, adapting itself to different contexts and escaping easy comprehension. Consequently, it is as difficult to understand Rousseau's meaning as it is facile to distort it.

Jean-Jacques begins with one of his striking, hyperbolic statements: "Man is born free, and everywhere he is in chains. He who believes himself the master of others is in fact more of a slave than they are" (I, 1, p. 351). Rousseau's book will explain how this change came about legally and legitimately. He will argue that although society did take away the absolute freedom that man enjoyed in the state of nature, it gave him in return a limited but more efficient political liberty.

The first chapters rehearse the usual explanations of society's origins: the authority of the father in the family and conquest through war. Conquest, however, cannot produce a legitimate society because it turns those conquered into slaves by depriving them of their liberty, notably the liberty to choose their ruler. Jean-Jacques makes a crucial point here. Liberty is what defines man: "[T]o renounce his liberty is to renounce his quality as a man, his human rights" (I, 4, p. 356). Man can never give up his right to freedom. Consequently, slavery is a type of war; slaves, like any conquered people, always have the right to overthrow their rulers.

How, then, can society be legitimate if neither the model of patriarchy nor the imposition of a conquering government is acceptable? Jean-Jacques claims there is a primitive convention, a fundamental act that constitutes society, an originating gesture that resolves this dilemma. The social contract he will present describes "that form of association which defends and protects with its common strength the person and the property of each member, and in which each individual, as he joins with all the others, obeys only himself and remains just as free as before" (I, 6, p. 360). This *association* is not a simple aggregation of individuals (359). On the contrary, it is of a radically different nature, and this passage to a higher level is what transforms the "natural liberty" of the isolated individual into the "conventional liberty" of social man (360). This transition is effected by the "total alienation of each associate and all his rights to the entire community" (360). Since everyone gives up the same rights, equality is maintained: "the union is as perfect as it can be and no associate has anything to complain about" (361). Rousseau becomes almost cryptic as he develops this symmetrical give-and-take: "Each giving himself to all gives himself to no one"

(361). Each individual holds over others the same rights that he has relinquished to others: "everyone gains the equivalent of what he has lost, and more force to preserve what he has" (361). The balance is neatly symmetrical, with gain compensating loss.

The act of association just described produces "a collective and moral being" (361), called the general will (*volonté générale*), that is composed of all its members, who are an "indivisible part of the whole" (360). The relationship of these indivisible parts to the whole is critical, as is the difference between the whole as a whole (the invisible and the unlocatable general will) and the simple sum of all the constituent members or particular wills. The whole, for Rousseau, is not only greater than the sum of all its parts but is of a different nature. The complexity of this new moral being that is the general will can be seen when Jean-Jacques tries to define it. All he really does is identify it in traditional terms that fail to express this extra quality, this supplementary dimension that is crucial to his concept:

> This public person which is formed by the union of all the other persons took in the past the name of *City* and takes now the name *Republic* or *body politic,* which is called by its members *State* when it is passive, *Sovereign* when it is active, and *Power* when compared to others like it. As for the associates, collectively they take the name *people,* and more precisely are called *Citizens* when they exercise their sovereign authority, and *Subjects* when they submit to the laws of the State. (361–62)

The entity that has stepped out of Rousseau's founding act of association is a terribly complicated one. All the aspects of its nature overlap. Which interactions receive priority? Which contexts help define the true functions of each of these parts?

It is important to understand that Jean-Jacques is not using here the mechanical metaphor that was so frequently employed in eighteenth-century political discourse. Government was often compared to a machine whose parts functioned together or in opposition (i.e., checks and balances), like so many pulleys and levers. These mechanical parts never changed; they remained the same before and after their functioning in the act of government. Rousseau envisions government more like a liquid. Once the drops flow together they cannot be separated or distinguished from one another. The final mixture is a composite whose consistency and density is different from the original brew and from every subsequent state of that mix. Each separate drop transforms the volatile whole no matter how slightly. Every single addition, no matter how microscopic, has its effect. Imagining that this general will can at times be a lumpy liquid containing discrete and not entirely homogeneous particles helps to explain why an individual's particular will might be "contrary or not identical to the general will that he has as a Citizen" (I, 7, p. 363). If we compare the individual's private will to a drop before mixing and the general will to the whole solution containing all the drops, we can understand how one citizen's "self-interest might speak to him differently than the common interest" (363). Nonetheless, the individual must follow the general will: "whoever will refuse to obey the general will shall be obliged to obey by the entire body; this means nothing more than the whole shall force him to be free" (363). For us today, that phrase is unfortunate, ringing with too many bad memories. Forcing someone to be free sounds like tyranny. Chemically speaking, however, a well-mixed liquid does force all its different components to become a single new compound. Although his notion is difficult to explain (but what political theory is not?), Rousseau does make an authentic effort to solve the eternal dilemma of the individual's obligation to obey society's laws vs. his own free will. Rousseau should be judged in the context of his experience and of the problems he considered primary and not anachronistically in the wake of our political failures.

This is the crux of Rousseau's system: how can one be free if he is forced to obey a general will that does not coincide with his own particular will? Earlier Jean-Jacques mentioned the individual who wanted to enjoy the "rights of a citizen" without fulfilling the "duties of a subject" (363). Each member of the state is both subject and citizen, and thus potentially divided between self-interest and the common good. Why do some citizens act selfishly for private gain while others behave generously for the benefit of all? No one has answered that question, but Jean-Jacques tries. The transition from nature to society produced profound changes in man. Justice replaced instinct; morality and the voice of duty supplanted physical impulse and appetites. The advantages of society more than compensate for any disadvantages. In society an individual can develop the faculties, ideas, and sentiments that would have been wasted in the state of nature. Rather than complain about any discrepancy between the particular and the general will, the individual "should unceasingly bless the happy moment that tore him from [the state of nature] forever, and that made an intelligent being and a man out of a stupid and benighted animal" (364). Rousseau draws up the balance sheet in favor of society: "[W]hat man loses by the social contract is his natural liberty and an unlimited right to all that tempts him and that he can reach; what he gains, is civil liberty and the property of [or legitimate title to] all he possesses" (I, 8, 364). This argument climaxes in a phrase that explains what Jean-Jacques means by forcing someone to be free. It also echoes the moral dimension of many of the terms he has already used. Moral liberty is more important than mere physical liberty because it "alone makes man the master of himself; for, the impulses of mere appetite are slavery, and obeying the law that one has prescribed for oneself is liberty" (365). The thorny problem of the general will can best be resolved as a spiritual, almost a theological concept. Commentators who discuss it only in terms of law, logic, or politics are doomed to misrepresent the *soul* of Jean-Jacques's argument.[3]

Despite the example of his own life, Jean-Jacques does not offer an apology of individualism or absolute freedom. Liberty is limited. The radical element of Rousseau's thought, which cannot be ignored, is that individual liberty should be restricted only by laws that citizens have chosen for themselves and not by the whim or decree of a monarch or aristocratic elite. Freedom means ruling over yourself and not being ruled over by others. Freedom is neither chaos nor license. Civilized man is not an animal nor a slave to base desires and appetites. Discipline is what makes him both fully human (civilized and social) and free.

This first book closes with a chapter on property. At first Rousseau seems to be a severe collectivist: "[R]egarding its members, the State is the master of all their goods [possessions] by virtue of the social contract" (I, 9, 365). Subsequent discussion seems to nuance this statement a great deal, however. In the end this chapter really emphasizes individual ownership. In the state of nature, an individual had possessions but no property; the social contract reverses that situation. Rather than taking over individuals' property, the state "assures [those individuals] a legitimate possession, changes usurpation into a real right, and a holding into property" (I, 9, p. 367). Let us recall that Rousseau had condemned private property in the first *Discourse* because it was a usurpation and the first step toward society and inequality; here the social contract undoes that original wrong and makes ownership legitimate. Only by recognizing the authority of the state over private property can the individual enter into full possession and legitimate title of what he claims to own: "Then the owners being considered as the depositaries of state property, their rights [are] respected by all members of the state and maintained by the state's full power against foreigners" (367). Once again, an exchange has taken place. The individual gives up something to the group only to receive something more valuable in return. Rousseau sums up his first book by repeating the exchanges that constitute the social contract and thus establish a legitimate society: "rather than destroying natural equality, the fundamental pact on the contrary substitutes a legitimate and moral equality for the physical inequality that nature gave to men; as a result, while perhaps being unequal in strength or intelligence, they all become equal by agreement and by law" (367).

Of course, these two liberties are not identical. Natural liberty is based on the inequality of the individual's personal strength: he can do whatever he can get away with. He has possession of his goods as long as he can hold on to them. Conventional liberty, on the other hand, makes the weak equal to the strong and assures them legal title to their goods. Most important, it gives them the freedom to enjoy their property.

Book Two

The major topics of the second book are the general will and the legislator. By returning to and expanding many of the points he made in book I about the nature and functioning of the general will, Rousseau nuances that already complex concept. But the price he pays is repetition. The legislator, on the other hand, is a new subject and one that develops naturally out of the discussion of the general will.

The general will "alone" runs the state for "the common good" (II, 1, p. 368). If discord among private interests has made society necessary, only the agreement of those same interests can make society possible. Sovereignty is the general will in action, and the sovereign (Rousseau follows the tradition that allows him to personify the powers of the state; cf. Machiavelli's Prince) is a "collective being" who can "only be represented by himself" (368). The general will, which is concerned with equality, is not always identical to the particular wills, which are concerned with the individual preferences that are most often opposed to equality for all. For this sovereign or general will to exist, the people must participate in self-government. When Rousseau says that sovereignty is inalienable, he means that it can not abdicate its responsibility to rule. Any failure of the people to make their own laws means that the contract and the state are destroyed. "If then the people promise simply to obey [and not to make laws], it dissolves itself by this very act and loses its essence as a people" (II, 1, p. 369).

Just as it is inalienable, so too is the sovereign or general will indivisible. It deals only with general issues and never with specific situations.

The latter are the province of particular wills or, on another level, of "decrees" or "acts of the magistrature." Here Rousseau distinguishes the state, which is animated by the general will or sovereign, from the government, which tends to the daily tasks of making specific laws and enforcing them. Unfortunately it is not until chapter 12 that Rousseau defines the different classes of laws and makes this important distinction evident.

Although the general will is by definition always right, the individual members who comprise that will can be mistaken. "They always desire what is good, but they do not always see it: the people are never corrupt, but they can be mistaken" (II, 3, p. 371). Furthermore, the will of all the people, which "touches on private interests and is only the sum of particular wills," is not identical to the general will, which regards only the common interest. Clearly Rousseau's distinctions and definitions are becoming more abstract even though he promised a practical treatise! Still, all these details are important because they nuance his depiction of sovereignty, and thus what civil freedoms are acquired when natural freedom is renounced.

But what conditions are required to reach this general will as opposed to the will of all or the sum of many particular wills? First, the people, "having been sufficiently informed, deliberates"; second, citizens should not communicate among themselves but deliver their individual and solitary opinion. Individuals reflect alone so they will not be persuaded to sell their vote or favor any individual scheme over the common good. When these conditions are satisfied, "out of the great number of small differences the general will would always emerge and the deliberation would always be valid." This deliberation, however, is not a political debate or even a counting of votes. Rousseau's general will is too much a moral concept or an ideal (should I say unreal?) notion. There is no practical way to determine its presence. Ideal but real, difficult to locate because it is omnipresent in the body politic, this nearly spiritual process is menaced, however, by concrete dangers. Rousseau feared combinations or groups of individuals whose private interests, when combined together, would thwart the common good. More specifically he condemned what today are called pressure groups or lobbies. "But when there are factions, partial associations at the expense of the whole, the will of each of these associations becomes . . . particular as regards the State. . . . then there is no more general will, and the opinion which carries is only a private one" (371–72). "It is crucial then that in order to hear the voice of the general will, there be no partial society [lobby, pressure group] within the State and that each citizen express only his own opinion" (372). Without such precautions, the people can make mistakes and the general will can be thwarted.

Returning to a previous point that seemed to make the state the owner of all property, Rousseau specifies that "by the social contract each individual alienates or surrenders only that portion of his power, goods, or liberty, as is needed by the community" (II, 4, p. 373). The citizen's sacrifice is limited to what the general good requires. Again the notion of exchange appears. The responsibility of the citizen to the state is reciprocal, so that "in fulfilling [these obligations], one cannot work for others without working for himself" (373). However difficult it is to formulate a practical model, in Rousseau's mind self-interest meets the general interest: there is no one "who does not think of himself while voting for all" (373).

An act of sovereignty or of the general will is "a convention of the whole body with each of its members. As a convention it is legitimate because it has as its basis the social contract; equitable, because it is common to everyone; useful, because it has no object other than the general good; and solid, because it is guaranteed by public force and supreme power. As long as the subjects submit only to such conventions, they obey no one but their own will . . . each one toward all and all toward each one" (374–75). Thus Rousseau claims that there is no real "alienation" here but rather "advantageous exchange of an uncertain and precarious existence for a better and safer life; of natural independence for liberty; of the power to harm others for one's own protection; of their power, which others might overcome, for a right that the social union makes invincible" (375).

In chapter 6, Rousseau defines law as the sovereign, which is also to say as the general will. But this general will deals only with general issues, never with specifics. Thus, "when all the people pronounce laws for all the people," the result is an "act that I call a law." Furthermore, Jean-Jacques continues, "when I say that the object of laws is always general, I mean that the law considers its subjects as a body and these actions as abstract, and never a man as an individual nor a specific action" (II, 6, p. 379). Rousseau considers any state ruled by laws a republic. By "republic" he means a legitimate government, because only in such a state are the people sovereign: only in a republic do they themselves enact the laws they obey.

The end of this chapter provides the transition to the book's other topic, the legislator. Here Rousseau enumerates a number of pointed questions about the practical matter of knowing the real general will: "In themselves, the people always want what is good, but by themselves they do not always see it. The general will is always right, the judgment that guides it is not always enlightened" (380). The practical need for some mechanism to distinguish the general will and to show citizens the good they really want brings us to the legislator.

Rousseau's legislator is an ideal and almost chimerical being. He has a superior intelligence, knows men's passions but is above them, understands our human nature without sharing it. He is almost divine: "It requires Gods to give laws to men" (II, 7, p. 381). This lawgiver will have to change men's nature and transform that solitary being who existed in the state of nature into a part of the higher moral order that is society. Finally, the legislator guides the state without really belonging to it. The obstacles he has to overcome and the qualities he has to possess make Rousseau's legislator an unreal, superhuman presence. Obliged to use a paradoxical authority that "can enlist [the people] without violence and persuade without convincing," the legislator nonetheless assures that men "obey with liberty and wear docilely the yoke of public felicity" (383). Returning to the religious tone of the book's opening, Rousseau ends this chapter by envisioning the lawgiver as a prophet and a voice of God. His is a self-validating mission whose success borders on the miraculous. Looking back over this chapter, I have little doubt as to why Rousseau is so difficult to understand. The rhetorical exuberance and the stylistic imprecision that make these ideas so fuzzy have given rise to the widely divergent interpretations that surround *The Social Contract*.

In contrast, the final five chapters are rather conventional in tone and content. Rousseau talks in typical eighteenth-century terms about such topics as the ratios between land mass, populations, and government efficiency. In a paragraph that recalls Montesquieu, he talks about the importance of "mores, customs, and especially public opinion" (II, 12, p. 394). When shared by the whole community, these moral values constitute the most important type of law because they "are engraved not on stone or brass, but in the hearts of citizens; and . . . comprise the true constitution of the state" (394).

Book Three

Book III contains some rather traditional discussions and some very radical concepts about government. Rousseau follows in the footsteps of

Montesquieu, for example, when he voices a few typical eighteenth-century notions about government. He discusses in chapters 4, 5, and 6 the usual types of government (democracy, aristocracy, monarchy); how Montesquieu's concepts, like virtue and moderation, fit different kinds of polities; and how physical factors, like climate, soil fertility, and population, influence the running of a state (chap. 8). Like Montesquieu, Jean-Jacques believes that each type of government is suitable to a different size and population (chap. 8). He attempts to determine with mathematical precision the ratios and proportions of interacting forces within the state (chap. 1). In the relativist tradition, Jean-Jacques claims that any form of government can be good, depending on what its citizens want. The test of good government—and here Rousseau's radicalism begins to appear—is whether it promotes the "conservation and prosperity of its members" (III, 9, p. 320). Other things being equal, the government under which "the citizens reproduce and multiply more is infallibly the best." The chapter ends defiantly: "Calculators, now it is up to you: count, measure, compare."

More interesting, however, are those passages in which Rousseau advances radical notions, even if they seem tame today. His contemporaries had no trouble recognizing the revolutionary implications of these ideas. Jean-Jacques separates government from sovereignty or the general will or the original contract that made society possible. He defines government as "an intermediary body established between the subjects and the Sovereign for their mutual interaction, and charged with executing laws and maintaining both civil and political liberty" (III, 1, p. 396). A second definition identifies it as "the supreme administration" and "the legitimate exercise of executive power." Government is an abstraction, a moral entity that must be distinguished from its real incarnation, the magistrate who is "the man or the group charged with this administration." Government, then, has two faces, one theoretical, the other practical. Moreover, it is a separate corporation within the body politic; it has its own collective existence. More importantly (and more dangerously), it has its own will, which is not the same as the general will (or the sovereign) of the whole state. Any specific government might at some time have a particular will that does not reflect the general will of the whole society (III, 2).

This gap between sovereign and government is gradually widened. The sovereign is the legislative power, whereas government is the executive. The former promulgates laws that are unanimous expressions of the general will; the latter deals in specific decrees and judicial acts that concern particular cases. This distinction is capital for Rousseau's theory even though it is difficult to draw that thin line between the corporeal presence of an actual government and the ethereal essence of the disembodied general will inspiring it.

Rousseau's ideal state becomes more and more complex as he imagines all these distinctions among the various aspects of a government's functioning. Throughout this book Jean-Jacques refers to situations in which the social contract is violated and the state dissolved. He knows, therefore, how difficult it is to have a good government, one that works for the best interests of its members. Although a practical necessity, any government is by definition a danger to the liberty of its citizens. Sovereign power, which means true liberty, presides only "when the people are assembled" and ready to legislate those laws which alone "are authentic acts of the general will" (III, 12, p. 425). If it was possible to assemble the people in ancient Rome, why is doing so considered a chimera today?

Such assemblies should be regularly scheduled ("fixed and periodic") so that the sovereign can by its very presence affirm its continued support for past laws and decide whether the government accurately reflects the general will of its citizens. Government loses all its authority as soon as the people assemble and for as long as the sovereign is in session. The citizens together are sovereign, and general will is the supreme authority; everything else must bend to them, or liberty and the conditions of the primitive contract are lost.

At this point Rousseau introduces a discussion on representation that brings out the radical element in his contrast between sovereignty and government.[4] Citizens cannot be represented, even by elected deputies, without losing their liberty and destroying the state. Sovereignty can only be exercised, never given away. Citizens have to participate in governing themselves or they automatically lose their freedom. For me this is the positive and democratic meaning of that unfortunate phrase in which Jean-Jacques spoke about forcing someone to be free: being free requires that the citizen participate in his own self-governance, or else he loses his freedom. Rousseau develops an extended metaphor that contrasts an inert metal (the French term he uses, *argent,* means both money and silver) with a living body. The state is near ruin when citizens choose to "use their purse rather than their body" for public service (III, 15, p. 428). "In a really free state, citizens do everything with their own arms and nothing with money" (429). To be free, citizens cannot delegate any duty that relates to their sovereignty; they have to embrace it themselves. Any representation, any substitution eliminates freedom and introduces slavery. Money of course is the ultimate substitution: a citizen buys the duty he is unwilling to perform. "It is the hurly-burly of business and the arts, it is the greedy desire for gain, it is softness and love for commodities that transform personal service into money" (429). Punning on the words *argent* (silver and money) and *fers* (iron and leg irons), Jean-Jacques denounces the irresponsible citizen who refuses to participate and thus to assume his own freedom: "Give silver/money and soon you will have (leg)iron(s). That word 'finance' is a slave's word" (429).

Rousseau opposes elections because they give only the illusion of sovereignty. Elected representatives cannot represent anyone because the general will cannot be anything but itself, which is to say all the members of the state active and assembled. "Any law that the People in person have not ratified is null; in fact, it is not even a law" (430). Although many have criticized Rousseau's general will as incipient totalitarianism, I understand it as a very demanding concept of direct, participatory democracy:[5] "As soon as anyone says about state business, 'what does it matter to me?' we have to recognize that the state is lost" (429).

The final chapter introduces an even more radical idea. The assembled people, as sovereign, can change their form of government whenever they wish. Government depends on the sovereign for its authority and not vice versa. Thus "the depositories of executive power are not the masters of the people but its officers, and the people can establish or destitute them whenever it chooses to do so" (III, 18, p. 434). In Rousseau's state, the power flows up from the people and not down from the ruler, even if he is a king by divine right. Monarchy offers only one of several possible forms of government. Now the definition of good government given earlier takes on its revolutionary significance. Citizens can judge for themselves whether their government is best for them, and they can change it if they are dissatisfied. Indeed, whether to continue the present form of government is one of the mandatory questions the citizens ask when they assemble as sovereign. Without explicit and continuous affirmation, government becomes illegitimate. Deliberating as the general will, citizens have the right to change their government whenever they so choose.

Behind the obtuse tone of its frequent abstractions and its commonplaces on types of government, this book hides a profoundly radical discourse that subverts monarchical authority and invests the people, the citizens and subjects of every state, with a very modern concept of political hegemony. When the authorities in France and elsewhere con-

demned and banned *The Social Contract* in 1762, they clearly understood
the implications of Rousseau's thinking for their political system.

Book Four

The fourth book focuses on how any state degenerates when the general
will is unable to express itself clearly or when its citizens fail to cooperate
to produce a valid general will, which amounts to the same thing. This
is a rather pessimistic conclusion to the *Social Contract,* which at first
promised a theoretical system of how an ideal state could function. It is
curious to note how often Jean-Jacques's optimistic schemes—Clarens
in *Julie,* the marriage of Emile and Sophie in *Emile,* and here in the *Social
Contract*—end in disappointment and apparent disaster.

The first chapter of book 4 details the many and various dangers that
can render the general will inoperative. As long as the citizens recognize
their solidarity, "there are no contradictory or confusing interests, the
common good is clearly visible everywhere and requires nothing but
common sense to be recognized" (IV, 1, p. 437).[6] Simple country folk are
more likely to avoid dangerous dissensions than are sophisticated city
dwellers; Jean-Jacques is only echoing a point he made in his *Discourses*.
Ambitious and exceptional individuals like Cromwell can thwart the
general will, but so can excessive self-interest in ordinary citizens.
Whenever "the social link is broken in [individuals'] hearts, the most
vile self-interest boldly assumes the sacred name of public good; then,
the general will falls silent" (IV, 1, p. 438). Moral degeneration leads to
the loss of civic consciousness that destroys the very soul of the state:

> But when the social connection comes undone and the State weakens;
> when private interests begin to win out and small groups influence the
> larger one, the common interest is altered and finds opponents. Unanim-
> ity no longer reigns in the votes, the general will is nothing but the will
> of all. This gives rise to contradictions and disputes, and even the best
> advice is contested. (IV, 1, p. 438)

Several chapters that appear to be odd digressions on the history of
Rome relate nonetheless to the overall theme of this book. They demonstrate how even Rome, which remained an ideal for Rousseau, was unable
to avoid the corruption of its general will as expressed in its *comices,* the regular assemblies at which Roman citizens met to conduct public business.

The two final chapters are most interesting because they relate the question of the state's corruption and degeneration to moral causes. Recalling the proportional analogies he used earlier, Jean-Jacques equates public opinion and the general will: "Just as the statement of the general will resides in the law, so too the statement of public judgment resides in censure" (IV, 7, p. 458). Rousseau is using the word *censure* in the sense of that Roman official the censor, who was a guardian of public morals. Every people's mores exercise a critical influence on their laws and political life. Mores and laws are interdependent; the corruption of one spreads to the other. The general will can therefore be affected negatively by unsuitable attitudes: "[A]lthough the law does not regulate mores, legislation does give birth to them; when laws grow weak, mores degenerate. But then the decisions of the Censors cannot accomplish what the force of laws has not already accomplished" (IV, 7, p. 459). While short and a bit cryptic, this chapter reveals Rousseau's insight into the moral causes of political decline.

The last chapter, on the need for civil religion and the dangers of existing religions, continues this discussion of the intangible side of politics. For Jean-Jacques, the best type of religion would be a return to the principles of Jesus and the gospel, a religion without dogma, "without Temples, altars, rituals, limited to a purely internal cult of the Supreme Being and to the eternal obligations of duty" (IV, 8, p. 464). In contrast, Rousseau attacks Catholicism ("Roman Christianity"); "founded on errors and lies, it deceives men, makes them credulous and superstitious, and drowns the real cult of divinity in vain ceremonies. It is once again bad when, becoming exclusive and tyrannical, it makes a people bloodthirsty and intolerant" (IV, 7, p. 465). Although he concentrates his anger on Catholicism, Rousseau is hostile to all formal and institutional religions. Christianity weakens the state by focusing man's attention on the other world: "[T]he Christian's fatherland is not in this world. He does his duty, it is true, but he does it with profound indifference as to whether his efforts succeed or not" (466). The Christian accepts God's will, whatever happens to his country. Such otherworldliness undermines the citizen's duty to participate actively and fully in the general will and in the sovereignty of the state. In case of war, Christians "do their duty, but without any passion for winning. They know how to die but not how to conquer." They would make poor soldiers against the Romans or Spartans, who were inspired by a "burning love of glory and fatherland." Because Christianity "preaches servitude and dependency" and has an innate tendency toward tyranny, "true Christians are made to be slaves . . . ; this short life has too little value in their eyes" (467).

Rousseau therefore proposes a purely civil religion that will keep the most positive dogmas of traditional Christianity: "[T]he existence of a Divinity that is powerful, intelligent, that does good, that is provident, prudent; the life to come; reward for good and punishment for evil; the sanctity of the Social Contract and Laws" (468). It will have one negative dogma: total hostility toward intolerance. Rousseau sees religious extremism as the cause and counterpart of civil and political intolerance: "It is impossible to live in peace with people you think are damned. To love them would mean you hate God who punishes them. You have either to convert them or torment them. Wherever theological intolerance is allowed, it necessarily has civil consequences" (469). Rousseau sees religion as a rival to the sovereign, a threat to the general will, and a faction that rebels against the legitimate political authority. With this bitter attack against religion the entire *Social Contract* concludes.

Overview

Just as book 4 did, the *Social Contract* as a whole leaves a very mixed and confusing impression. It begins as an abstract and theoretical consideration of an ideal form of government, yet it often gets lost in practical matters and overly specific historical examples. It offers some interesting concepts, such as that of the general will or the legislator, but either drops them in mid-discussion or depicts them so abstractly or metaphorically that the reader has difficulty imagining how they would function in reality. The subtle argument of how the general will involves and transcends those particular wills that (temporarily) oppose it, or how it is not to be confused with the will of all, seems to degenerate into that old principle of majority rules: "Except as regards this original contract, the voice of the majority always speaks for everyone else" (IV, 2, p. 440). Finally, numerous points are unclear or can be interpreted variously. Rousseau has been particularly unlucky in that later commentators have read the *Social Contract* as a blueprint for totalitarian excesses, such as the Reign of Terror during the French Revolution and Nazi Germany under Hitler. Rousseau should not be blamed anachronistically for aberrations that he could not have foreseen. Still, he is responsible for ambiguous ideas that do seem to provide the ideological pedigree for subsequent political and human disasters.

On the positive side of the ledger, however, I insist on noting that Rousseau was a convinced democrat in an age of monarchy. Even as forward looking a document as our own Constitution and as liberal a group as our Founding Fathers register only as moderate, middle-of-the-road republicans on the political spectrum, whereas Rousseau stands isolated as an extreme democrat. He spoke up for the common man in an age of aristocratic privilege. He dared to suggest that political power originated in the union and cooperation of common men when other theorists barely recognized them as anything more than mobs and subjects. Whatever its shortcomings—and they are many—the *Social Contract* marks an important step in the evolution of modern political thought.

Chapter Six
Emile (1762)

Emile, the most controversial of Rousseau's works, incurred the anathema of the Protestant Petit Conseil in Geneva and the Catholic Sorbonne in Paris on its publication in 1762. Civil condemnation by Parlement followed immediately. Fear of legal pursuit forced Jean-Jacques into exile. Once considered so confrontational and incendiary that it was burned in public, this book has lost most of its ability to shock. In this chapter I will try to recapture some of that lost spark.

Pedagogy

Not too long ago *Emile* was required reading for courses in colleges of education. Directly influencing such innovative educators as Maria Montessori, Rousseau's pedagogical insights seem so commonplace today that we can easily fail to recognize how radical they were in their time. Most were implemented, in theory if not always in practice, by the early twentieth century. What remains most potent in *Emile,* however, is the way Rousseau connects pedagogy to his moral and political concerns. Indeed, for many critics, *Emile* is much more than pedagogy and politics. It is Rousseau's "most important philosophical work," his most complex and complete statement about man in society.[1]

Preceding the pedagogical treatise proper is a philosophical preamble whose opening paragraph presents an explosive condemnation of man's miseducation:

> Everything is good coming from the hands of the author of things; everything degenerates in the hands of man. He forces one soil to nourish the products of another; one tree to bear the fruits of another. He mixes and confuses climates, elements, seasons. He mutilates his dog, his horse, his slave. He upsets everything, he disfigures everything: he likes deformities, monsters. He wants nothing to be as nature made it, not even man; he wants to break man as he breaks a horse; he wants to prune man like a tree in his garden.[2]

In addition to the ornamental disfigurement of animals (cropping horses' tails and dogs' ears), mutilation means either literal or figurative castration for men. Equally disturbing is the reference to the elaborate topiary work that was typical of French formal gardens, pruning that cut ordinary hedges and trees into fantastical shapes. The violence of these mutilations, disfigurements, and miscegenations is shattering.

Rousseau proposes at first the education of a man, not of a citizen.[3] This stark alternative must be softened. Later Rousseau will admit that Emile is being educated to take his place in society as a citizen: "Emile is not made to remain solitary for ever. A member of society, he must fulfill its obligations. Made to live among men he must know them" (654). Not only will he live in society but Emile will participate in its governance. The tutor exhorts him: "If the Prince or the State calls you to serve the fatherland, drop everything and go satisfy the honorable function of Citizen in whatever position you are assigned" (860).

For the moment, however, this disassociation of man and citizen reveals Rousseau's deepest aim in *Emile:* to reconcile the natural man of the state of nature, which no longer exists, with the actual man or citizen who does live in society and who must deal with the social and political alienation that living in society entails. Man exists for himself alone, while the citizen lives for the state. Educating a man is an ideal process, whereas educating a citizen is tainted by existing human institutions. Citizens are trained to fill the place assigned to them by society; men, on the other hand, are educated to realize their personal value. A citizen receives a limited, technical instruction while a human being deserves an authentic liberal arts education (248–50). Rousseau's pedagogy is frankly impractical: "our real study is the human condition" (252). How to live is what Jean-Jacques will teach his student.

This preamble identifies two specific educational practices that Jean-Jacques wants to reform. First he condemns the swaddling clothes that were tightly wrapped around the limbs of newborn babies and kept them immobile. Rousseau denounces this maillot as unhealthy because it constricts infants so much they become deformed, hunchbacked, and lame (254), and as unjust because it places adults' convenience above the infant's basic human rights. Swaddled babies are "more unfortunate than a criminal in irons" (254); they are forced to live in "chains" and "torments" (255). Jean-Jacques even describes one such infant as "crucified," suffocating to death. Human institutions like the maillot explain why "civil man is born, lives, and dies in slavery" (253). As a remedy

Jean-Jacques will propose in *Emile* a natural pedagogy that accentuates living in freedom: "Living is not just breathing, it is moving; it is using our organs, our senses, our physical faculties, all the parts of our body that give us the feeling that we exist." Dressing an infant might seem innocuous, but in Jean-Jacques's hands it turns into a powerful critique of dehumanizing social behavior.

The second cultural practice he denounces is the failure of eighteenth-century mothers to breast-feed their babies. In aristocratic circles, which followed the royal example, children were not directly raised by their parents. Usually they were sent out to a wet nurse at birth. If as adolescents they were not educated away from home, they did nonetheless live quite separately from their parents. In contrast, around the middle of the century bourgeois mothers began to have the leisure to devote themselves to caring for their children. Jean-Jacques articulated perfectly this new attitude toward children and championed the family virtues of the bourgeois home. Rousseau noticed the close connection between breast-feeding and maternal bonding: "[T]here is no substitute for maternal involvement" with children (257). Domestic motherhood stands opposed to the social whirl that distracted noblewomen from rearing their children. "But when mothers deign to feed their children themselves, social mores will be reformed on their own, the sentiment of nature will be reborn in all hearts, and the state will be repopulated. This initial point, this single point will accomplish all that. The appeal of domestic life is the best antidote to a corrupt culture" (258). Like the use of the maillot, breast-feeding is a moral issue. Changing these practices would produce spiritual regeneration: "Thus from this single abuse corrected, a general reformation will result. Soon nature will have recovered all its rights. Let women become mothers once again, and soon men will become fathers and husbands" (258). When women assume their rightful place in the family, men will return to their domestic obligations and abandon their wayward habits. Adultery, which was endemic in aristocratic circles, would then disappear, in Rousseau's estimation.

To modern feminists Jean-Jacques seems reactionary when he encourages women to abandon society and return to the home. Few women in the eighteenth century had any real independence, however. They usually enjoyed their fortune and status through some man, a father, a husband, a brother, or a lover. Furthermore, running a large bourgeois household then was the equivalent of managing a small business today. By exalting motherhood Rousseau in fact gave women unprecedented status and importance. A long note that recognized their primary role in educating their children also assigned them a critical task (245–46). For Jean-Jacques it was women and not men who held the key to society's moral rejuvenation. Even if it required him to "brave the empire of fashion and the shouts of the fair sex" (258), Rousseau would subordinate current feminist concern with economic parity or job equality to moral reform and family values.

After laying out his cards, so to speak, in the preamble, Jean-Jacques formally introduces his pedagogical treatise. His enterprise is ideal: "[I]nstead of doing what is necessary, I will make an effort to say it" (264). This fictional experiment is based on Emile, "an imaginary student" whom the author will tutor.

The pedagogical presentation of book 1 is not well constructed. Rousseau often drops an idea, only to pick it up again in a different context, many pages later; or he loses his train of thought and slides off into digressions. Nonetheless, his ideas are provocative. Many were at the forefront of progressive pedagogical thought in his time.[4] Here I can mention only a few, for there is not enough space to delve into all their nuances.

Choosing a tutor and a wet nurse presents a problem. Ideally, the parents should perform both tasks themselves. No amount of money is adequate to recompense a good tutor. More than a job, tutoring is a sacred duty for either the father or his best friend, as well as a lifelong commitment (265). In an imperfect world, however, compromises must be made (273). Although he despises doctors and their "lying art" (270), Jean-Jacques prizes good health, which depends on a vegetarian diet and cleanliness, even to the point of bathing in cold water all year long (274–75, 278). Pure country air is better than the fetid atmosphere of the city (276–78), which is "the abyss of the human species" where overcrowding produces both "infirmities of the body as well as vices of the soul" (277). Jean-Jacques repeats his condemnation of the maillot. A baby's clothes should be large and loose and "leave all his limbs in liberty" (278). Free in his clothes, every baby should be allowed to crawl about and so develop his muscles as well as his enjoyment of freedom.

Liberty is always both the end and the means. The tutor does not command, he allows the student to decide and develop on his own (266). Rousseau instructs the tutor to "[p]repare well in advance the reign of liberty" (282). Free of physical deformity, free of habits that might limit or constrain, free of any physical dependency or weakness, the child progresses toward "the state of always being master of himself," which is the maximum amount of freedom anyone can enjoy.

A discussion of language, always a concern of Rousseau's, concludes this first book. Although Jean-Jacques, following the Lockean tradition, considers the infant a tabula rasa who must learn everything (280), he also believes the baby possesses an innate, natural language. "Children speak before knowing how to speak"; their "language is not articulated, but it is accentuated, sonorous, and intelligible" (285). Infants understand not the sense but the accent of words. For both Rousseau's fictional infant and his ideal language, cognition and signification are subordinate to emotion and intuition.

Crying is at once a manifestation of this original language and the child's introduction to socialization: "[H]ere is forged the first link in the long chain that constitutes the social order" (286). An infant cries to express his needs. If punished for expressing those needs, the infant experiences injustice. If, on the other hand, adults respond too readily to his cries, the baby becomes a tyrant. Beseeching turns into ordering: infants "begin by seeking assistance, they end up by being obeyed. Thus out of their own weakness, which comes first from feeling their own dependency, is born the idea of empire and domination" (287). Even newborns are involved in this struggle of weakness that begets resentment that in turn leads to the desire to dominate others. The origins of injustice date from man's earliest experiences in society.

Returning to his antithesis of city and country, Rousseau claims that country kids, who are also taller, stronger, and healthier, enunciate better than their urban counterparts, who mumble (292–97). Mumbling is not an innocent linguistic tic; it is, rather, a potential vice. A child who speaks clearly and intelligibly can speak for himself. He has no need of an intermediary or interpreter and thus avoids the risk of having his words falsified (295). Freedom of expression for Rousseau, who was himself haunted by the fear of misinterpretation, is not simply a question of content. More importantly and quite literally, it deals with the issue of speaking in your own voice and making yourself heard.

A lengthy book 2 deals with adolescence, from the time when the infant learns to speak, to about age 12. This book is also loosely constructed, with Rousseau repeating himself and indulging his penchant for extended digressions. Nonetheless, I propose organizing the material into three large sections.

The first explores the connections among suffering, happiness, and freedom. "Suffering is the first thing [Emile] should learn" (300). Both senses of the term are operative: Emile should undergo pain as well as learn how to put up with inconveniences. Only by accepting the hard-

ships that the natural order imposes can Emile be free. Thus the child
should play freely and risk the bumps and hurts that rough playing
entails. Otherwise he will be forever timid, unaccustomed to cold and
rain, incapable of living as he chooses because he fears bodily harm.

In a moving paean to adolescence (302), Jean-Jacques begs that children be treated like children and not like miniature adults. Childhood
has to be recognized as a unique time of life. "Men, be human. . . . Love
youth; encourage its games, its pleasures, its amiable instinct. . . .
Fathers, do you know the moment when death awaits your children?"
(302). Jean-Jacques repeats something he said in the first book, that half
of all children in the eighteenth century died before the age of eight
(259)! In the face of such high infant mortality, he wants childhood to
be a happy time. If children must die young, they will at least have
enjoyed their brief life (306).

Imagination produces human misery. Reduce the child's expectation
of happiness and it is easier for him to be happy: "O man! shrink your
existence inside yourself and you will no longer be miserable" (308).
Freedom is internal and depends on attitude. Since he accepts the natural order and resists the insatiable urges that society encourages, "the
truly free man desires only what he can do, and does only what he
wants" (309). On this point Jean-Jacques disagrees with the poet:
when our reach exceeds our grasp we experience a dissatisfaction that
destroys our freedom because then we become the prisoners of desires
we cannot satisfy. "Your liberty and your power extend only as far as
your natural strength and not beyond; all the rest is only slavery, illusion, prestige" (308).

The second section sets out Rousseau's famous notion of "negative"
education, of knowing how to lose rather than gain time (323). It is
more effective to go slowly and learn basic mental operations than to
cover quickly material that children cannot absorb. Instead of seeking
such lofty abstractions as virtue and truth, Rousseau proposes a much
more pragmatic goal: to "protect the heart from vice and the mind from
error" by teaching through direct experience and concrete objects (323).
Lessons are based "more in actions than in talk" (333). The notion of
incorporating the child's own experiences into his instruction is perhaps
Jean-Jacques's most important contribution to modern pedagogy. He
offers a series of examples that illustrate how to do so, the most famous
being the scene in which Robert the gardener teaches Emile about property rights and injustice. Because he proposes direct knowledge of
things and not of words, which are only secondhand reflections of pri-

mary experiences, Jean-Jacques opposes early foreign language instruction. Incapable of real reflection, children would learn only terms and external signs, becoming dictionaries without understanding the reality behind words (347). Similarly, children confuse geography, which should be grounded in a direct contact with the land, with the maps and globes that only represent (and hence falsify) physical reality. In pedagogy as in politics, Rousseau fears this split between reality and the conventional, arbitrary, human signs we use to designate reality.

Long before Piaget did so, Rousseau realized that children are not ready to learn abstractions before a certain age and that to attempt such instruction too soon is fruitless. This period of apparent delay is really a time to prepare "a storehouse of knowledge" (351), or rather of experiences that will subsequently become knowledge. By patiently awaiting the proper moment, Jean-Jacques's "inactive method" (359) will fuel the child's own desire to learn once the spark of interest has been struck. Self-motivation alone can sustain authentic learning: "The immediate interest, that is the great motivation, the only one that leads far and safe" (358).

Rousseau also denigrates memorization and "useless" reading. In a close analysis similar to what he proposed elsewhere for Lully's Armide and Molière's Alceste, he condemns the fables of La Fontaine, which at the time were widely used as pedagogical tools. He finds them contrary to reality, confusing to children, and morally perverse.

The third section elaborates the notion of negative education in a way that deserves a separate heading. Rousseau calls such education the art of "being ignorant" (370): he wants to develop not knowledge itself (science) but the instrument by which we acquire knowledge, our own body. This is *la raison sensitive* (370), cognition developed by sense stimuli. Our feet, hands, and eyes are our teachers long before books are. Jean-Jacques's emphasis on learning through the senses explains why he is so attentive to good health and physical coordination. Emile will combine "strength of body and that of the mind; the reason of a scholar with the strength of an athlete" (362). Rousseau's ideal student is far from current and unfortunately too-prevalent stereotypes of the muscle-bound dolt and the puny "brain."

Rousseau examines each of the five senses in turn. Emile's sense of touch, for example, is sharpened by nocturnal activities without benefit of artificial light. As a corollary these exercises increase Emile's freedom because he learns to be independent, doing for himself and doing without external assistance. "What! always machines! Who guarantees that they will follow you everywhere just in case? For myself I prefer that Emile possess eyes at the tips of his fingers rather than in a candle shop" (381).

Book 2 ends triumphantly with an enthusiastic portrait of Emile as he finishes this unusual course of study. Isn't it, Jean-Jacques asks rhetorically, "a sweet and charming spectacle to behold a handsome child, content and serene, with a bright merry eye and an open, smiling countenance, all of it prepared by playing at the most serious things or profoundly occupied with the most frivolous amusements?" (423). Jean-Jacques fairly glows with paternal pride as he enumerates the virtues of his ideal 12-year-old who combines the best of town and country without either's defects. This negative education has brought Emile far. Not only is he capable of acting politically, but he has transcended class barriers. His merits and talents easily overcome any social disadvantage or prejudice. "He is made to guide, to govern his equals: talent and experience take the place of right and authority. Give him the clothes and the name you choose, it makes no difference. He will come out first anywhere, he will become the leader of others. They will always feel his superiority over them. Without wanting to command he will be the master, they will obey without knowing they obey" (423).

Book 3 covers the short but critical period just before Emile reaches puberty, when adolescent sexual urges will distract him from any thoughts of learning (435–36). This age is "the most precious in life" (427), when the child's desires are in balance with his strengths. "No imaginary need torments him . . . [;] his desires are no longer than his arm" (426). This is childhood's golden age, and it recalls that fictional state of nature where Rousseau placed his natural man.

The bulk of this book is devoted to illustrating Rousseau's concept of useful education (429). This is practical education, emphasizing "accurate and clear ideas" (435) rather than the recital of trivial facts. How Jean-Jacques would pillory today's fill-in-the-blank mentality and multiple-choice exams! He prefers actions to words, doing to telling: "You have to speak as much as possible in actions and only say what you cannot do" (451). He reminds the tutor to base his lesson on the student's abilities and not to teach a prearranged, one-size-fits-all syllabus.

As in the previous books, Jean-Jacques weaves in and out of his main topic with both digressions and fictionalized anecdotes. Among the latter, two stand out. In one, Emile learns that astronomy is useful when, lost in the woods near Montmorency, he reorients himself by the sun (448–50). In the other, whose undertone is ambiguous, Emile exposes a

carnival trick with magnetic ducks, only to be fooled himself the following day. Critics have emphasized the troublesome quality of this anecdote: the whole moral lesson is based on trickery; the action is artificial
and stilted (even for Rousseau); the tutor, who always preaches advance
preparation, seems strangely unready and complacent; and Emile is cru-
elly humiliated in public (437–41). Although a hidden agenda is possible here,[5] this anecdote does illustrate Rousseau's avowed point that the
student learns best when he is participating in the learning experience
and when he recognizes how useful knowledge can be to him personally.

Usefulness is the key concept throughout, even as Jean-Jacques
repeats ideas he has presented before. Concrete objects, real things are
superior to mere words in teaching geography: "[W]hy all these repre-
sentations! Why don't you begin by showing him the object itself?"
(430). Later, he says, "[N]ever substitute the sign for the thing. . . . the
sign absorbs the child's attention and makes him forget the thing represented" (434). And again, "Things, things! I can never repeat it enough,
we give too much power to words. With our talky education we are only
producing talkers" (447). Rousseau prefers doers to talkers, things to
words, the concrete to the abstract. "To fit him out with a few vain
instruments which he will never use, you take away from him man's
most universal instrument which is his common sense" (445). From
words to instruments, the link is clear. Jean-Jacques prefers that men
use their own limbs rather than tools: "[T]he more ingenious our tools
are, the more our organs become gross and clumsy; to the degree we
gather machines around us, we no longer find them in us" (442–43). In
addition to its literal meaning, "machine" was a common eighteenth-
century synonym for the human body.

Rousseau, a voracious reader himself, then exclaims, "I hate books"
(454). The only one he allows Emile to read is *Robinson Crusoe* because
DeFoe's shipwrecked sailor was alone on an isolated island that approxi-
mated the state of nature. Like Jean-Jacques the pedagogue, the solitary
Robinson is interested only in what is useful.

Jean-Jacques returns to the issue of signs vs. reality as he condemns
modern economics. Money is a "conventional equality" that replaces
"natural equality" so that the exchange of different materials, which is
the essence of society, can take place (461). Barter is an authentic
exchange of real objects. In contrast, money only represents authentic
objects and their real value. The transactions money makes possible are
therefore only illusions or fictions that take place at a remove from actu-
ality. Grounded in falseness, almost in fraud, money has deleterious

moral effects. Can we explain to children "how signs cause us to neglect things, and how money gives birth to all the fantasies of [public] opinion" (462)?

Despite his idealization of nature and condemnation of society, Jean-Jacques admits that Emile is being educated to live in society and not in the state of nature. Learning how to deal with his fellow men will therefore be part of his study (467). Earlier contrasts between natural man and the citizen have to be modified. Emile is being trained to retain as much of the natural state as possible even though he will be a part of modern society with all of its inevitable failings.

The abstract discussion of money now becomes concrete as Rousseau fiercely denounces wealth and the gap between the rich and the poor. Although some critics harp on Rousseau's potential for totalitarianism, I insist on pointing out how democratic and courageous he is when he criticizes these abuses. "Man is the same in all states; the rich do not have a larger stomach than the poor and do not digest any better than they do; the master does not have longer or stronger arms than his slave; an aristocrat is not more grand than a man of the people; finally, all natural needs being the same everywhere, the means of satisfying them should be equal" (468). Absent such equality, "this [social] order is subject to inevitable revolutions" (469). He even compares to brigands the wealthy who live off their investments and do not work (470).

For Jean-Jacques, every individual has a personal obligation to be useful to the state. This duty cannot be satisfied by anyone else, nor can it be paid off with money: "[H]e who eats in idleness what he has not earned himself is stealing it" (470). Everyone must fulfill this obligation personally, or justice will disappear from the state. "Working is then the indispensable duty of every social man. Rich or poor, powerful or weak, the idle citizen is a scoundrel."

Consequently Emile learns a trade. Not, however, one in the corrupting luxury arts, not one that is sedentary or effeminate (476), not one requiring a base and odious soul (473), but a trade that would be useful to Robinson Crusoe (474), "in which the hands work more than the head, and which does not lead to wealth, but allows you to do without [money]" (471). Having a trade means independence and freedom. The artisan is not dependent on fortune or other men because he is mobile and able to hire out his skill (470). "He depends only on his work; he is as free as the laborer [i.e., the unskilled worker who is attached to the land or to a master] is a slave." This encomium of manual crafts condemns aristocratic and bourgeois prejudice just as it extols the value of a job well done (477, 480). Consistent with his rejection of signs that replace things, Jean-Jacques exalts the product of the skilled artisan's *travail* (work), the well-wrought object, over *titres* (titles) or empty words. Titles are false values that attempt to disguise an inferior product, just as aristocratic rank, based on titles and not merit, is fraudulent because it cannot produce an artisan's masterpiece. Connecting this whole sequence of ideas with his notion of negative education, Rousseau proudly claims that Emile "will have lived free, healthy, true, hard working, just: it is not losing your time to earn it this way" (475).

This long discussion of useful education prepares the next pedagogical stage: becoming "a thinking and active being" (481) who knows how to distinguish "good and evil" and recognize what is "good and fitting" (429). A sketchy theory of cognition shows why Emile can think. Ideas are comparisons or judgments based on physical sensations and experience (481). "The art of judging and the art of reasoning are exactly the same" (486). Thanks to his extensive basis of sense experiences acquired slowly but accurately, Emile possesses the means he needs to make judgments and thus to become a rational being.

Like the previous one, book 3 concludes with a glowing evocation of Emile, now age 15. He might know only a few things, but he knows nothing halfway (487). His knowledge is deep and personal because it is based on his own experience and because he has found his own answers. He has no truck with theory or abstractions. Emile "is alone in human society, he counts only on himself alone" (488). Taking "the easy road to knowledge, in fact, but [one that is] long, immense, and slow to travel" has made Emile a unique individual and an unusual citizen, "content, happy, and free" (486, 488).

The very long book 4 can be divided into three roughly equal sections. In the center stands the "Profession de foi du Vicaire Savoyard" ("Profession of Faith of the Savoyard Priest"), which is a powerful statement of Rousseau's religious views. This lyrical exposition of natural religion, that is to say deism or an agnostic recognition of a divine presence in the world, also contains criticisms, direct and indirect, of the liturgy and doctrines of the more formal Christian religions. It was principally this "Profession" that provoked the anger of the religious establishment in Paris and Geneva, and caused *Emile* to be banned and burned.

Book 4 begins with the awakening of Emile's sexual urges, "the murmur of nascent passions" (490). Puberty is Emile's second birth, his passage from solitary to social existence. His new life will require an education that is different from what has preceded. Sex and society are dangers that Emile, and indeed every modern person, must learn to deal with.

Jean-Jacques accepts that passions are natural and cannot be eliminated. Good passions are "the instruments of our liberty"; bad ones "subjugate us and destroy us" (491). The tutor's task now becomes to "control" Emile's passions and to "revise God's work." Rousseau distinguishes between two fundamental passions, a positive "love of self," which is a natural instinct for self-preservation, and a negative "self-love," which is a product of society (523). Sex is obviously a natural passion, but since it involves human interaction it is also a social phenomenon. Emile comes to grips with puberty at the same time that he is preparing to enter society. Intertwined, love and society are twin perils for the young Emile (502).

Rousseau's discussion of the passions leads in many directions: the importance of pity as a humanizing passion, the deleterious physical consequences of precocious sexuality, the masks men wear in society, to mention only a few (505–8, 519). "Let [Emile] know that man is naturally good . . . but let him see how society depraves and perverts men, let him find in man's prejudices the source of all his vices; let him esteem every individual but despise the multitude, let him see that all men wear the same mask" (525).

Jean-Jacques also reworks his ideas about natural equality and how it is lost in society. "There is in the state of Nature a factual equality that is real and indestructible because it is impossible that in this state the differences between men become large enough so that one man depends on another. There is in the civil state a legal equality that is imaginary and vain because . . . public force, which is added to the stronger to oppress the weaker, breaks the equilibrium that Nature had placed between them" (524). To learn about the society he will live in, Emile reads history. Books are now deemed appropriate because reading history educates Emile about men while protecting him from being corrupted by close association with them (526). Jean-Jacques offers a critique of historians, of historical methods (e.g., the use of such literary devices as the portrait; the unreliability of so-called historical facts), and of the dubious moral value of history's lessons (527–34).

By the middle of the book Emile is ready to deal with abstractions. Religion is the study that will crown his pedagogical and moral development. It is presented in one long abstract speech by the Savoyard Priest that contrasts with the short, concrete anecdotes of the tutor in the earlier books. By presenting the "Profession" as a verbatim transcription of the Savoyard Priest's own words, Rousseau pretends that he is not speaking here. The autobiographical reminiscences are too strong, however: the Savoyard's beliefs are Rousseau's. This game of hiding behind another's words with a telescoping sequence of first-person narrators (Rousseau as author; Jean-Jacques as Emile's tutor; the Savoyard's disciple, who recounts this whole episode; the Savoyard Priest, who is speaking) was totally ineffective since Rousseau was condemned and turned into a fugitive because of the ideas expressed by his fictional mouthpieces.

The Savoyard Priest's speech to his disciple (replicating the situation of the tutor and Emile) divides into three parts. First, the Savoyard expounds his basic religious principles, which are based on his own personal lights and not on ecclesiastical authority (569). Since the *vicaire* is a Catholic priest (the French term means the principal curate in a parish; the English word *vicar* is a false cognate because it designates a Protestant clergyman), his rejection of the church's traditions and dogma in favor of his personal beliefs constitutes heresy. Refuting materialism, he postulates that a Will must exist in order to move matter (575). Unconvinced by the theory that an infinite number of tries might produce the universe, he proclaims that this Will is intelligent (578). "Everything is one and proclaims a single intelligence. . . . I call it God" (581). God, however, is unknowable. "I perceive God everywhere in his works; I feel him within me, I see him all around me. But as soon as I want to contemplate him in himself, as soon as I want to seek out where he is, what he is, what substance he is, he escapes me, and my troubled mind no longer perceives anything." Because he is an avowed agnostic, the Savoyard, like Rousseau, is nondogmatic and nonauthoritarian. He prefers his own error to another's truth (569). Later he will claim to propose ideas, not impose them (630). He is content to believe with a sincere heart and accept incertitude in matters he does not fully understand (570). His final principle is that man is free. God is not responsible for the evil done by man's freedom. "Moral evil is incontestably our own handiwork" (587). Physical catastrophes belong to the larger order of the universe and cannot be considered evil.

The second part of the Savoyard's speech shows how to live according to these principles. Conscience is our infallible guide; its principles are found "at the bottom of my heart written by nature in ineradicable letters. I only have to consult myself about what I want to do: everything that I feel is good is good, and all that I feel is evil is evil" (594). No matter how gently expressed, the proposition that an individual can judge for himself without relying on external authority challenged the foundations of both church and civil government. It is no wonder that the hierarchical eighteenth century considered *Emile* subversive.

The last section comprises the priest's answers to his disciple's questions, a technique that allows Rousseau to emphasize some key ideas. Since God is felt through our emotions and not through our reason ("The cult that God demands is that of the heart"; 608), any intellectual effort to prove his existence diminishes him. Therefore the Savoyard dismisses revelations, accounts of miracles, and books about religion. "How many men between God and me!" (610). Like Jean-Jacques, the Savoyard brooks no intermediaries, no barriers, no impediments that would block his direct access to God. He emphasizes the need for works of charity, calls upon us all to follow the gospel's message (629), preaches submission to civil authority, and denounces intolerance (628). He mixes the most orthodox religious principles with a most radical affirmation of the rights of individual conscience. This amazing profession ends quietly and almost devoutly. "The abuse of knowledge produces unbelief. . . . Proud philosophy leads to atheism just as blind devotion leads to fanaticism. Avoid these extremes. . . . Dare to acknowledge God among the philosophers; dare to preach humanity to the intolerant" (633–34).

The final third of book 4 finds Emile ready to seek a bride at the ideal age of 20 (640). The study of religion has prepared him to live in society among his fellow men—and women, despite the danger of sexual seduction that they present. Significantly, his relationship with his tutor is changing. No longer is it the dependent and unbalanced relationship of teacher and student; now they are equals. "He is still your disciple, but he is no longer your student. He is your friend, he is a man, treat him like one from now on" (639). Confidence and friendship are the bonds that link them, not authority or stratagem. This personal transformation has political ramifications. Emile begins to recognize his new responsibilities as a man and a citizen as well as the dilemma presented by freedom: "I want to obey your laws, I want to do so always. That is my constant will. If ever I disobey, it will be despite myself. Make me free by protecting me against my own passions, which do me violence. Prevent me from being their slave and force me to be my own master by not obeying my senses, but my reason" (652). This apparent contradiction, which is another formulation of the *Social Contract*'s submission to the general will, recalls the earlier discussion of the bad passion. The man who lives by self-love is self-destructive. He is not free because he is in thrall to his senses, his passions, his urges. Emile's true freedom lies elsewhere, not in the license of anything goes but in the sober freedom of self-control and self-mastery.

Long and patiently prepared, Emile finally stands ready to enter society. But first there is a long digression in which Jean-Jacques deplores bad taste (671–77). Paradoxically, good taste coexists with bad, so Emile will travel to Paris. "There is perhaps today not one civilized spot on the earth where the general taste is worse than in Paris. Nonetheless, it is in this capital that good taste is cultivated" (674).

Book 4 terminates with a curious maneuver. Jean-Jacques displaces Emile and imagines himself entering society. "Permit me, in order to develop my idea, to leave for a moment Emile whose pure and healthy heart can no longer serve as model to anyone, and to seek in myself an example that is more touching and closer to the reader's mores" (678). In this quite literal rewriting of his life as a young man, Jean-Jacques underscores a number of his favorite themes: healthy diet, country festivals, living without servants and other intermediaries who invariably spoil rather than enhance communication (680), having a country house and a group of close friends for company (687), walking in and thus enjoying a park rather than owning it (690).

In the final paragraph, Emile and Jean-Jacques leave Paris, fleeing its social life dominated by public opinion and its bad taste fashioned by too many women. Sophie, the ideal woman and Emile's future mate, cannot be found in this brilliant but corrupt metropolis. Jean-Jacques and Emile will seek her elsewhere.

Fiction

In the fifth book, the only one with its own title, "Sophie, or Woman," Rousseau's educational treatise veers off into fiction. Presented as a sustained narrative, the courtship of Emile and Sophie occupies a third of the book (56 of 179 pages in the Pléiade edition). Rousseau himself called this portion of *Emile* a novel, "a rather handsome one, the novel of human nature" (777), a description that has been widely accepted. Critics, however, have tended to oppose treatise and novel, and usually denigrate the former by considering it the latter.

The opening third of book 5 continues the didactic tone of the pedagogical treatise and focuses on Sophie, the female counterpart to Emile. At this time, despite a few notable exceptions (which only prove the rule), girls were educated in convents to do household tasks and received little formal instruction at all. Rousseau was therefore quite liberal in proposing any serious education for a woman. Even if Sophie gets only one book to Emile's four, her education is conceived as parallel to his and as equally important. But before specifying what constitutes an ideal female education, Jean-Jacques plunges into a general discussion of the two sexes and their relationship to each other.

Men and women are similar as members of the same species but dissimilar because of their sexuality. Rousseau insists they are equal in what they share but incomparable because of their differences: they should *not* resemble each other (693). How the sexes can be both different and equal is the conundrum Jean-Jacques tries to solve. Even though his position incurs feminists' wrath, Jean-Jacques insists that women are better off when they do not imitate men: "[W]oman is worth more as a woman and less as a man; wherever she exercises her [female] rights she has the advantage; wherever she tries to usurp ours [i.e., men's], she is beneath us" (701). Women need public recognition, men do not. Men can ignore public opinion, whereas women have to protect their reputation: "[o]pinion is the tomb of virtue for men, and its throne for women" (702–3). On the other hand, Rousseau claims that women govern men. Feminine wiles make her man's companion, not his slave (712). Her apparent docility counterbalances his physical force: "[S]he governs him while obeying him." Rousseau reiterates this paradox of female weakness being more powerful than man's strength. Overtaking Sophie in a foot race, Emile carries her across the finish line. Falling at her feet, he "admits he was beaten" (807). Earlier the tutor observed another struggle of strength and weakness culminating in the latter's victory: "[W]hatever she orders, he does not demur, and often as he leaves to obey, his eyes full of joy tell me: look how she has taken possession of me. Meanwhile, the proud girl observes him slyly, and smiles secretly at the pride of her slave" (789–90). When their engagement is announced, "far from seeming to be haughty over her conquest, Sophie became even more friendly and less demanding of everyone. . . . She triumphs modestly in a victory that cost her her freedom" (795). After being presented as narrative, this same idea recurs in the style of a philosophical maxim: "Unfortunate the times in which women lose their ascendancy, and men no longer accept their judgments! That is the highest degree of depravation. All peoples who have had [decent] mores have respected women" (742). Another page praises the "empire" of the "honest, lovable, and wise" woman who can send her man to "combat, to glory, to death, wherever she pleases" (745). Finally, a woman "should rule in her home like a minister in the state, by having herself commanded to do what she wants to do. . . . the best families are those in which the woman has the most authority" (766–77).

Having set out his concept of the male-female relationship, Jean-Jacques turns to the principles that should govern a young girl's education. Although some critics disparage Sophie's education as entirely conventional,[6] the principles behind it resemble what Rousseau proposed for Emile. She should learn what is appropriate and useful to her state. "Does it follow that she should be raised in ignorance of everything and limited only to household functions? Will man make a servant out of his companion, will he deprive himself when he is near her of society's greatest charms? . . . No, of course. . . . [Young girls] should learn many things, but only those which it is fitting they know" (701–2). Characteristically Jean-Jacques avoids giving too many specifics about what is pertinent to her female condition. Paying attention to the body before the mind is primary (704 ff). A girl's attraction to finery (*parure*) is natural and constitutes part of the female character: "[S]he is more hungry for finery than for food" (707). Clothes are "a supplement" to a graceful body (713). But *parure* is also ambiguous because it speaks to the inherent coquetry in women. Clothes do not make the woman (713), but they can hide physical defects, thus creating one of the many ruses that make women the equal of men. Like Emile, Sophie has to learn self-control and submission: "[T]hey have to get used to constraint, so that it is never hard to control their fantasies and submit to the will of others" (709). Religion completes her education even though Rousseau fears it might turn into fanaticism (720). Religion should be taught by her mother with examples and not by preaching (720–29). At its best religion consists of good works, not dogma (729). According to Jean-Jacques, women are of mediocre intelligence at best. Weak in the exact sciences, they are experts in the human heart, a stereotype that is still very much with us.

Now the didactic exposition ends and Sophie appears. The fictionalization of the treatise hits full stride. The detailed portrait Rousseau paints of this young woman is more active than static, more dramatic than descriptive. Sophie loves food, practices all the domestic arts, even runs the household for her mother (748). Normally reserved, she can be rambunctious (750). At 15, she is as mature as a 20-year-old (754). She is also passing through the same puberty crisis as Emile.

Curiously, at this point Jean-Jacques seems to play with his fiction. He pretends that Sophie is real and not an invention like Emile: "If I told them [his readers] that Sophie is not at all an imaginary being, that

I have only invented her name, that her education, her behavior, her character, even her face all really existed, and that her memory still draws tears from an honest family . . ." (759). Unwieldy syntax is as confusing as the intention. Here Rousseau confuses this real girl with his fictional Sophie: "The young person whose temperament I have given to Sophie shared with her besides all the similarities that name could merit for her, and so I leave it to her." He then recounts an incident from this "false" Sophie's life. Like the real Sophie, she has parents who once were rich and now are destitute, and her favorite book is Fénelon's novel, *The Voyages of Telemachus*. What do "false" and "real" mean here if both Sophies are identical, as they are according to Rousseau? And what is his point in introducing an extra one? His "false" Sophie is frustrated because she has fallen in love with Telemachus, the fictitious hero in her novel! But Jean-Jacques quickly abandons this incipient plot line. "Shall I bring this sad story to its climax? . . . Shall I describe this unfortunate girl . . . slowly proceeding toward death and descending into the grave at the very moment when she seems headed toward the altar? No, I push away these morbid visions" (763). The novelist conscious of his own fictional devices reappears a paragraph later: "Let us return to Emile and his Sophie; let us resuscitate this lovely girl and give her a less lively imagination and a happier fate. . . . I lost my own way. Let us double back on our steps." And so the two become one, the false Sophie is reabsorbed back into the real one.

Rousseau's elaborate game serves little purpose but to advertise the arbitrary and fictional nature of his pedagogical experiment. Sophie represents a multiple vision of the ideal woman, just as Emile emerged as a composite of various experiences and anecdotes. The uncertainties lying just below the surface and the possibility that the plot can take an unexpected turn foreshadow the real novel that will follow *Emile*.

The courtship of Emile and Sophie, which fills the middle third of book 5, is told in a novelistic manner. While Emile prepares to seek his ideal mate, the tutor, always a manipulator, has already found Sophie. He then arranges a "false search" that will bring these young people together (765). And so "we leave Paris" (770), the fictional narrative picking up exactly where book 4 ended.

Jean-Jacques shares Sophie's tastes in novels, blending Fénelon's mythological backdrop into his own narrative. Emile and his tutor arrive at Sophie's house "like Telemachus and Mentor on the Isle of Calypso" and discover the "charms of Eucharis" (775). All the details of this courtship replay the pedagogical discussions that have preceded. On the day after their first meeting, both Emile and Sophie dress in a way that gives voice to their nascent passion. Emile is a bit laughable in his affectation, while Sophie is more wily. She has dressed more simply than the day before. In this unspoken sartorial "declaration" (779), Jean-Jacques discerns a number of contradictions, of which Sophie herself is not fully aware: her clothes are seductive but plain, studied yet casual; she draws attention to herself while seeming unaware of her effects. How natural and inborn those female ruses are!

A few fully realized episodes bring out the character of these two model individuals. After seeing Emile at work one day, Sophie invites him home. He cannot accept, however, even though he wants desperately to do so, because he has promised to help an artisan meet a deadline. Duty prevails over desire (809). In another episode, Emile arrives at Sophie's house a day later than expected. To show her intense displeasure, she is polite but cool. All is forgiven when Emile explains that he was delayed only because he performed a heroic good deed. The "rights of humanity" are even more sacred than those of love (812–13). Like true Cornelian heroes, their mutual love is based on and yet subordinate to higher values, without which it could not exist.

The last test of their young love is the two-year separation the tutor imposes on them. There is no adequate explanation for this delay: Emile is already 22, Sophie almost 18 (822). After three to six months of daily courting they are ready to marry. Following his own psychological reflex, however, Jean-Jacques wants to postpone the pleasure he is about to enjoy. He explains to Emile that the expectation created by separation will pique his imagination and his desire. Waiting for such a prize is better than actually enjoying it: "Even in climaxing his happiness, I would destroy its greatest charm. Supreme bliss is a hundred times sweeter to wait for than to obtain. We enjoy better when we wait than when we finally taste it" (782). In terms of character, Emile "has to leave her in order to return worthy of her" (823). In a long speech, the tutor explains that to be truly free, Emile must be free of his passions too, that is to say even of his love for Sophie. Only then can he love her fully and freely. Self is the enemy; we must control even the "appetites of our heart" (816).

Covering these two years of travel, the final portion of the book is rather disappointing after Emile and Sophie's romance (in both the literal and literary sense). Here Rousseau pens a long defense of the educational value of travel. The world is better than books, seeing is better than reading (828, 827). Because he wants to find out where he can "live independent and free" (835), Emile will study various forms of government during his travels. This section is comprised of a loosely connected series of pages taken from the *Social Contract,* most of which touch on the issue of individual freedom within the constraints of society.

After recounting a story remembered from his own travels in Venice, Jean-Jacques brings his lovers back together with a typical novelistic flourish. "It is time to end. Let's bring back Lord John to Miss Lucy, that is to say, Emile to Sophie" (854). Almost three years after their first meeting (821), the marriage finally takes place. In a last instructional gasp, Jean-Jacques lectures the newlyweds about sex the day after their wedding. However incongruous it might at first sound, sex and politics meet in his advice about how to make true love endure within the state of matrimony. Marriage can become a constraint, so Emile and Sophie should remain lovers even when they are married. Love means independence, whereas conjugal rights imply constrictions. Each partner in the marriage should remain free to be as loving as he or she chooses (863). Rousseau is too demure to state explicitly that "loving" here means sexually aggressive or demanding, and I have difficulty understanding how any difference of opinion on this might be resolved without one yielding to the other. "Remember always that even in marriage pleasure is legitimate only when the desire is shared." Sophie obeys Emile, who in turn is guided by her: her authority is over his heart, his over her body (865). In this conjugal balance of powers, which recalls the individual vis-à-vis the general will, each remains loving and free. Making such generalizations is as easy as resolving specific cases would be difficult. Not surprisingly Rousseau offers plenty of the former but avoids the latter.

Book 5 and *Emile* end as Sophie replaces the tutor and becomes Emile's new "governor" (867). This final scene, as full of pathos and emotion as a Greuze painting, stirs Rousseau's heart: "How many times do I join their hands in mine, bless Providence, and emit an ardent sigh! How many kisses do I bestow on those intertwined hands!"

Although *Emile* is complete, Rousseau did nonetheless return to his two lovers and followed them into married life in a short epistolary novel, *Emile et Sophie, ou Les Solitaires (Emile and Sophie, or the Solitary Ones).* Never completed, this fragment was probably written in 1762 but not published until 1780. In a sense it actualizes the impulse I already mentioned to explore additional narratives outside the didactic frame of *Emile.* The letters are written by Emile to his tutor perhaps ten years later (888–89). He explains how tragically his marriage to Sophie has ended. After the death of their daughter and then of Sophie's parents, Emile and Sophie moved to Paris, the "fatal city," for a "poisoned stay" of two years (885). During that time both lost them-selves in the social whirl, to the point of no longer having sexual rela-tions (889). It takes some time, but Emile finally notices how pro-foundly Sophie has changed. She confesses that she has been seduced by another man and is pregnant by him. Out of shame and her own sense of guilt and honor, Sophie can no longer live with Emile. Crushed, Emile wanders off (899). Seeking consolation, he takes up his old trade, which helps him find his bearings. "Submitting to the law of necessity I stopped my vain murmuring, I bent my will to the inevitable yoke. . . . peacefully I began to work as if I had been the happiest of men." One day, unknown to him, Sophie comes to the shop and sees that work has reestablished his equilibrium (907). She is relieved, for then she knows that Emile will not try to take their son away from her. Emile continues his travels, eventually being made prisoner by pirates. The novel, only two letters long, ends at this point. There are indications, however, that both Sophie and Emile's son may have died (884, 910). As he writes these letters, Emile expresses his uncertainty about whether his tutor is still alive and able to guide him.

It would seem that this novel stamps "failure" all over the pedagogi-cal program so painstakingly set out in *Emile*. If these two individuals, so wonderfully prepared by their ideal education, cannot succeed in life, who can? Is there no hope? Does Rousseau's addition of this sequel to his treatise indicate that he too despaired that even a perfect education could save man (and woman) from the perils of life in a corrupt society?

Convinced there are positive answers to these questions, I notice that *The Solitary Ones* consciously echoes *Emile*. But fiction avoids the obvious didacticism of the treatise. For example, Sophie's secret visit to Emile's workplace recalls a similar visit in book 5 that served to illustrate a moral lesson. Although a slave and in prison, Emile remains philosophi-cal. He knows how to submit to forces greater than himself and still maintain his own sense of freedom. "I am more free than before! I con-tinued. Well, in what sense? Have I lost my primitive freedom? Was I not born a slave to necessity? What new yoke can men place upon me?" (916–17). He even finds use for the political knowledge he acquired in his travels. He organizes his fellow slaves and leads a strike for better working conditions that is rationally, and successfully, aimed at his mas-ter's self-interest (923 ff). The novel climaxes with Emile implementing ideas taken from the *Social Contract*. What had at first seemed Emile's abject failure and a refutation of Rousseau's pedagogical experiment turns out to be another test of Emile's character and another fictional application of Rousseau's principle: "he who knows best how to want what [necessity] orders is the most free, because he is never forced to do what he does not want to do" (917).

Still, the larger question of *Emile* as pedagogical treatise or novel or both remains problematic.[7] A serious essay seems incompatible with a frivolous novel, especially in light of Rousseau's own screeds against the deception and illusion that all fiction and indeed all art is based upon.

Emile is filled with narratives and stories: I have already mentioned that curious episode of the "false" Sophie who may be his "real" heroine and who may have died. Just as there are several tutors whose pedagogical experiences are retold and vaguely assimilated to those of the prime tutor, so too are there several students, or "Emiles," whose education is described. Proliferation of this kind and the creation of a single composite out of several models belong to the realm of fiction. Novels willfully play tricks with "reality" or alternative narratives, whereas a treatise generally offers unequivocal information.

Furthermore, there are major ambiguities regarding the narrator of *Emile*. Although Jean-Jacques describes his experience as tutor in the first-person singular, he frequently addresses another apprentice tutor as "you" and explains to him how he should deal with Emile. Since the earliest draft of *Emile* is in the third-person singular, this shift from "he" to "you" and "I" indicates the kind of fabulation that characterizes fiction more than the expository essay. I have already pointed out the telescoping narrative point of view in the "Profession of Faith," in which Rousseau, Jean-Jacques, the disciple, and the priest each use the same pronoun, "I," to designate a separate individual and his distinct voice. However slight, those distinctions are real and significant. Again, ambiguity can enhance a fiction, whereas it only undermines a didactic treatise.

If Rousseau the author who signed *Emile* is real, Jean-Jacques the tutor inside that work is fictional. I think that most if not all those didactic anecdotes in which the tutor plays so important a role are either invented or borrowed from others' experiences. Rousseau tutored the Dupin boy for only 10 days in 1743, and his tenure as tutor with the Mably family in Lyon (1741–1742) was a complete disaster. On the other hand, real life does enter into the treatise, but unexpectedly. Jean-Jacques recounts an actual supper party at which a young pupil performs his tutor's lesson rather successfully. When Jean-Jacques tries to ask the young boy some questions, he is shouted down by the other guests. One woman finally whispers to him: "Keep quiet, Jean-Jacques!" (348–50).

Later he confirms that the pupil "understood nothing at all about the story he had recounted so well" concerning Alexander the Great's eloquence (349). By collapsing the distance between the real and the imaginary Jean-Jacques and confusing the concentric series of tutors and pupils, such anecdotes undermine any claim of scientific truth and push this treatise toward the personal and subjective realm of autobiography.[8] This does not of course invalidate what Rousseau has to say about pedagogy. It just makes it more difficult to identify the voice that made these pronouncements and to weigh its credibility.

How much more interesting—and so thoroughly modern—it would be to read *Emile* as the product of an *unreliable* narrator, one whose story is not entirely truthful and one that readers must weigh carefully before they accept it at face value. Indeed, this seems to be the crux of the difficulty. Accepting Rousseau's texts as straightforward, critics have traditionally sought out his contradictions and attributed them to bad faith. If his narrator is unreliable, however, such inconsistencies become postmodern experimentation, literary games playing with multiple versions of reality. "Bad faith" is no longer the issue, which becomes rather a question of literary tricks and technique. Jean-Jacques as tutor manipulates his student continually, concocting situations that lead Emile to do what he wants or to some moral lesson. The narrative of the magnet and the ducks at the carnival is only the most famous of such secret machinations. Might Jean-Jacques the author be manipulating his readers, willfully presenting events that are not what they seem, plot developments that do not take place? As tutor Jean-Jacques informs Emile that Sophie is dead before ordering that two-year separation from her. As narrator Jean-Jacques has introduced a false Sophie and her false death. Are these gestures in any way similar? Finally, I would add that the Emile in *The Solitary Ones* is the autobiographical reflection of Rousseau, just as the tutor was in *Emile*. Only Jean-Jacques could imagine himself—that is to say, fictionalize himself—as both characters, each so different, simultaneously the student and his own tutor.

The ultimate failure of *Emile*'s pedagogical project—if failure it is—should not come as a surprise. Jean-Jacques warned his readers that the chances of success were remote: "Surrounded by ever increasing perils, [Emile] is going to elude me whatever I do. At the first opportunity, and this opportunity will soon arrive, he will follow the blind instinct of his senses; it is a thousand to one bet that he will lose his way" (640–41). A similar premonition spoiled the otherwise happy nuptials. A few days after the wedding a misunderstanding, obliquely presented but involving sex, required the tutor's intervention. A residual pessimism prevents a happy outcome in almost all of Rousseau's works, especially when there is some autobiographical resonance. In the utopian Clarens the happiness of Saint-Preux and Julie is either frustrated or short lived; the chances of finding a Legislator or implementing a functional (as opposed to theoretical) general will in the *Social Contract* seem remote. Emile's ideal education, as well as Sophie's, is thwarted by the pressures of living among men in a necessarily corrupt society.

But there is another explanation, and it is a more positive one. Although man is good in the state of nature, he can be virtuous only in society. To claim virtue, as opposed to mere natural goodness, Emile must be tested. Since *The Solitary Ones* is incomplete, it is possible that Emile will eventually triumph after these necessary trials and temporary defeats.[9] Clearly Rousseau recognizes the dramatic importance of defeat in striving toward virtue. More than realization and enjoyment, his focus is on anticipation, expectation, and waiting. Rousseau's personal preference here approaches the kind of attitude that characterizes a good reader of fiction.

Chapter Seven
The Confessions (1772)

Rousseau first conceived the idea of writing his life story in 1759 and 1760, finishing the first part (books 1 to 6) around 1767 during his exile in England and the second part in 1769. The *Confessions* were not published until after his death, however. From 1770 until early 1771, Rousseau gave public readings of his text, which upset his former friends (who had become his enemies) because they feared his treatment of them in the sections still not made public. Their uneasiness was mirrored in Rousseau's own fear that they were plotting to suppress or bowdlerize his book.

One of the most controversial aspects of the *Confessions* is the question of its veracity. Simply put, is Rousseau telling the truth? Starting with his contemporaries, many have over the years accused Rousseau of lying or of fabricating large parts of his autobiography. Let us remember that Rousseau was working mostly from memory, with few written documents, long after the events he describes. The 1760s were emotionally tense years for Jean-Jacques, and it is not surprising to see, especially in the second part, how those intense emotions affected his retelling of events. Nonetheless, most critics now agree that Rousseau gave a remarkably accurate account of his life despite a few errors in dating or in small details. Beyond the factual question of simply what happened when, the real interest of the *Confessions* lies in their artistic value: how Rousseau arranged those true facts into a moving narration of his emotions and personality.

It would be foolish to try to summarize the *Confessions*. What would be the purpose of repeating a story that Jean-Jacques tells so much better? The alternative I propose is to analyze his life story from two perspectives: first the structure of each book and then the themes that interweave through several books. In his autobiography Jean-Jacques gives us more than the facts of his life and does more than enumerate events, encounters, friends, publications. He also dramatizes. What interests me is this self-dramatization. How does Rousseau shape this biographical information into a narrative? how does he articulate the defining events? how does he find the fiction in the facts, the novel in his life? By examining both narrative architecture and thematics I hope to explain what is happening beneath the surface of Rousseau's narrative. Readers can use these analytic perspectives as tools to explore these *Confessions* on their own.

Narrative Architecture

Book 1 covers a time of life that writers before Rousseau rarely treated: childhood. With some justice it is said that Rousseau "invented" childhood as a literary topic, one that would know enormous success with the nineteenth-century romantics. This opening book climaxes with the drama of the adolescent Jean-Jacques being locked out of Geneva. This is a turning point for the 16-year-old, who is thereby thrust out into the world, simultaneously rejected and freed by the adult authority that the child-man Rousseau will confront for the rest of his life. Leading up to that emotional high point is a series of childhood incidents whose principal purpose is to depict the joy and happiness of being young and alive: Rousseau reading through the night with his father or enjoying an idyllic stay in the countryside playing with his cousin Bernard and impossibly in love with his aunt Mlle. Lambercier.

The eight months of 1728 covered in the second book are critical to Rousseau's moral and emotional development. He articulates them in four strong beats. "Free and master of myself" upon leaving Geneva (first beat), Rousseau is awed at his first meeting with Mme. de Warens (second beat). This woman who will be his lifelong love persuades him to abjure his Protestantism and become a Catholic. The third beat contains a mixed sequence of sexual incidents: Jean-Jacques's homosexual encounter at the convent in Turin and his puerile infatuations with other women (Mme. Basile, the Comtesse de Vercellis) that mark the distance between Mme. de Warens and everyone else. The last and most intense beat falls on the story of how Jean-Jacques falsely accused Marion, a fellow servant, of stealing a ribbon. What for anyone else would be a minor incident becomes for Rousseau a crisis worthy of his public penitence. Convinced he has ruined Marion's life, Jean-Jacques confesses to his readers what he claims to be the most serious fault in his life.

Book 3 (December 1728 to April 1730) has a picaresque tone with its emphasis on physical movement, Jean-Jacques traveling on foot along highways and byways with his not-always-reputable friends. Emotionally unstable (he leaves Mme. de Warens twice but returns repentant each time), Rousseau reveals his sexual peccadilloes, flashing and masturbating in public. He balances his negative picaresque behavior with his positive experience of music. Duality structures this book: Jean-Jacques discovers his precocious musical talent thanks to his roguish friend Venture de Villeneuve but ignominiously abandons his teacher Le Maître when the latter falls into an epileptic fit.

Encompassing the short period from April 1730 to October 1731, the leisurely paced book 4 opens with the beautiful retelling of a single memorable and ideal day when Jean-Jacques gathered cherries with two young ladies. This is a golden moment, dominating the whole chapter, fixed in Rousseau's memory as if it were yesterday. The youthful innocence of this unchaperoned meeting pulsates with sexual innuendo. A young man caught between two equally desirable yet unattainable women is a pattern Rousseau both lived and dramatized in his writing. The slow narrative pace of this short day, which is all light and emotion, captured in minute detail and recounted at length, contrasts with a rapid sequence of other events: a trip to Fribourg, a concert at Lausanne, a meeting with a preacher collecting alms for the Holy Sepulcher. An encounter with a poor peasant closes the book. The peasant has hidden his modest food supplies from the rapacious tax collector but shares them with Jean-Jacques, whose honesty and discretion he immediately recognizes. This is a fine example of the "transparency" Rousseau always yearned for yet seldom enjoyed. Placed at the chapter's climactic endpoint, this incident encapsulates all the social inequities of the ancien régime. Two very different meals, one an idyllic picnic with cherries and a pair of charming young ladies, the other a clandestine repast furtively shared with an impoverished peasant, mark the dramatic, emotional poles of this chapter.

Book 5 covers a longer period, from Rousseau's return to Mme. de Warens at Chambéry (October 1731) until they move to Les Charmettes in the summer of 1736. Passion is the principal theme, expressed in Rousseau's love of music and of Mme. de Warens. He makes physical love to her near the center, the "heart," of this book, although most of the time they are living together with Claude Anet in a bizarre but harmonious ménage à trois. The book opens with an account of how Anet accidentally poisoned himself but was lovingly cured by Mme. de Warens. Just past the midpoint of the chapter, Anet does die and Jean-Jacques recounts his first sexually consummated experience with Maman. Despite Rousseau's praise for his rival, Anet's twin deaths seem to express a deeper and more hostile attitude. In the final quarter, Jean-Jacques himself falls dangerously ill, recalling the poisoned Anet of the beginning. He regains his health as a new, less sexual relationship with Maman begins at Les Charmettes.

Right in the middle of Book 6 Jean-Jacques again appears as a comic, unsophisticated picaro. He recounts with deadpan humor a carriage trip he took to Montpellier. During it he seduces an attractive, older woman, Mme. de Larnage, or more accurately, she seduces him. Rousseau is so ridiculously naive that at first he does not understand the meaning of Mme. de Larnage's bold advances and then he does not know how to take advantage of them. The ludic tone hides this episode's deeper and more serious meaning.

Before embarking on this trip, Jean-Jacques describes his idyllic existence at Les Charmettes with Mme. de Warens now that Anet is gone: his daily routine, his studies, his music. The only sour note is that curious illness, an echo of the previous book, which confines him to bed. Returning from the trip and its sexual adventure, Jean-Jacques is shocked to find that in his absence Mme. de Warens has taken another lover. The denouement of this idyll is catastrophic; Rousseau's comic tale has turned unexpectedly to tragedy.

I would point out, however, that Jean-Jacques has rearranged the chronology here and thus shaped biographical facts into a dramatic story. His rival in love, Wintzenried, was admitted to Mme. de Warens's bed before the trip to Montpellier, a fact that would both explain that trip and motivate Rousseau's own infidelity. Discouraged, disconsolate, his dream destroyed, Rousseau decides to seek his fortune in Paris. At this point, the first part of the *Confessions* ends. Having reached age 25, the legal age in Geneva, Rousseau is an adult. His childhood, recounted in these first six books, is over, and he is entering the world of grown-ups.

Book 7 opens with a brief but powerful evocation of a Rousseau persecuted by his former friends and driven to despair by misfortune. Only part of this screed is due to Rousseau's paranoia: Jean-Jacques was in fact pursued by the police and chased into exile. The themes of plot and persecution will color the rest of the *Confessions* with their somber tone. Indeed, several other books open with similarly emotional incipits that denounce the plot and his enemies.

This seventh book, which is much longer than the others, covers a period (1742–1749) when Jean-Jacques was struggling to survive. Like the preceding book, this one is dominated by a single episode that is recounted at a length disproportionate to its real elapsed time but appropriate to its emotional and symbolic importance. Rousseau's year-long employment as secretary to the French ambassador in Venice estab-

lishes a pattern that will be repeated throughout his life: an initially brilliant situation turns unexpectedly and inexplicably into bitter disappointment. Rousseau's hopes for a diplomatic career seem at first plausi-
ble thanks to his effective secretarial work and his clever negotiating
skills. He acquires notions of rank and honor, even thinking that his
position "ennobles" him. In a highly dramatic confrontation with the
lazy and incompetent ambassador, M. de Montaigu, the timid Jean-
Jacques asserts his dignity and quits his job.

This pattern is underlined by other incidents that Rousseau recounts
after his climactic confrontation with Montaigu, that is to say out of
their chronological sequence. Each begins auspiciously, only to end in
deception, disappointment, and embarrassment. The beautiful singing
he hears in a cloister is done by ugly girls; a night with a prostitute leads
to fears of infection. Julietta, widely recognized as the most beautiful
courtesan in the city, entices the handsome Jean-Jacques into her bed,
but finding a slight blemish on her breast extinguishes his sexual ardor.
Finally, he buys a 13-year-old girl and plans to share her sexually with a
friend, only to develop paternal feelings toward her. Upset by the hint of
incest, Jean-Jacques abandons the girl and his sordid plan.

Book 8 narrates a series of crises that occurred between October
1749 and April 1756. Looking back on his rise to fame, Rousseau finds
here the beginnings of the inevitable quarrels that alienated him from
all his old friends. Of course he never blames himself. No matter how
genuine these friendships were at the time, Jean-Jacques sees them in
retrospect as contaminated by the approaching betrayal. He is convinced that a plot against him exists and that it had begun long before
he ever suspected it.

Curiously Rousseau does not emphasize the events that might seem
the most important. For example, he gives only a short account of his
"illumination" along the road to Vincennes that led to the first *Discourse*.[1] Other incidents are presented like a string of disjointed frag-
ments. Only in the center of the book is there a coherent narrative
block. It deals with a minor work, *Le Devin du Village* (*The Village Soothsayer*), an opera for which Rousseau wrote both the words and the music,
its production at Fontainebleau for the king, and Rousseau's disastrous
reaction to his own triumph. Music at this time was something of a code
for other more serious issues that divided the court and Paris into two
warring camps. The King's Corner, filled with political conservatives
and even reactionaries, favored French music, whereas the Queen's Corner, grouping all the philosophes, the *encyclopédistes,* and such liberals as

Rousseau, Diderot, Grimm, and their friends, supported the more lyrical and emotional Italian music. Rousseau narrates this "War of the *Bouffons*" from the inside, as a participant.

Symmetrically balanced on either side of this operatic centerpiece are two incidents that at first glance seem lost in the otherwise uninflected sequence of discrete events. They are critical, however, because they bear witness to the profound transformations taking place in Rousseau's psyche. In the first, Jean-Jacques changes his clothes, abandoning normal attire and distinguishing himself sartorially, just as his first *Discourse* marked out his new ideological position. The second is his conversion back to Protestantism from Catholicism, which was motivated by his desire to be recognized as a citizen of Geneva. A bit too flippantly Jean-Jacques justifies his apostasy by stating "that for a reasonable man there were not two ways of being a christian."[2] Such an explanation could not but incense both religious groups and do Jean-Jacques irreparable harm, as will be seen later.

If book 8 was choppy and hurried, book 9 is a leisurely, multileveled, and complex narrative that focuses intensely on the short period (April 1756 to December 1757) that Rousseau spent at the Hermitage as the guest of Mme. d'Epinay. His retelling is complicated by a double perspective: although most of the story is told from the point of view of the actor Jean-Jacques, who did not always understand what was happening, occasionally the narrator Rousseau, writing years later, intervenes with his knowledge of subsequent events. In addition, Jean-Jacques elides some facts, conflating events, confusing dates, and in the end composing a narrative that is undeniably dramatic and effective but also self-serving. How Rousseau shapes this retelling of his life is more important than the facts, which are difficult to recover or judge today. More than any book in the *Confessions,* this one illustrates the narrow line between autobiography and novel, truth and fiction.

Once back in the countryside, Rousseau finds peace and consolation in nature: "The more I examined this charming retreat, the more I felt it was made for me. This place, more solitary than wild, transported me mentally to the ends of the earth. It possessed those touching beauties that are rarely found near cities" (IX, 403 – 4). Inspired by his surroundings—"I had these meditations in the finest season of the year, in the month of June, under shady trees, to the sound of singing nightingales and babbling brooks" (426)—his work advances, especially his novel *Julie.* He records a moment that is both magical and typically Rousseauian as the fiction he is imagining comes to life:

Soon I saw gathered around me all those objects [women] who had moved me as a young man. . . . I saw myself surrounded by a harem of beautiful women whom I had known. . . . My blood pumps and boils, my head turns despite my graying hair. . . . The impossibility of attaining real women threw me into the land of dreams . . . and I nourished my delirium in an ideal world that my creative imagination rapidly peopled with living beings fashioned after my heart. (427)

This is one of Rousseau's most characteristic and suggestive themes, the power of imagination over reality.

Even as he creates this imaginary world for his novel, the real world begins to look imaginary. An unexpected visit ignites an overpowering passion. Sophie d'Houdetot, Mme. d'Epinay's sister-in-law, enters his life like a character stepping out of a fiction: "[T]his visit seemed a bit like the beginning of a novel" (432). Since Sophie is both married and the mistress of his friend Saint-Lambert, Rousseau's life imitates the pattern of the ménage à trois that appears in the novel he was then writing and the themes inherent in that pattern: the "intimate and sweet society" of three friends (441), love that cannot be consummated, the exaltation of both love and friendship between the sexes.

But disaster lurks, in life as in fiction. The tone turns somber in the middle of the book as Rousseau, the retrospective narrator, sees the plot against him develop. "These were the last fine days given to me on earth; here begins the long skein of my misfortunes which will have little interruption" (446). Like his creation Saint-Preux, Rousseau has to be expelled from paradise. Like Saint-Preux, Rousseau's love for Sophie climaxes not in sexual consummation but by rising to the level of platonic friendship. "We formed the charming project of a close group of the three of us" (479). Pique, misunderstandings, and insults both real and imagined drive a wedge between Rousseau and Mme. d'Epinay, Diderot, and Grimm. The final quarter of the book denounces these former friends and the plot that Grimm in particular has inspired. The breakup is both dramatic and definitive. Rousseau insists on leaving the Hermitage "even if I had to sleep in the woods and on the snow which then covered the ground" (487).

At the beginning of book 10 Rousseau's newest friends, the Maréchal and Maréchale de Luxembourg, rescue him from his plight and lodge him at their estate at Montmorency, which was not far from either the Hermitage or Paris. The proletarian Rousseau had a conflicted reaction to his numerous aristocratic acquaintances. On the one hand, he complained that the generosity of rich friends cost him dearly: "[B]ut me, alone, without my own servants, I was at the mercy of those in the house whose good graces I had to win over, so as not to suffer too much" (514). Too sensitive to ignore these servants and what they might be saying behind his back, Jean-Jacques felt obliged to tip them extravagantly. Then he would rage against such impositions on his purse: "These expenses are inevitable for a man of my temperament who neither knows how to finagle or to scheme, nor how to put up with the face of a servant who complains or who sulks while waiting on you" (515). On the other hand, Jean-Jacques was also very proud to hobnob in such distinguished company. "I have always been all or nothing; soon I was all, and seeing myself wined and dined by people of that rank, I went over the top and felt for them the kind of friendship that one should not have for any but his equals" (522).

On the evidence that Rousseau himself recounts, this period should have been a happy one. He was in the countryside he loved, either at Montlouis or the main chateau at Montmorency: "I was there in an earthly Paradise; there I lived with as much innocence, and there I tasted the same happiness" (521). Despite a few inconveniences, he could enjoy his solitude and was without any financial worries: "I was then perhaps the best and the most agreeably lodged individual in Europe" (526).

As in the previous book, the subtle distinction between Jean-Jacques as narrator or actor articulates his growing perception of the plot against him. "Disillusioned by chimerical friendship, detached from everything that allowed me to love life, I saw nothing that could make life agreeable; I saw nothing but the pains and miseries that prevented me from enjoying. . . . But let's pick up the chain of events" (489). At every turn he now sees the impending doom he was blind to then: "[I]n the midst of this temporary prosperity germinated the catastrophe that was to make it end" (528). Since he is so convinced that things will turn out badly, Jean-Jacques is often his own worst enemy: "Could I expect from so distinguished a Lady [i.e., the Maréchale de Luxembourg] a faithfulness that was proof against my own inability to sustain it? I was unable to hide from her the dark foreboding that disturbed me and made me even more sullen" (532–33). All this bad humor and brooding petulance derive in Rousseau's mind from the cabal of former friends who have become enemies plotting his downfall. "It is therefore here that I locate the foundation of the system that those who took advantage of me adopted with such rapid success that it would seem a miracle to anyone who does not know how everything favors whatever evil men want to do. I must try and explain in a few words how this deep and hidden system appeared to my eyes" (491).

Pace is the defining feature of book 11. Right at its center the narrative slows to fully emphasize a major crisis. Jean-Jacques fell seriously ill in the fall of 1761. At the same time he was under maximum stress from the frustrating task of seeing *Julie, The Social Contract,* and especially *Emile* through press to publication. Under these physical and mental strains Rousseau blamed all his problems on that convenient scapegoat, the plot against him:

> my natural penchant is to fear shadows, I hate and dread their blackness; mystery always upsets me. . . . So my imagination, fired up by this long silence, began to create ghosts for me. The more I yearned for the publication of my latest and best work, the more I tortured myself by seeking whatever was blocking it. Always going to extremes, I thought I saw in the printing delay the suppression of my Book. However, unable to imagine how or why, I was left in the most cruel uncertainty. I wrote letter after letter. . . . I became overexcited, I fell into a frenzy [je délirois]. (566)

Jean-Jacques relives his illness and persecution in slow detail. He evokes possible enemies (is it the Jesuits?), unable to decide, yet certain he is being victimized. "I felt myself dying. . . . Even today as I observe that plot advancing to its blackest execution, the most horrible plot that ever was hatched against the memory of a man, I will die much more calmly knowing that I leave behind in my writings a witness that will sooner or later triumph over the plots of men" (568). An open door, a book he cannot locate, any casual detail both indicates and hides this persecution: "After having feared the Jesuits, I was afraid of the Jansenists and the philosophes. An enemy of anything resembling a party, faction, or cabal, I never expected anything good from those who belonged to them" (570). Some days he is calm, but the sense of tragic destiny is always hovering over him: "[T]he dull rumblings that precede the storm began to be heard and everyone with any sense easily understood that some plot about me and my book was being hatched and that it would soon explode" (575).

Offended by the religious ideas expressed in *Emile,* the conservative Paris Parlement ordered that the author be arrested and the book confiscated. Awakened in the middle of the night by the Luxembourgs,

Rousseau had barely enough time to escape. Once again on the road, once again chased from his home, Rousseau ends book 11 with a dramatic gesture that echoes his rapid departure from the Hermitage at the end of book 9: "Upon entering the territory of Berne, I stopped the coach. I climbed out, I lay down, I embraced, I kissed the earth, I cried out in my emotion. Heavenly protector of virtue, I praise you, I am reaching a land of freedom" (587).

Book 12 covers the period from June 1762, when Jean-Jacques was chased from France, to October 1765, when he fled from Switzerland to England. (Three of the last six books in the second part of the *Confessions* end with catastrophic departures.) Rousseau's conviction that he is the object of a sinister plot dominates this final book. The opening paragraph practically explodes with fear and paranoia, as did the incipit of book 7:

> Here begins the work of shadows in which I have been buried for eight years without being able, no matter what I have done, to pierce the frightening obscurity. In the abyss of evil where I am submerged, I feel the blows that strike me, I see their immediate cause, but I cannot see either the hand that guides them or the means being used. Opprobrium and sorrow fall on me as if by themselves and without seeming to. When my broken heart groans, I seem to be a man who complains without cause, and the authors of my ruin have discovered the unimaginable art of making the public an accomplice in their plot while the public does not even suspect it or notice the results. (589)

The intensity of Rousseau's pain reaches the breaking point as he repeats his laments about the plot: "This chorus of barking whose motivations continued under a veil were sinister and frightening" (605). Even in his retreat at Neuchâtel, Rousseau notices that "they had begun to foment the people through underground maneuvers" so that "the population secretly incited to revolt by I know not who" gradually was moved to "fury," insulting him "publicly, in broad-daylight," both in the fields and on the streets (624). Rousseau is doubly distressed to see that "the families of my friends or those who had that name enter[ed] quite openly into the league of my persecutors" (631). The agitation around him is so intense that "from then on I was enveloped in those thick shadows through which I could not perceive any sort of truth" (633).

The plot (both the narrative story line and Rousseau's persecution) culminates in "my catastrophe at Môtiers" (634). In the dark of night, rocks were thrown at Rousseau's house, breaking windows and frightening everyone out of bed (634–35). "The spectacle of the people's hatred so broke my heart that I could no longer stand it" (636). Rousseau was once again chased from his refuge.

Being the victim of such persecution prevents Rousseau from understanding his predicament. "In narrating the events that concern me, the treatment I have suffered, and everything that has happened to me, I am incapable of finding the directing hand and of ascertaining causes while recounting the facts" (589). Despite his confusion, he weaves this complex series of overlapping events into an effective narrative. "I have such a confused memory of this whole affair that I cannot put it in order or find any link among the ideas that remain; I can only present them separately and isolated as they occur to me" (627). Rousseau shapes his story through details that, while true, are most effectively placed. Thus each crisis, either persecution or exile, is followed by a calming release: after the lapidation at Môtiers comes the sweet idyll on Saint-Pierre island. The list of the true friends he has "lost" (the Duc de Luxembourg and Maman had died, while Lord Keith had moved to Berlin) provides a somber background for these events. His quarrels with local authorities start a fatal drumroll of expulsions: Berne, Môtiers, Saint-Pierre, Bienne. Disgusted by the "terrible fermentation concerning me," Jean-Jacques finally determines to leave "this homicidal land" (655). This final book climaxes on another pathetic departure. Thinking that he is leaving to join Lord Keith in Berlin, Jean-Jacques, hounded by intolerant religious authorities and haunted by the shadowy plot that was both real and imaginary, will in fact end up in exile in England. This time there is no resolution, no calming closure. The *Confessions* end abruptly, broken off in midlife, in mid-crisis, in mid-flight.

Thematics

Having looked at the structure of individual books, I now turn to the larger patterns that weave in and out of the entire text. Patterns are neither easily defined nor clearly distinguishable units. Pervasive yet vague, they do not have a single locus even though they saturate the whole work. By contrasting narrative architecture and thematics, horizontal and vertical readings, my binary approach tries to make sense of this most complex composition. At the same time I do not want to impose too simplistic an analysis. I do not intend to cut up a work as rich as the *Confessions* into neat compartments. Rousseau's text is a complicated combination of various parts that, like a gourmet dish, cannot be reduced to the list of its ingredients. No recipe can compare to eating a fine meal, though it might whet our appetite and alert us to some culinary delights we might otherwise have missed.

Rousseau was not the first to write about his own life or to attempt an autobiography. The title of his work is an acknowledgment and an imitation of Saint Augustine, who wrote his *Confessions* in the fourth century A.D. Augustine's title as well as his depiction of himself as a sinner admitting his wrongs and thus moving to a higher spiritual level surely appealed to Rousseau. Montaigne, however, is the most immediate as well as the most powerful French model. His *Essays* delineated a portrait of himself, of his ideas, and of his mental life. Still, as revealing and intimate as the *Essays* were, they were not a retelling of the various incidents of his life and thus not the kind of coherent narrative detailing people, places, and events that is recognized as (auto)biography. Closer to Rousseau's time was the growing number of novels published as "memoirs." These novels imitated the fairly common genre of real memoirs, in which notable individuals left an account of their lives. Memoirs, whether real or fictional, were potential (auto)biographies that help define how a life could be transformed into a narrative.

How might that transformation be managed? I begin with a few narrative techniques that offer some insight into how Rousseau approached that critical question. Even as Jean-Jacques anchors his life story in an exact time frame, chronology often blurs or disappears as a fixed measure of passing events. Time expands and contracts from book to book according to the needs of the narrative. Some books are presented as a panorama, sweeping over many years (e.g., 1712 to 1728 in book 1, 1742 to 1749 in book 4). Details appear for a brief instant and then fade. In contrast, book 2 deals with only eight months in 1728, and book 9 focuses on the year and a half spent at the Hermitage. At several points in that book, time either stands still or moves with agonizing slowness. A palpable tension rises as Jean-Jacques and Mme. d'Epinay exchange letters they insist on interpreting for the worst. As if in cinematic slow motion, many of these letters are reproduced in full. Narrative pace slows to almost a full stop just before this once-happy relationship explodes in recriminations and mutual accusations.

Jean-Jacques is not just the principal actor in this script in which he plays himself. The first-person singular pronoun *I* denotes both the author and the actor in this life story. As the narrator, Rousseau tells his story from a more distant perspective and with a foreknowledge of consequences that he, as participant in these adventures, could never have had. Addressing us directly, located outside the time frame he is narrating, Jean-Jacques shapes our reading of his narrative and tells us how to react to the story in front of us.

This double perspective is of course familiar to readers of eighteenth-century memoir novels. Critics have theorized extensively about these distinctions between narrator and personage as well as between the story told and the telling of that story.[3] Rousseau's text, however, acquires an extra emotional charge because we readers know we are witnessing a real life and not a fiction, especially when he connects innocent experiences with later consequences. The entry of the genial fraud Venture de Villeneuve is announced with almost tragic portent: "I was distracted, dreamy; I was gasping; what could I do about it? Nothing that I could do myself was lacking for my progress. But for me to commit new foolishness all that was missing was a subject to inspire them. The subject arrived. Chance arranged things, and as you will see later on, my foolish head did the rest" (III, 123). Most memorable are those passages, many of which I examined in the first half of this chapter, where the retrospective narrator denounces the conspirators who were plotting against him when he was an unaware participant.

Even though Jean-Jacques is writing an autobiography and not fiction, he blurs that crucial distinction between document and novel when he incorporates fictional devices into his tale of truth. As the reader's guide and interlocutor, Jean-Jacques often pauses to offer a commentary on the tale he is telling. "No accident disturbed my trip; I was in the most fortunate state of mind and body that I have ever been in my life. Young, vigorous, full of health, security, and confidence in myself and in others, I was in that short but precious moment of life when its expansive fullness stretches, so to speak, our being through all our sensations and embellishes in our eyes all of nature with the charm of our own existence" (II, 58). At other times he admits the difficulty of trying to make sense of the confusing series of events he wants to meld into a coherent narrative: "The more I advance in my story, the less I can find order and coherence. The agitation of the rest of my life has not given events the time to arrange themselves in my head. They have been too numerous, too mixed up, too disagreeable to be told without confusion" (XII, 622).

On occasion Jean-Jacques sees himself from the outside, as others do. Almost invariably these passages are comic as the narrator denigrates the younger but not wiser fellow he used to be. "The result of his observations was that despite what my person and animated physiognomy promised, I was if not completely inept, at least a boy of no wit and no parts, one who having learned almost nothing was extremely limited in every sense, and for whom the honor of becoming one day a poor parish priest was the highest fortune I had any right to expect" (III, 113). What he wins on one hand—dramatic premonitions, enthusiastic personal effusions, comic characterization—he loses on the other by confusing the genres. Those accusations that Rousseau lied in his *Confessions* stem in large part from his very effective but too liberal use of fictional devices.

One outstanding quality Rousseau brought to his narrative was a conviction that he was unique and that his personal life story would interest everyone. This sense of his uniqueness meshed well with his double role as both narrator and actor. The audacity of Rousseau's concept of self, his overweening conceit that all eyes should focus on him, and the powerful rhetoric that sustains this conviction are all captured memorably on the opening page of the *Confessions:*

> I am initiating an enterprise that never has had a precedent and whose execution will have no imitator. I want to show my fellows a man in all the truth of nature; and that man will be me.
>
> Me alone. . . . I am made like no one I have ever seen; I dare to believe that I am made like no one else alive. If I am not better, at least I am different. . . .
>
> Let the trumpet of the last judgment sound when it will. I will come before my sovereign judge with this book in my hand. I will say out loud: here is what I have done, what I have thought, what I was. I have told the good and the bad with equal frankness. I have hid nothing that was bad, added nothing that was good. . . . I have revealed myself as I was, despicable and vile when I was that, good, generous, sublime when I was that. . . . Eternal Being, gather around me the numberless crowd of my fellows: let them listen to my confessions, let them groan at my indignities, let them blush at my miseries. Let everyone of them in turn reveal his heart at the foot of your throne with the same sincerity. And let anyone then say to you, if he dare: I was better than that man. (I, 6)

Some contemporaries reacted negatively to this solipsistic display as well as to Rousseau's cavalier attitude toward the God of Judgment Day. But time was on Jean-Jacques's side. His conception of the sacred and unique individual would soon become one of the major tenets of romanticism. And so Rousseau's special sense of self, his unshakable conviction that he was a unique individual, operated a major transformation in literary history. In the wake of his writings, the classical concern with general and abstract human nature, with the human (stereo)type that is valid in all times and places, yielded to romantic individualism and to the unique hero who resembled no one but himself.

One measure of proof that Rousseau was correct to consider himself so special and noteworthy is the fascination that his *Confessions* have excited among psychoanalysts. With a frequency and an attention to detail not granted to many writers, Jean-Jacques has been the subject (might I say the victim?) of innumerable psychological analyses. That he is so often chosen as a case study in abnormal psychology serves to confirm his own conviction that he was different from the usual run of men.

In addition to himself, Rousseau brought another topic to his *Confessions* that was quite new and refreshing. He "invented" childhood, or rather the possibility of talking about adolescence as a critical and unique time of life. Before Rousseau, writers simply did not talk about their childhood; before Rousseau, children were seen but not heard. Rousseau's memories of childhood prepared the way for Wordsworth's phrase that the child was the father of the man. Today, such ideas as the innocence of children and childhood as a kind of paradise have become so common that we can hardly imagine we ever thought otherwise. This revolutionary new sense of childhood as a worthwhile artistic subject can be illustrated by passages like the following, in which Jean-Jacques simply but effectively describes the aunt who raised him:

> I was always with my aunt, watching her embroider, listening to her sing, sitting or standing next to her, and I was happy. Her sprightliness, her sweetness, her kind face left me with such powerful impressions that I still see her look, her attitude, her expression. I remember her kind words. I would tell how she was dressed and how she wore her hair, without forgetting the two hooks of her dark hair against her forehead, as was the fashion at that time. (I, 11)

When he talks about the songs she sang, he creates a real nostalgia for those forgotten words. The words themselves are not important; all that counts is that wonderful feeling of a happy, carefree time, the past recaptured by memory: "The attraction her singing had for me was such that not only did I remember several of her songs, but that others come back to me, now that I have lost her; totally forgotten since my infancy, they return as I grow older, and with a charm I cannot express. Can anyone imagine that me, old fool that I am, worn out by worry and pain, that I am surprised to find myself crying like a baby as I mumble those old melodies in a broken and trembling voice?" (I, 11).

Writing an autobiography naturally demands that the author remember the incidents he wants to retell. Jean-Jacques goes one step further and emphasizes that the simple act of remembering, of recalling one's past, is a special activity: "This welter of objects boldly depicted has enchanted me a hundred times in my memory, as much and even more than in reality. I have always had a soft spot for a certain air of *Conditor alma Syderum* in iambic rhythm because one Sunday in Advent lying in my bed I heard this hymn being sung before dawn on the steps of the cathedral according to the rite of that church" (III, 122–23). Remembering is not a mechanical recall of past events. More importantly, it is a sentimental activity that is a pleasure in itself: "More than 30 years have passed since I left Bossey without remembering that period agreeably through a network of memories. But having passed my prime I am descending into old age, now I feel that these same memories come to life while others disappear, and they etch themselves into my memory in a way whose charm and strength increase from day to day" (I, 21).

Rousseau remembers not for informational purposes; he remembers for pleasure. What for a historian would be an intellectual reconstruction becomes for Jean-Jacques an emotional adventure, a sentimental reliving of the past: "The smallest incidents from then please me simply because they date from that time. I recall all the details about places, people, or what time it was. I see the servant girl or the valet busy in the room, a swallow flying in through the window, a fly land on my hand while I was reciting my lesson. I see the entire lay-out of the room where we were. . . . I know that the reader does not need to know all that; but it is I who need to tell him all that. Do I dare tell likewise all those anecdotes from that happy age which still make me tremble with pleasure when I remember them" (21–22).[4] Jean-Jacques wants to tell five or six such anecdotes but knows he cannot. So he proposes to tell just one, "provided that you let me tell it at great length, just to prolong my pleasure." Autobiography here is more than getting the facts of one's life on record. It supposes that those facts will be presented with a special emotional charge, for both the author and the reader. Indeed, that emotional charge will affect especially the author, whose obvious emotional commitment conditions the reader's own affective response.

Rousseau promised that he would tell his life without embroidery, without hiding the disagreeable side of his personality. Part of the shock

of Rousseau's autobiography is the discovery that the child is not perfectly innocent and that sex is a fact of life. Jean-Jacques admitted to
sexual urges that later, more puritanical ages did not want to recognize:
his ambiguous homosexual experience in the convent in Turin (II,
66–68), erotic games that today we would describe as flashing or, more
accurately, mooning (III, 88–90), his masturbation, "that dangerous
supplement" (III, 109) that Jacques Derrida has commented upon so
famously.[5] Surrounded by a whole tradition of libertine and scurrilous
writing that flourished in the eighteenth century, Rousseau did not share
that Victorian reluctance (which was still prevalent until quite recently)
to discuss private sexuality in public. Some of Rousseau's most moving
pages recount his adolescent passions: that delightful afternoon picking
cherries, and the series of older, married women, such as Mme. Basile,
whom he adored so chastely and yet so comically: "Without having
reached that point [i.e., any physical intimacy], next to her I tasted
inexpressible delight. Nothing of what I experienced from physically
possessing a women can equal the few minutes I spent at her feet without daring to touch her dress" (II, 76–77).

His relationship with Mme. de Warens combined both the ineffable
and the physical. He met her at age 16 in a theatrical moment that
transformed his life completely. In recounting that first meeting
Rousseau suddenly changes verb tenses from the expected past to the
dramatic present. "Ready to enter [the church] through that door,
Mme. de Warens turns around upon hearing my voice. What did I
become upon seeing her!" (II, 49). A few years later he entered her bed.
His emotional attachment long outlasted their physical relationship,
which indelibly marked his youth. That same sudden shift from past to
present tense intensifies one of his bittersweet homecomings: "How my
heart beat as I approached Mme. de Warens' house! My legs were trembling beneath me, my eyes seemed covered by a veil, I could see nothing, I heard nothing, I would not have recognized anyone. I was forced
to stop several times to breathe and gather my senses. . . . I tremble at
the first sound of her voice, I throw myself at her feet, and in a frenzy of
overwhelming joy I attach my mouth to her hand" (III, 103).

This not-so-innocent child leads quite easily to the question of guilt
and of exactly what Jean-Jacques confessed. In terms of its length and
dramatic impact, the greatest fault Jean-Jacques acknowledges is the
lie he told to the Comte de La Roque when he was suspected of stealing
a ribbon (book 2). Now, as narrator, he confesses his remorse at having
accused another servant of this theft. Marion, the young girl in ques-

tion, was, as Jean-Jacques now admits, completely innocent. Rousseau asks pardon because he feels that his accusation, and the dismissal it entailed, ruined Marion's life. The story is moving. The guilt Jean-Jacques has borne for some 50 years taps into the emotional dialectic that flows through all the *Confessions*. To do evil is wrong, but to confess having done evil is good. Confessing absolves the fault, turns guilt into empathy so that sin disappears in forgiveness. Instinctively Rousseau knows how to manipulate the dynamics of sin and repentance. Unerringly he touches his reader at her most vulnerable point: her desire to forgive, her maternal instinct to pardon her wayward son. Let us not forget that Rousseau's most enthusiastic readers were female. Rousseau's seductive charm over women was most effective not in aristocratic salons or public spaces, where timidity paralyzed him, but in more intimate settings, where he dominated his interlocutor, as he did on the written page.

There is, however, another side to guilt and confession. By admitting small failings Jean-Jacques disculpates himself from much more serious faults. He beats his breast contritely at the thought of having ruined Marion, but he glides lightly over abandoning all his own children to an orphanage as soon as they were born (XI, 557–59). Orphanages were dismal institutions in the eighteenth century; almost all children there died before their fifth birthday. Because there was little possibility of adoption, surrendering a child to an orphanage was tantamount to infanticide. Nonetheless, so powerful is the confessional mode that Jean-Jacques almost succeeds in transforming his most grievous fault into an accusation against those who revealed his own despicable action.[6]

Rousseau's guilt, both for the serious offense he slides over and for the minor peccadilloes to which he confesses so effectively, touches on something discussed in the previous section: all those passages about the plot and how he has been marked both by destiny and by his fellow man. A good deal of Rousseau's fascination with the plot stems from his megalomania, his paranoia (which is not too strong a term for Rousseau's state of mind), and his overwhelming desire to be different. I am not forgetting that the plot was real. Although the morbidly sensitive and thin-skinned Jean-Jacques was often enough at fault in dealing with his friends, he was also the victim of real persecution. Even though he was not as innocent as his short list of faults would imply, he was not so evil as to deserve the harsh anger of such former friends as Diderot and Mme. d'Epinay or the organized pursuit of ideological adversaries in church and government who drove him into exile.

The theme that, after childhood, is probably most associated with Jean-Jacques is his innovative and very personal treatment of nature. Before Rousseau, French classical writers were largely indifferent to any depiction of nature. After Rousseau, the romantics were defined in part by their ability to describe nature as a reflection of their inner feelings, as a landscape of the soul. Jean-Jacques is the writer who operated this major transformation in our way of, literally, *seeing* nature. When he describes his room at Chambéry chez Maman, he captures both its natural setting and its sentimental value: "This room opened onto the narrow street I have spoken about where our first meeting took place, and beyond the stream and the gardens you could see the countryside. This view was not an indifferent thing for its young lodger. It was the first time since Bossey that I had some greenery in front of my window. . . . How sweet and stimulating this novelty was for me! It greatly increased my penchant toward being moved emotionally" (III, 105).

Unlike almost any other writer of his time or before, Jean-Jacques belongs to nature, in nature. "The joy with which I saw the first buds cannot be expressed. To see spring again is for me to be resuscitated in paradise" (VI, 233). It was Rousseau who "discovered" such natural phenomena as mountains. In what others before him had considered a frightening geological phenomenon, he saw a sentimental ally, a point of communication between the human observer and the nature he observed. During his short stay on Saint-Pierre island Jean-Jacques would rush outside early in the morning "to sniff the cool and healthy morning air and let my eyes rove along the horizon of this beautiful lake [the lac de Bienne], whose banks and the mountains that lined them enchanted my sight" (XII, 642). Jean-Jacques walked long distances, traveling on foot from Geneva to Chambéry in Savoy and eventually to Paris. He was the poet of the open road, of carefree wanderings, of almost mystic communication with the environment surrounding him. "I would rise every morning before the sun. I would walk through a near-by orchard along a pretty little path which was above the vineyard and which followed the hill up to Chambéry. There as I walked I would offer a prayer that consisted not in the vain babble of lips but in the sincere elevation of my heart toward the author of this loving nature whose beauties were spread before my eyes. I have never liked to pray in a room. . . . I like to contemplate [God] in his works as my heart rises toward him" (VI, 236). Alone among his contemporaries, Jean-Jacques records the exhilaration of sleeping under the stars:

I even remember having spent a wonderful night outside the town along
a road that followed the Rhone or the Saone, I forget which. Terraced
gardens lined the road on the other side. It had been quite hot that day;
the afternoon was charming; dew was moistening the wilted grass; no
wind, a quiet night; the air was crisp without being cold; after setting the
sun had left in the sky some red vapors whose reflection turned the water
rose-colored; the trees on the terraces were filled with nightingales
exchanging calls. I was walking in a kind of ecstasy opening my senses
and my heart to all this, sighing only a bit regretfully at enjoying it
alone. . . . I lay down voluptuously on the threshold of a niche or fake
doorway cut into the retaining wall. The canopy of my bed was formed
by the topmost branches of the trees, a nightingale was directly above
me. I fell asleep listening to his song. Sleep was sweet, and awakening
was even sweeter. (IV, 168 – 69)

Recounting his frequent trips, Rousseau mixes his striking appreciation of the natural world with the picaresque adventures he experienced
either alone or with such companions as Venture de Villeneuve or Bâcle,
his amorous encounters on the road (with Mme. de Larnage, among
others), and his obvious joy in being free (that great political, moral, and
physical value: freedom) and in following whatever path seemed most
inviting. When he abandoned Geneva at age 16 and took to the open
road, he mused, "The independence I thought I had acquired was the
only sentiment that affected me. Free and master of myself, I thought I
could do anything, reach anywhere; I had only to spring to rise up and
fly through the air. With confidence I was entering the vast space of the
world" (II, 45).

Love is another major theme that runs through the different periods
of Rousseau's life and inspires a number of his most moving pages. Love
appears in the *Confessions* in all its various moods. Innocent, adolescent
love pervades that entire afternoon in book 4 when a handsome young
Jean-Jacques met two young ladies on horseback in the countryside. He
shared a picnic with them and together they spent the day picking cherries. Excited and amorous, Jean-Jacques was attracted to both Mlle. de
Graffenried and Mlle. Galley, but he was unable to choose between
them. Desiring both and yet unwilling to give up one to embrace the
other, Rousseau was happily blocked in the middle, innocent and chaste
in his erotic dream. This triangulation of potential lovers is something of
a constant both in Rousseau's own life (Maman, Claude Anet, and Petit;
Saint-Lambert, Sophie, and Jean-Jacques) and in his fiction (Julie,

Claire, and Saint-Preux). Filled with desire and yet frustrated, unsa-
tiated amid apparent satisfaction, Jean-Jacques experienced both joy
and bitterness in this idyllic passion.

But love has more impetuous moments, too. Sophie d'Houdetot
bursts into Rousseau's retreat at the Hermitage in dramatic fashion:
"This visit seemed a bit like the beginning of a novel" (IX, 432). This is
literary and literal passion. Dressed like a man on her second visit (more
grist for the psychoanalytic mill!), both a married woman and the mistress of one of Rousseau's best friends, Sophie inspired "the first and the
only [love] in all my life, and . . . its consequences will make it forever
unforgettable and terrible in my memory" (IX, 439). Sophie gave her
name to the heroine of *Emile* and was at least a partial model for Julie: "I
saw my Julie in Mme. d'Houdetot" (440).

Love is also filial devotion directed at that maternal ideal, Maman.
Jean-Jacques first saw Mme. de Warens in a splendid springtime revelation. It was a literal and figurative lightning bolt whose intensity was
never matched and that lasted throughout his life. "It was Palm Sunday
1728. I run after her: I see her, I catch up with her, I speak to her. . . . I
should remember the place, I have since then often wet it with my tears
and covered it with my kisses. Oh if I could surround with a golden rail
that happy place! if I could direct the homage of all the earth to it!
Whoever wants to honor monuments to the salvation of men should
only approach them on his knees" (II, 48–49; ellipses in the original).

Finally, love can involve bitter betrayal. Book 9 recounts the
heartrending dispute between Jean-Jacques and Diderot. Also involved
in this famous quarrel were other friends, principally Grimm and Mme.
d'Epinay. But Jean-Jacques and Denis share the principal roles here.
Inseparable friends and soul mates ever since they met in Paris in the
late 1740s seeking their fortune, they had a falling out due to a series of
real and imagined slights. Miscues on both sides destroyed their friendship. Whom to blame, the caustic Diderot or the morbidly sensitive
Jean-Jacques? What most interests me here is the pain, almost the
lover's deception, that shook Rousseau to the depths of his soul. "Without noticing it I described [in the *Letter to d'Alembert on the Theater*] my
current situation. I depicted Grimm, Mme d'Epinay, Mme d'Houdetot,
Saint-Lambert, myself. Writing it I shed such delicious tears! Alas! it's
too obvious that love, that fatal love I tried to cure myself of had not yet
left my heart" (X, 495–96). The only name missing in this account, and
thus emphasized by its absence, is Diderot's. In the *Letter,* however, the
only one Rousseau really had in mind was Diderot, with whom he pub-

licly broke: "I will regret him unceasingly and my heart will miss him more than my writings" (*Oeuvres complètes,* V, p. 7). This "lover's quarrel," if I can be permitted such a term without implying anything sexual, shows its unabated hurt upon the written page with the same intensity today as it had 200 years ago.

Chapter Eight
The Reveries (1778)

The *Rêveries d'un Promeneur solitaire* (*Reveries of a Solitary Walker*) is Rousseau's last work: he was writing the tenth promenade when he died in June 1778. Like the *Confessions,* the *Reveries* are personal and autobiographical.[1] The work's short length and its generally optimistic outlook (for Rousseau, that is) make it an ideal text for anyone reading Jean-Jacques for the first time or wanting to experience the power of his poetic prose. Chronologically the last of his works, thematically the culmination of many typically Rousseauian concerns, the *Reveries* provides a logical point at which to conclude my study of Jean-Jacques.

Rousseau described these promenades as "a formless journal of my reveries" because of the "strange ideas which pass through my head as I walk along."[2] Hence the title and the free composition of these essays. Some are circular, doubling back at the end to their point of departure; others repeat the same idea, turning it over several times and examining it from multiple vantage points. Not only repetitive, they are also paradoxical, which is quite in harmony with Rousseau's character. My intention in this chapter is to follow Rousseau as he treads along these paths of memory and to indicate his principal ideas and how he moves from one to another.

The first promenade begins with Rousseau's eternal complaint about being the outsider, ostracized from society and victimized by mankind. He sees himself as blameless, while all others are leagued against him: "Here I am then alone on this earth, no longer having a brother, a fellow creature, a friend, or any society but myself. The most social and loving of men has been proscribed by unanimous agreement" (995). Although he will return in the course of the *Reveries* to denounce what he considers a hidden conspiracy against him, this opening serves nonetheless to introduce the underlying optimism of the text. Despite the plot against him, Jean-Jacques has discovered peace and calm. "It was not even two months ago that a deep calm settled into my heart. . . . An event as sad as it was unexpected has just erased from my heart that feeble ray of hope. . . . Henceforth I resigned myself entirely and I found peace" (997). No one is sure what this "sad and unexpected event" was. Perhaps it was the episode he will recount in the second promenade; perhaps it was the death of the Prince de Conti, one of his powerful protectors, which made Rousseau realize that he could not overcome his enemies. Whatever it was, it produced this incredible change in his attitude. He continues to see himself as the blameless victim, of course, but he no longer cares.

More importantly, he decides to cease struggling against his fate. In the final years of his life, Rousseau discovers that the only effective strategy against his foes is to ignore them. "Whether they do me harm or good, everything about them is indifferent to me; whatever they do, my contemporaries will never be anything for me" (998). Paradoxically, Rousseau wins his struggle when he stops fighting. Passivity becomes a successful and effective defense. "Henceforth I am nothing among men" (1000). More than nothing, or perhaps more accurately, less than nothing: Jean-Jacques aspires to real absence. "No longer able to perform any good action that does not turn bad, no longer able to act without harming myself or others, abstaining has become my sole duty."

As Rousseau develops his strategy of nonresistance, he explains the value of writing these *Reveries*. "Since I find only in myself consolation, hope, and peace, I should and I want to be concerned only with myself" (999). He proposes to study himself and prepare the final reckoning with his creator that he will soon be called upon to give. In addition, he foresees the pleasure writing will give him: "I will set down in writing those [daily promenades] which might yet happen to me; each time I reread them will repeat the pleasure." Not only will he find pleasure in rereading what he has written, but writing will in some degree replace living. Writing about the perfect moments will make them available to be lived a second time and will compensate for the sadness of his real life: "In my old age as my departure approaches, . . . reading them will remind me of the sweetness I tasted in writing them, and by recreating for me the past will so to speak double my existence" (1001).

These two themes fuse as the promenade draws to its conclusion. Writing had been part of Rousseau's struggle, and he was always worried that his enemies might destroy what he had written, alter the historical record of his life, and thus defeat him.[3] Now he brings his new-found peace to his concerns about the ultimate fate of his writings. "If they take them away from me while I'm alive, they will not take away either the pleasure of having written them, or the memory of their contents, or the solitary meditations of which they are the fruit" (1001). In a radical change of position, Rousseau is no longer concerned with the fate of what he has written. Now he focuses on the act of writing and the pleasure he derives from it because that augments the peace of mind he has just discovered: "[E]ven if they [his enemies] enjoy my discomfort fully, they will not prevent me from enjoying my innocence and from ending my days in peace despite them." The tone is still one of hurt and defensiveness, but Rousseau has reached a significant level of peace with himself and with his life.

The second promenade is mainly concerned with an accident that injured Rousseau rather severely on 24 October 1776. Before recounting that incident, however, he talks of walking back to Paris after an afternoon of observing wild plants and flowers in the countryside. As dusk approaches, he sees a field that has been harvested. The whole scene strikes him as an expression of his own feelings.

> The harvest had been finished a few days before; those on excursions from the city had returned there; even the peasants had left their fields until winter tasks were due. The countryside, still green and gay but already losing its leaves and almost entirely deserted, presented everywhere an image of solitude and of approaching winter. It thus produced a mixed impression, both sweet and sad, that was too similar to my age and my situation for me not to recognize it. (1004)

Here is a fine example of the pathetic fallacy, the romantic doctrine that nature has a necessary connection with the observer's personal life. Completely in tune with this melancholy countryside, Jean-Jacques laments that, late in the seasons of his life, he has not accomplished as much as he wished: "Sighing I said to myself, What have I done here below? I was made to live, and I'm dying without having lived."

This autumn scene sets the mood for the dire and ominous events that follow. Immediately after describing these desolate fields and implicitly comparing them to his soul, Rousseau is knocked down by a huge dog chasing a speeding carriage. Crossing the streets was no safer in eighteenth-century Paris than it is today! When Rousseau regains consciousness, he sees the world anew, just as if he had been reborn. I do not think it too strong to claim that here Rousseau records the kind of near-death and rebirth experience that such thanatologists as Kubler-Ross have studied. "It was night when I regained consciousness. . . . It was getting darker. I saw the sky, a few stars, some green. That first sensation was a wonderful moment. I felt nothing but that. I was being reborn to life at that instant" (1005). Only when he finally arrives home does Jean-Jacques realize the full extent of his injuries. Rumors start to fly that he was killed. Jean-Jacques is shocked to read his own obituary and the public reactions to his demise. The importance of Rousseau's accident emerges from this cleverly constructed sequence of disparate incidents: the autumnal field at twilight, his consciousness of an awakening or rebirth, and the report of death that turns out to be false. Significantly, this promenade ends with another evocation of the plot against him: "[T]hose black shadows that continually unfurled over me rekindled all the horror that they inspire in me naturally" (1009). Reborn through this death experience, however, Jean-Jacques recovers his calm and resignation in the final lines: "Rather than being cruel and cutting, that idea consoles me, calms me down, and helps me to resign myself. . . . God is just; he wants me to suffer; he knows I am innocent. . . . Let men and fortune do what they will; let us learn to suffer without murmuring. Everything must in the end fit into place, and my turn will come sooner or later" (1010).

Continuing the serious vein of the previous essay, the third promenade is a philosophical and at times religious meditation on a quotation from the Greek lawgiver Solon to the effect that only in old age do we learn how to live or, rather, how we should have lived. Rousseau's need to study himself, his actions, and most importantly his motivations informs all the *Reveries*. The entire central portion of this essay is devoted to the "grand revolution" that took place in Jean-Jacques in 1752 at age 40. "From my youth I had fixed the age of 40 as the end point of my efforts to succeed" (1014). Like many revolutionaries, he first made what would be called today a fashion statement:

> escaping from all temptations, from all vain hopes, I gave myself up to the neglect and the mental relaxation that was always my dominant taste and my strongest penchant. I left the world and its pomp. I renounced all finery: no more sword, no more watch, no more white stockings, gilt, hairdos; only a simple wig, a suit of good homespun, and better than all that, I rooted out of my heart the cupidity and the covetousness that gave value to all I had left behind.

Going beyond sartorial appearances, Jean-Jacques radically alters his attitude toward society. As he desperately seeks certainty, Rousseau cleans his philosophical house, discarding the tricks of argument and settling on what he feels is most truthful. "At first I was lost in such a labyrinth of perplexities, difficulties, objections, tortured thinking, and shadows that, tempted 20 times to abandon everything, I was ready to limit my deliberations to the rules of common prudence and, renouncing vain efforts, to stop further investigation into those principles that I had so much difficulty understanding" (1016–17). With characteristic hyperbole, Jean-Jacques describes his search for those beliefs that satisfied his heart rather than his head: "After the most passionate and the most sincere efforts that had ever been made by any mortal, I decided for my whole life upon those sentiments that mattered to me" (1014). All this philosophizing would eventually culminate in the profession of faith of the Savoyard Priest, the centerpiece of his *Emile,* which left Rousseau at peace with his personal revolution: "Imperturbable since then in the principles that I had adopted after so long and careful a meditation, I made them the immutable rule of my behavior and my faith, never again worrying either about the objections I could not resolve nor those I could not foresee" (1018).

This faith did not prepare him, however, for the conspiracy that was silently engulfing him: "[W]hile my open and unsuspecting heart overflowed with my friends and brothers, those traitors silently wrapped me up in nets woven in the depths of hell" (1019). Shaken by the extent and ferocity of the plot against him, Jean-Jacques at times doubted even himself: "It is true that in the middle of numberless outrages and huge indignities that crushed me on every side, periods of doubt and disquiet came from time to time to shake my hope and disturb my tranquillity" (1020). Nonetheless, the position taken in the strength and vigor of youth should not be abandoned in decrepit old age: "No, I am not now wiser, nor more educated, nor of better faith than when I decided these great questions" (1021). The calm Rousseau described in the earlier promenades returns. This essay, like an easy stroll, comes full circle as Jean-Jacques returns to the initial citation from Solon. "It is to this sole and useful study that I devote the rest of my old age. Happy if, through my progress on myself, I learn to leave this life not better, for that is not possible, but more virtuous than when I entered it" (1023).

With sincerity and veracity as its topics, the fourth promenade has unfortunately but rightfully earned Rousseau his reputation as one who did not hesitate to stretch the truth to fit his needs. The first main section deals with Rousseau's principles for defining truth. He chops a good deal of logic while avoiding the main issue. He tries to define truth as utility and as what we owe others. He objects to literary fiction as a lie, just as he takes simple politeness and social etiquette to task. Such were

the "rules of conscience on lies and truth" that his "heart followed
mechanically" (1032).

In the second section, which is even more tortuous than the first,
Jean-Jacques claims that his feeling about truth is more valid than his
thinking about it, "for I have rarely behaved according to rules or followed in anything any rule other than my natural impulsions" (1033).
He who earlier condemned fables and fictions and protested his fidelity
to the "holy truth that [his] heart adores" (1032) admits to having lied.
For himself, however, he finds excuses. He was unable to avoid lying
because he was too slow in conversation, too timid or ashamed to tell
the truth (1033). His claim on our sympathy is weakened when he
admits that "I sincerely repent my mistake, without however daring to
correct it" (1034). Far from having "dissimulated" anything in his *Confessions*, Jean-Jacques praises himself for having lied "in the opposite
direction by accusing myself too severely rather than by excusing myself
too indulgently" (1035). Writing the *Confessions* from memory, he did
"fill in the gaps with details which I imagined as a supplement to my
memories but which never contradicted them." This strange apology
climaxes when Jean-Jacques claims to have hidden truths that would
have put him in too good a light. "No, when I spoke against the truth
that I did know, it was only in indifferent matters and it was more by
the embarrassment of talking or the pleasure of writing than by any
motive of self-interest, or personal advantage, or harm to others"
(1038). In this ramble around truth, Rousseau finally arrives at the
desired point but leaves me puzzled as to how he got there: "I have
often uttered fables but I have very rarely lied."

The fifth promenade, probably the most famous of them all, can be
considered one of the defining texts of romanticism, or to be more accurate, a text that already embodied the tone and the themes that romantic writers would embrace as their own. Jean-Jacques returns in time to
1765, when, living on the island of Saint-Pierre in the lac de Bienne, in
Switzerland, he enjoyed a brief interlude of tranquillity during the very
troubled exile that followed the publication of *Emile*. His evocative
description contains the geographic and sentimental elements that
would shortly define a typical romantic site:

> The shores of Lake Bienne are more wild and romantic than those of
> Lake Geneva because the rocks and the woods there come closer to the
> shoreline. Still, they are no less inviting. If there are fewer cultivated

fields and vineyards, fewer towns and houses, there is more greenery, more meadows, more shady copses, more frequent contrasts, and more various topography. . . . the area is little frequented by travelers. (1040)

After the physical description comes the moral aspect of his brief idyllic residence. Free from social constraints, free to do nothing (the dear *"far niente"* he celebrates rejects any outside compulsion), Jean-Jacques indulges his passion for nature by gathering botanical specimens.

The middle section of the promenade contains a poetic evocation of Rousseau's typical day. Here Jean-Jacques melds all his days into one, compacting his six-week experience. Temporal adverbs ("often," "other times") and the imperfect verb tense establish the iterative nature of this romantic day par excellence as Rousseau's various activities all center around his contact with the water and his marvelous appreciation of its soothing effect: dreaming in a drifting boat, sitting on the shore at dusk, strolling along the banks with his companions after dinner. Twelve years after his stay there, Rousseau's memory of it is so powerful that "it is still impossible for me to think about this dear abode without feeling myself transported there every time by the wings of desire" (1045).

Most appropriately, in the final third of this promenade Jean-Jacques inquires into the nature of happiness. For him, happiness consists not in "those short moments of frenzy and passion, no matter how strong they are," but in a "simple and permanent state" (1046). Although alone, Jean-Jacques finds all he needs to be happy in himself: "[A]s long as that state lasts, one is self-sufficient like God" (1047). Like the waters of the lake whose soothing motion he has described, happiness requires a subdued but regular movement. Revery and reality, consciousness and dream, nature and self, are all assimilated in Rousseau's beatific vision of his island paradise:

> Coming out of a long and pleasant dream, seeing myself surrounded by greenery, flowers, and birds, and letting my eyes roam to the distant romantic shores that bordered a vast expanse of crystal clear water, I mixed all these lovable objects with my fictions and, finally led back to myself and to what surrounded me, I could not tell the point of demarcation between fiction and reality; so much did everything conspire to endear to me the sheltered and solitary life I was leading in that beautiful dwelling. (1048)

In the end, Rousseau's promenade and his essay are powerful enough to elude time. Just as his supercharged day overlaps and subsumes all the

other days on the island, writing this essay allows Jean-Jacques to slip out
of time, to go back in time, to relive out of time that time when he was so
happy: "But they [his enemies] will not prevent me from transporting
myself there every time on the wings of imagination and to enjoy for a few
hours the same pleasures as if I were still living there. . . . The objects [of
his dreams] would often escape from me in these raptures, and now the
deeper my revery, the more it paints them vividly. I am often more among
them, and more agreeably, than when I really was there" (1049).

The sixth promenade begins with Rousseau going off to the countryside, passing through the gate in the city's walls not far from today's
major intersection at Denfert-Rochereau, and automatically taking a
particular path. Asking himself why he would take that path and not
another launches a discussion about how an act of charity, originally
done freely and spontaneously, became an oppressive obligation. This
kind of paradox, examining how freedom can insensibly lead to constraint, is typically Rousseauian.

Although he claims always to have found pleasure in doing good,
Jean-Jacques often felt trapped by his initial good action: "The pleasure
that incrementally became a habit was transformed, I do not know how,
into a kind of duty whose constriction I soon felt" (1050). Every kind
gesture locked him into subsequent obligations: "I often felt however
the weight of my own good deeds because of the chain of obligations
that they brought in their wake" (1051). The extent of Rousseau's outrage comes across in the images and vocabulary he uses to describe his
dilemma: "Once any *unfortunate* individual caught me with the *grappling
hook* of a good deed done, it was all over. That first good deed, free and
voluntary, became an *unlimited* right to all those that he might need in
the future. . . . That is how the sweetest pleasures were transmuted into
onerous enslavement for me" (1052; my italics). Rousseau's generous heart
is free to act only when it is absolutely free from any compulsion to act.
"That is what makes painful for me those good deeds that others
demand and that I would do myself if others did not demand them"
(1053). Jean-Jacques compares his predicament to a contract. Once the
giver has entered into this contract, he cannot refuse subsequent acts of
charity, because he has encouraged the receiver to expect them. Better
never to have entered into the contract! Although Rousseau's point is a
bit strained, it nonetheless provides a valid insight into the antagonistic
relationship of charity and (in)gratitude.

Rousseau's solution for this dilemma is to abstain, a strategy he
advanced in the first promenade. To avoid those traps set for his gen-

erosity, "I abstain from acting" (1056). The notion of traps naturally provokes the oft-repeated complaint that Jean-Jacques is being harassed by his former friends turned enemies. Another variation of this strategy is avoidance: "I prefer avoiding them to hating them." A third form of escape from such obligations involves the wish to be invisible. If he were unseen, Rousseau could act generously and still avoid any expectations that his generosity aroused: "I would exercise over them [i.e., his fellow human beings] a universal and perfectly disinterested benevolence. . . . without the yoke of duty, I would do for them, freely and of my own volition, everything that they themselves, inspired by self-love and constrained by laws, have so much difficulty in doing" (1057). Jean-Jacques concludes by affirming how poorly adapted he is to civil society, "where everything is hindrance, obligation, duty" (1059). Again he complains that as soon as he feels the yoke of obligation, "I rebel and become mulish, then I am nothing. . . . I abstain from acting." Just as countless times he took that same path through the gate at the Denfer barrier to the Bièvre river, Rousseau repeats how any compulsion always had a chilling effect on his warm generosity.

The seventh promenade has a scientific tone and content. At age 65, Jean-Jacques resumed his study of botany.[4] This renewed interest, which transformed an old man into a young schoolboy again, is "a bizarre fact I wanted to explain about myself" (1061). It is another opportunity to acquire more self-knowledge. Rousseau prefers dreaming to real study: "[D]reaming relaxes and amuses me, thinking wears me out and makes me sad; reflection was always for me a difficult activity without any attraction" (1062). This same paragraph contains an excellent definition of the reverie as a literary genre: "Sometimes my reveries end in meditation, but more often my meditations end in reveries. During these wanderings my soul roams through the universe and soars on the wings of imagination in raptures that transcend any other pleasure." Jean-Jacques sings the praises of the "spectacle of nature" whose rich variety comforts him in distress. He criticizes those who seek in nature only what is useful or practical, "drugs and remedies" (1063), and who fail to understand that "the vegetable kingdom can of itself merit our attention" (1064). Seeing nature as a "pharmacy" reduces something truly grand to the lowest level of man's selfish, material interest.

The next section evokes in succession the beauties of the three natural kingdoms, the mineral, the animal, and the vegetable (the last reduced to flowers), and the difficulties encountered in studying them. Talking of minerals and mining, Jean-Jacques paints an ecological nightmare, linking the discontents of civilization to its mistakes in dealing with nature. To his great misfortune, man

> digs in the intestines of the earth; in its center, at the risk of his own life and at the expense of his health, he seeks imaginary goods in place of the actual goods that the earth offers him when he knows how to enjoy her. He flees the sun and the daylight he is unworthy to see; he buries himself alive, and that's good since he no longer deserves to live in the light of day. Over there, quarries, chasms, forges, furnaces, a whole machinery of hammers and anvils, smoke and fire, replace the sweet images of rustic labor. Blackened ironsmiths, hideous cyclopes, the emaciated faces of those unfortunates who languish in the infected atmosphere of mines, are all spectacles that mining wreaks on the earth, replacing those of greenery and flowers, blue skies, shepherds in love, and vigorous peasants. (1067)

Defending nature quickly turns to attacking industry, which was of course another manifestation of the society Rousseau detested. His critique includes not only the mechanical aspects of industry but also its intellectual pretensions: "From all this sad and exhausting work there results usually much less knowledge than pride. Where is the most mediocre chemist who does not think he has understood all the operations of nature when he has found by accident a couple of tricks of his art?" Jean-Jacques would certainly not appreciate the research laboratories on our university campuses today!

The vegetable kingdom does afford real pleasure. That pleasure, however, exists only when man limits himself to "low-tech" activities, like botanizing. "But once you add self-interest or vanity, either to find a job or to write a book, as soon as you learn in order to teach others, when you botanize only to become an author or a professor, all that pleasant charm evaporates, you see plants only as the instruments of your own passions" (1069). Rousseau's screed against man's imperious desire to use everything for his own satisfaction culminates in the opposition of city and nature, study and pleasure: "By denaturing this lovely study, they transplant it to the center of cities and academies where it degenerates just like those exotic plants in botanical gardens" (1070). For Jean-Jacques, nature is a sanctuary, a refuge where he can hide from his enemies: "It seems that in the shade of a forest I can be forgotten, as free and peaceful as if I never had an enemy or as if the leaves of the trees would protect me from their attacks." After an amusing anecdote in which, thinking himself alone in the remote mountains, he comes upon a stocking factory, Rousseau claims that only Switzerland has been able to reconcile nature and industry.

The promenade ends on three notes that recapitulate the essay and suggest how its main themes can be prolonged. First, Rousseau reiterates his love of nature, "this beautiful countryside, these forests, these lakes, these copses, these rocks, these mountains whose view has always touched my heart" (1073). Second, he celebrates the power of memory and imagination: "[N]ow that I can no longer travel in those happy lands, I have only to open my book of dried plants and immediately it transports me there." Finally, he finds peace and consolation in the correct, disinterested study of nature: "It reminds me both of my youth and my innocent pleasures, it allows me to enjoy them anew, and makes me happy."

The eighth promenade gives new formulations to a paradox and a complaint that Jean-Jacques has expressed before. The happy periods of Rousseau's life have left little or no trace, whereas the difficult times produced some pleasure. "The varied duration of my brief prosperity has hardly left me any agreeable memory . . . and on the contrary in all the miseries of my life I felt myself constantly filled with tender, touching, and delicious feelings" (1074). Jean-Jacques has reached his present state of indifference and calm in the face of adversity: "[A]fter lengthy anguish, instead of the despair which should finally have been my lot, I found again serenity, tranquillity, peace, and even happiness" (1077).

But how? First, he "learned to wear the yoke of necessity without murmuring" (1077). Next, he distinguished between the intention to harm and actual harm itself. This distinction permits him to "look at all the details of my destiny as so many acts of pure fatality to which I could not assign direction, intention, or moral cause, and so I had to submit without quarrelling and without resisting since that would have been useless" (1079). Finally, he had to overcome his "self-love" (*amour propre*): "In whatever situation we find ourselves, it is only because of [self-love] that we are consistently unhappy" (1080). Peace comes when and only because Rousseau has recovered his true nature: "I will continue, whatever they do, to be, in spite of them, what I am. . . . I have only myself as a resource."

This peace of mind is another variation on the passivity and absence that Rousseau mentioned in the first and sixth promenades as his strategy for escaping the plot: "I worry about nothing, whatever happens, I am indifferent to it all" (1081). His enemies and their machinations have unwittingly given him peace: "By making me insensitive to adversity, they have done me more kindness than if they had spared me their attacks." Nonetheless, Rousseau's equilibrium is precarious. A prisoner of his senses and of the physical impact they record, he can at times react violently to the slightest stimulus. "But I rarely escape the evident attack, and when I'm thinking the least about it, a sinister look I notice, a poisoned word I overhear, a wicked person I meet, is enough to bowl me over. All that I can do in such a case is to forget quickly and flee. The agitation of my heart disappears with the object that caused it and I regain my calm as soon as I am alone" (1082). Flight is but another form of abstinence and escape.

The ninth promenade touches on a delicate subject: the five children Jean-Jacques placed in an orphanage after they were born. Like the essay on lying, this promenade does not leave a good impression because of the way Rousseau deflects and distorts the issue. The accusation of abandoning his children (which was true) is transformed into one of "being an unnatural father and of hating children" (1087). Not only does that original and very serious charge disappear as a fault, but it almost becomes praiseworthy: "I would do it again with even less hesitation if it were to do over, and I know that no father is more kind than I would have been for them." Thus amended and modified, the accusation is much easier to refute, which is of course why Rousseau has made the substitution. That rhetorical sleight of hand taints what otherwise would be an extraordinary evocation of the past.

Jean-Jacques points to the serious study he made of children: "[I]t would obviously be the most incredible thing in the world if *Heloise* and *Emile* were the work of a man who did not love children" (1088). He observes that he wanted children to enjoy being with him, whereas most adults selfishly think only of their own enjoyment when they are with youngsters. He then recounts in detail three episodes that prove his affection for children. In the first, he embraces a child in the street but is frightened away by a "spy" who, he thinks, is denouncing him to the child's father (1090). For us today, Rousseau's behavior is quite disturbing because we are so aware of passers-by who molest or kidnap children. We also remember that stealing children was throughout the eighteenth century a common crime, one that was a source of permanent anxiety to parents. Rousseau's paranoia leads him to misinterpret the father's understandable caution. The second story tells how, out walking one Sunday afternoon with Thérèse, Jean-Jacques buys treats for a group of orphan girls. In the third, he purchases apples for a few boys. "Then I enjoyed one of the sweetest spectacles that can flatter a man's heart, that of seeing joy united with youthful innocence spread out around me" (1093). Rousseau sounds a note of real social criticism, since his joyful act stands in stark contrast to the brutal and degrading tricks that a few aristocrats, guests at the same chateau as Jean-Jacques, were playing on the same peasants.

The last section of the essay continues to examine the pleasure Rousseau experiences either seeing or doing good. Jean-Jacques especially likes to see the faces of people when they are happy. He contrasts the sad demeanor of Parisians with the cheerful and smiling Swiss, Switzerland remaining his ideal in so many arguments. He wishes he could be invisible or unrecognizable so that he could have the pleasure of seeing others smile. This pleasure has been denied him by unseen enemies who denounce him. Soldiers near the Ecole Militaire (Military School) who used to salute him now display "a repugnant air, a sullen look" (1095). With a final anecdote about an old soldier whose ferry passage across the Seine he pays, and which leads to a rebuke of those whose generosity has been corrupted by money, Rousseau ends the discussion of the children he abandoned.

The tenth promenade goes further back in time than any other. Jean-Jacques returns, day for day, to his first meeting with the woman he loved throughout his life: "Today, Palm Sunday, precisely 50 years ago, my first meeting with Mme. de Warens" (1098). Although she was much older than he and not always faithful to him, he evokes their love as an idyllic, magical moment, a brief, tranquil pause in a life destined to be troubled: "I convinced mama to live in the country. A house isolated on the side of a valley was our refuge, and it is there that in the space of four or five years I enjoyed a century of life and of happiness so pure and full that it covers with its charm all that my destiny held of horror" (1099).

Only a fragment, this essay was never finished. It is moving to think that Jean-Jacques died while attempting to recapture and relive his past by writing about it. "Not a day passes that I do not recall with joy and feeling that short and unique time in my life when I was fully myself without dilution or obstacle, when I can truly say that I have lived" (1098–99). This theme of reliving life through writing was repeated several times in the previous promenades. Here it acquires real pathos because it is no idle image. Without exaggeration I suggest that Rousseau died as he was writing about living, as he was reliving his life by writing about it. Precisely because this last promenade terminates abruptly, almost in mid-phrase, it offers a poignant reminder both of human mortality and of the immortality that a great writer like Rousseau can attain.

Chapter Nine
Conclusions

According to the dictionary, the verb *conclude* is defined as "to decide, determine, or resolve."[1] It would be foolhardy to suppose that at the end of this short study I could seriously *resolve* the many questions that I hope to have raised in it.

Nevertheless, I think I have clearly delineated some pertinent themes and issues: the power of imagination; the antithesis between countryside and city, modern decadence and healthy antiquity; the opposition between emotion and cognition, primitive speech and modern jargon, vowels and consonants; dreams about the past vs. harsh experiences in the present; the critique of modern mores and lifestyle; the celebration of every individual as unique; the absolute need for freedom and the consequent hatred of any constraint or limitation; a yearning for transparency, which means that the act of representation is always adequate to whatever is represented; childhood as a privileged period of magical moments; a natural world that remains in sympathy with its human observer.

Rousseau's literary production is so diffuse that it cannot be reduced to any simple labels. In addition to the letters, essays, novel(s), and treatises I have analyzed—most of which do not fit easily into traditional literary molds—there are poems, plays, essays, articles, an opera (libretto and music), and an immense private correspondence that I have not discussed at all.

A conclusion being necessary, however, I focus on the modernity of Jean-Jacques. Even after 200 years Rousseau's writings are still controversial, still able to rouse passions. Rousseau continues to speak to the issues behind today's headlines in a voice that is amazingly current and contemporary. Whether or not the term is in vogue today, Rousseau's concerns are primarily *moral* ones. He is worried about group pressures that squelch individuality, societal norms that deform individual differences, political lobbies that thwart the commonweal. Uncannily he discovers the struggles between appearance and essence, between self-love that is egotistical and self-serving and love of self that is honest and generous. He addresses the thorny problem of how an individual should be educated to live in a hostile society. In very personal terms he investigates love: whether obeying a general moral code or true to the individual's heart, whether platonic friendship or physical passion, love is fraught with paradox, the most prominent, perhaps, being that frustration and irritation are its most potent inspiration. He sees connections that others do not perceive: the role of language in politics, the connections between speech and society, music and mores, clothes and conduct. He articulates the responsibilities that every citizen must shoulder if government is to be just. He adumbrates a politics of ecological stewardship. He criticizes institutions, even benevolent ones, in order to empower the individual.

Is he a liberal or a conservative? It seems impossible to make even as fundamental a distinction as this with any certainty. An authentic democrat who always questioned authority, he has been indicted as totalitarian and authoritarian. As modern and up to date as his ideas are, he advances them in the name of a program that harks back to the past, to the "basics," to a long-gone, nostalgic world that was, he is convinced, better than the present one.

Rousseau is so various, multifaceted, and polyvalent that he easily escapes all my efforts to reduce him to a few pages. Jean-Jacques is not a writer that we read and then check off our list of things to do. His is not a calming presence. On the contrary, he confronts us and involves us in discussions that give no quarter. We ignore him at our peril, simply because he almost always has something interesting to say on those critical issues that most interest us. The vigorous dialogue in which Jean-Jacques engages with his readers is evidenced in the bibliography that follows. Critics have, if anything, increased their interpretative interaction with Jean-Jacques over the past two decades. I can find no better way to conclude than to invite my readers to revisit Rousseau through these secondary readings.

Notes and References

Chapter One

Since Rousseau's *Confessions* are autobiographical, this biographical sketch should be read in conjunction with my chapter on that work. I have tried to arrange my discussions so that each chapter complements and does not repeat the other.

1. Maurice Cranston, *Jean-Jacques: The Early Life and Work of Jean-Jacques Rousseau, 1712–1754* (New York: Penguin Books, 1983), 40.

2. Critics are not sure what his illness was; probably it involved the embarrassment of incontinence. See Cranston, who believes the illness was a "malformation of the penis which impeded his sex life and made him subject to chronic urinary pain, inflammation and infection" (212).

3. Lester Crocker, *Jean-Jacques Rousseau: The Prophetic Voice, 1758–1778* (New York: Macmillan, 1973), 265–92.

4. Ronald Grimsley, *Jean-Jacques Rousseau* (Totowa, N.J.: Barnes and Noble, 1983), 160.

5. For an account of this episode and a positive reading of the *Dialogues,* a text that has been largely neglected, see James F. Jones Jr., *Rousseau's "Dialogues": An Interpretive Essay* (Geneva: Droz, 1991).

Chapter Two

1. *Oeuvres complètes,* vol. 3 (Paris: Gallimard, 1964), 36. All citations from Rousseau will be taken from this Pléiade edition of his works; all translations are my own. Subsequent references to volume 3 will be given parenthetically with page numbers only.

2. On this rhetorical set piece see Jean Starobinski, "La Prosopopée de Fabricius," *Revue des Sciences Humaines* 41 (1976): 83–96.

3. On this point see Walter Rex, "On the Background of Rousseau's First Discourse," *Studies on Eighteenth-Century Culture* 9 (1979): 131–50.

4. Robert Wokler, "Perfectible Apes in Decadent Cultures: Rousseau's Anthropology Revisited," *Daedalus* 107 (1978): 107–34.

5. See G. A. Wells, "Condillac, Rousseau, and Herder on the Origin of Language," *Studies on Voltaire and the Eighteenth Century* 230 (1985): 233–46.

6. The term *democrat* is of course anachronistic in a discussion of eighteenth-century politics. Some critics disagree that Rousseau was a democrat,

pointing to his distrust of the people and his paternalistic politics. On the other hand, no one champions the common man as aggressively as Rousseau did.

7. Jacques Derrida, *De la grammatologie* (Paris: Editions de Minuit, 1967). Collection "Critique."

8. *Oeuvres complètes,* volume 5, 375. Subsequent references to this *Essay* will be given parenthetically with page numbers only.

9. For a good discussion of the disagreement between Rousseau and Rameau, see Michael O'Dea, *Jean-Jacques Rousseau: Music, Illusion, and Desire* (New York: St. Martin's Press, 1995).

Chapter Three

1. *Oeuvres complètes,* volume 5, 293–94. Other citations in this chapter that contain only page numbers will refer to this fifth volume. A roman numeral preceding the page number will indicate another volume in the Pléiade edition.

2. For a good discussion of this see Patrick Coleman, *Rousseau's Political Imagination: Rule and Representation in the "Lettre à d'Alembert"* (Geneva: Droz, 1984), 155–86.

Chapter Four

1. *Julie* is found in volume 2 of the *Oeuvres complètes,* and all my references will be to that volume. For ease of reference with other editions, I will give the book number in roman numerals, the letter in arabic, and then page numbers preceded by "p."

2. There is a good deal of work on this topic, from Daniel Mornet, *La Nouvelle Héloise,* 4 vols. (Paris: Hachette, 1925), to Robert Darnton, "Readers Respond to Rousseau: The Fabrication of Romantic Sensitivity," in Darnton, *The Great Cat Massacre* (New York: Basic Books, 1984), 215–56.

3. Georges May, *Rousseau* (Paris: Seuil, 1961), 139.

4. "Emile," in *Oeuvres complètes,* 4:3, 453.

5. Jean Starobinski, *L'Oeil vivant* (Paris: Gallimard, 1961).

6. A similar shadow of latent totalitarianism hangs over the *Social Contract,* a text that Rousseau was writing at the same time as *Julie.* Many critics have noticed the resemblance between Wolmar and the Legislator.

7. See, for example, Nancy Miller, *The Heroine's Text* (New York: Columbia University Press, 1980), 96–115. Miller sees *Julie* as a "dysphoric" text. Julie herself is a failure as both a daughter and a wife.

8. Albert Camus, *Le mythe de Sisyphe* (Paris: Gallimard, 1943): "We have to imagine that Sisyphus is happy."

Chapter Five

1. For the general parameters of the debate around *The Social Contract,* see, among many others, Robert Wokler, ed., *Rousseau and Liberty* (Manchester,

England: Manchester University Press, 1995); John Noone, *Rousseau's "Social Contract": A Conceptual Analysis* (Athens: University of Georgia Press, 1980); and Judith Shklar, *Men and Citizens* (Cambridge, England: Cambridge University Press, 1969).

2. *Oeuvres complètes,* volume 3. Again, all translations are my own. To make consulting other editions easier, my parenthetical references give the book number in roman numerals, the chapter in arabic (when appropriate), and then the page number preceded by "p."

3. See, for example, Zev Trachtenberg, *Making Citizens: Rousseau's Political Theory of Culture* (New York: Routledge, 1993).

4. See Richard Fralin, *Rousseau and Representation* (New York: Columbia University Press, 1978), on the question of representation in the *Social Contract*.

5. For a discussion of Rousseau's modern reinterpretation of democracy and an affirmation of his status as a radical democrat, see James Miller, *Rousseau: Dreamer of Democracy* (New Haven, Conn.: Yale University Press, 1984).

6. Given the kind of difficulties we experience today in determining what is the common good, I think Jean-Jacques is more than a bit naive when he claims that the general will is obvious or easily recognized. Perhaps this is due to his lack of practical experience with participatory government. On the other hand, it might prove how right he was in warning us (book 3, discussed earlier) how private and selfish interests can thwart the general will.

Chapter Six

1. Peter Jimack, *Rousseau: Emile* (London: Grant and Cutler, 1983), 10.

2. "Emile," in *Oeuvres complètes,* (Paris: Pléiade, 1969), 4:245. All parenthetical citations will refer to this volume and provide page numbers only.

3. As was typical of his time, Rousseau proposes the education of a *male* child. Since all his references to his imaginary student are masculine, I will respect that usage in my translations. Today, some might find this male bias shocking. In Rousseau's defense, let us notice that he does devote his last book to Sophie, the female counterpart of Emile.

4. See Jean Bloch, *Rousseauism and Education in eighteenth-century France,* in *Studies on Voltaire and the Eighteenth Century,* vol. 325 (1995), for an appraisal of the pedagogical context of *Emile*.

5. See Joan DeJean, *Literary Fortifications: Rousseau, Laclos, Sade* (Princeton, N.J.: Princeton University Press, 1984), 155–61, for an example of such a deconstructive analysis.

6. Peter Jimack, for example, refuses even to discuss book 5 in his study of *Emile*.

7. For the background and the main issues on this distinction between "document" and "fiction," see Jeanine Eon, *"Emile* ou le Roman de la Nature Humaine,"* in *Jean-Jacques Rousseau et la Crise Contemporaine de la Conscience* (Paris:

Beauchesne, 1980), 115-40, and Judith Still, "From the Philosophy of Man to the Fiction of Women: Rousseau's *Emile,*" *Romance Studies* 18 (Summer 1991): 75–87.

8. My own practice in this chapter is similarly ambiguous, since I use the terms "Jean-Jacques" and "tutor" interchangeably even though I thereby blur the distinction between the author who creates and the fictional character who is created.

9. Several contemporary accounts by friends of Rousseau record this eventually happy outcome. See the *Oeuvres complètes,* 4:clxi–clxvii for these texts.

Chapter Seven

1. Jean-Jacques wrote a much more detailed account of this major event in the third *Letter to Malesherbes.* Indeed, this is the excuse Rousseau offers. But it also serves to show that he was consciously selecting which events to retell and how much weight to give each one.

2. *Les Confessions,* in *Oeuvres complètes* (Paris: Pléiade, 1959), 1:392. All my references to this edition will be parenthetical. Arabic numbers indicate the page; when necessary, a roman numeral will indicate the book in the *Confessions* and not the Pléiade volume.

3. This classic distinction between *discourse* and *story* is now a commonplace of literary criticism. See, for example, Seymour Chatman, *Story and Discourse: Narrative Structure in Fiction and Film* (Ithaca, N.Y.: Cornell University Press, 1978); Emile Benveniste, *Problèmes de linguistique générale* (Paris: Gallimard, 1966); and Gérard Genette, *Figures,* 3 vols. (Paris: Seuil, 1966–1972).

4. For a fine analysis of this passage, see Jack Undank, "A Fly on His Hand: Interpreting Rousseau's 'Useless' Sensations," *French Review* 62.2 (December 1988): 259–74.

5. Famously but perhaps not accurately or correctly. See the pertinent critique in Aram Vartanian, "Derrida, Rousseau, and the Difference," *Studies in Eighteenth-Century Culture* 19 (1989): 129–51.

6. In the ninth promenade of the *Reveries,* Rousseau returns to the subject of his abandoned children and offers again an insufficient explanation of his motives.

Chapter Eight

1. See Eugene Stelzig, "Rousseau's Reveries: Autobiography as Revision," *Auto/Biography Studies* 4.2 (Winter 1988): 97–106.

2. *Les Rêveries,* in *Oeuvres complètes* (Paris: Pléiade, 1959), 1:1000. All translations are my own; page references will be indicated parenthetically.

3. For a discussion of Rousseau's paranoia about his texts in 1776, just before writing the *Reveries,* and the impact it had on his autobiographical writing, see James F. Jones, *Rousseau's "Dialogues": An Interpretative Essay* (Geneva: Droz, 1991).

4. Rousseau's interest in botany is not a much-studied topic. See, however, Pierre Saint-Amand, "Rousseau contre la science," *Studies on Voltaire and the Eighteenth-Century* 219 (1983): 159–67, as well as Lisa Gasbarrone, "From the Part to the Whole: Nature and Machine in Rousseau's *Rêveries,*" *Studies on Voltaire and the Eighteenth Century* 267 (1989): 217–29. See also Thomas Kavanagh, *Writing the Truth* (Berkeley: University of California Press, 1987), chapter 7, "Anthologies of Desire."

Chapter Nine

1. Jess Stein, ed., *The Random House Dictionary of the English Language,* unabridged edition (New York: Random House, 1967) 305.

Selected Bibliography

Since the amount of critical work on Rousseau is enormous, the following is a very selective bibliography that covers only the past 20 to 25 years. My comments are intended to help readers identify the items closest to their own interests.

PRIMARY SOURCE

Oeuvres complètes. Ed. Bernard Gagnebin and Marcel Raymond. 5 vols. Paris: Gallimard, 1959–1969; 1995. Editions de la Pléiade. This standard edition in French, with an important critical apparatus, has recently been completed with the publication of the long-awaited fifth and last volume.

SECONDARY SOURCES

Books

Arico, Santo L. *Rousseau's Art of Persuasion in "La Nouvelle Héloise."* Lanham, Md.: University Press of America, 1994. Extensive use of traditional rhetorical devices (*inventio, disposito,* and *elocutio*) shows that the various letter writers are not spontaneous or artless. Rousseau's art is to appear free of rhetoric and yet to use it effectively.

Baud-Bovy, Samuel. *Jean-Jacques Rousseau et la musique.* Neuchâtel: La Baconnière, 1988. This somewhat repetitive series of essays, some previously unpublished, focuses on the conflict between Rousseau and Rameau. Although Baud-Bovy overrates Rousseau as a musician, his discussion of musical details and examples is excellent.

Behbahani, Nouchine. "Paysages rêvés, paysages vécus dans *La Nouvelle Héloise." Studies on Voltaire and the Eighteenth Century* 271 (1989): 7–180. The first part compares the real sites with those Rousseau imagined. The second establishes a repertory of elements (mountains, water, Julie's garden) that constitute his emotional landscape.

Coleman, Patrick. *Rousseau's Political Imagination: Rule and Representation in the "Lettre à d'Alembert."* Geneva: Droz, 1984. Attentive to small details, this close reading expands the *Letter's* topic from theater to wider questions about authentic culture and legitimate political order.

Cranston, Maurice. *Jean-Jacques Rousseau: The Early Life and Work of Jean-Jacques Rousseau, 1712–1754.* New York: Norton, 1983. A self-described Lock-

ean biography, based on evidence and manuscript sources, this excellent
retelling of Rousseau's life is filled with minute details.

————. *The Noble Savage*. Chicago: University of Chicago Press, 1991. The second volume of Cranston's three, this is as good as the first.

————. *The Solitary Self: Jean-Jacques Rousseau in Exile and Adversity*. Chicago:
University of Chicago Press, 1997. Published posthumously (the author
died in 1993), this third volume completes Cranston's excellent biography.

Crocker, Lester. *Jean-Jacques Rousseau*. 2 vols. New York: 1968, 1973. Another
excellent biography of Jean-Jacques and critical discussion of his writings, with a marked psychological emphasis on Rousseau's paranoia and
neuroses.

DeJean, Joan. *Literary Fortifications: Rousseau, Laclos, Sade*. Princeton, N.J.:
Princeton University Press, 1984. Transfers Vauban's military architecture into the rhetorical swerves, zigzags, and other defensive maneuvers
these writers use to protect their meaning. Argues that Rousseau's defensive *clinamen* in *Emile* subverts and deconstructs his pedagogy.

De Man, Paul. *Allegories of Reading: Figural Language in Rousseau, Nietzche, Rilke,
and Proust*. New Haven, Conn.: Yale University Press, 1979. A deconstructive reading: language and its production are preferred to referen-
tiality and historical meaning. In the *Second Discourse* "the political destiny of man is structured like and derived from a linguistic model" (156).
In the *Confessions,* there is "an absolute randomness of language prior to
any . . . meaning" (299).

Ferrara, Alessandro. *Modernity and Authenticity: A Study of the Social and Ethical
Thought of Jean-Jacques Rousseau*. Albany: State University of New York
Press, 1993. This philosophical and sociological discussion of ethics and
authenticity examines our contemporary culture through Rousseau's
social theory, especially his critique of Western modernity as represented
by neoconservatives writing today.

Fralin, Richard. *Rousseau and Representation: A Study of the Development of His Concept of Political Institutions*. New York: Columbia University Press, 1978.
Focusing on the *Social Contract,* Fralin examines the evolution and the
ambiguities in Rousseau's thinking about confining political authority to
representatives and about the extent of citizens' participation in their
government.

France, Peter. *Rousseau: Confessions*. Cambridge, England: Cambridge University
Press, 1987. Landmarks of World Literature. A satisfying discussion,
given the series format, of the *Confessions* as a novel and how Rousseau
incorporates novelistic techniques into his nonfiction autobiography.

Gouhier, Henri. *Rousseau et Voltaire: Portraits dans deux miroirs*. Paris: J. Vrin,
1983. This is, in the author's own words, a "strictly historical analysis of
the facts" and not a comparative biography. Gouhier examines specific

texts and events to see how Rousseau and Voltaire read and understood each other rather than how we read them both today.

Grimsley, Ronald. *Jean-Jacques Rousseau*. Totowa, N.J.: Barnes and Noble Books, 1983. Discusses the philosophical and political contexts of Rousseau's works and connects all the works through his biography.

Hamilton, James. *Rousseau's Theory of Literature: The Poetics of Art and Nature*. York, S.C.: French Literature Publishing Company, 1979. Examining the interactions of art and nature, terms whose precise connotations fluctuate, Hamilton sees literary theory as a unifying consciousness that holds the key to Rousseau's concept of society, politics, and morality.

Harvey, Simon, et al. *Reappraisals of Rousseau: Studies in Honour of R. A. Leigh*. New York: Barnes and Noble, 1980. Sixteen essays cover a wide range of topics, including music, Fénelon, Moses, Rousseau's ideas on literary criticism, and the lessons of some previously unpublished drafts.

Horowitz, Asher. *Rousseau, Nature, and History*. Toronto: University of Toronto Press, 1987. This "Marcusean reading" brings psychological and philosophical concepts to bear on "underdeveloped" dimensions of Rousseau's social and political thought, principally "how Rousseau's historical anthropology generates his critique of human civilization" in *Julie, Emile,* and the *Social Contract*.

Howells, R.J. *Rousseau: La Nouvelle Héloise*. London: Grant and Cutler, Ltd., 1986. Critical Guides to French Texts, no. 62. A brief, pertinent analysis that focuses on the ideology and philosophy of the novel, especially as they touch on such issues as love, happiness, time, and memory.

Howlett, Marc-Vincent. *L'Homme qui croyait en l'homme: Jean-Jacques Rousseau*. Paris: Gallimard, 1989. Découvertes, no. 66. A compact and sprightly written biographical sketch along with an excellent selection of contemporary pictures and engravings to illustrate Rousseau's life and times.

Hulliung, Mark. *The Autocritique of Enlightenment: Rousseau and the Philosophes*. Cambridge, Mass.: Harvard University Press, 1994. This sympathetic treatment of Rousseau argues that by moving a number of the philosophes' most cherished ideas to their logical conclusion, Jean-Jacques undermined them and the Enlightenment itself; thus the sense of autocritique.

Jean-Jacques Rousseau et la crise contemporaine de la conscience. Paris: Beauchesne, 1980. Colloque International du deuxième centenaire de la mort de J-J Rousseau, Chantilly, 1978. Twelve articles by French and Swiss critics, including these topics: the Genevan brand of Calvinism during Rousseau's childhood (Leuba); the theological arguments against *Emile* (Armogathe); the contradiction of authoritarianism and spontaneity in pedagogy and politics (Rousset); and the psychology of Rousseau's feelings of guilt and innocence (Clément).

Jimack, Peter. *Rousseau: Emile*. London: Grant and Cutler, 1983. Critical Guides to French Texts, no. 28. This concise summary discusses both the educational treatise and the philosophical tract, emphasizing the intricacies, ambiguities, and inconsistencies of Rousseau's thought.

Jones, James F. *Rousseau's Dialogues: An Interpretive Essay*. Geneva: Droz, 1991. A successful effort to rehabilitate a text long neglected and often considered demented. Jones examines how the *Dialogues* enacts modern theories of autobiography.

Kamuf, Peggy. *Fictions of Feminine Desire*. Lincoln: University of Nebraska Press, 1979. Part of a longer analysis on the Heloise-Abelard relationship, the chapter on *Julie* uses wordplay, psychoanalysis, and poststructuralism to discuss the violent paternal authority that drives Julie underground.

Kavanagh, Thomas. *Writing the Truth: Authority and Desire in Rousseau*. Berkeley: University of California Press, 1987. Inspired by Lacan (relationship of father and son) and Girard (the scapegoat and victimization) and dealing with minor works or minor details, Kavanagh investigates the major problems of truth and lies, speech and writing, intermediary and transparency as keys to all of Rousseau's work.

Launay, Michel. *Rousseau*. Paris: Presses Universitaires de France, 1968. SUP philosophes. This short but dense essay emphasizes Rousseau the philosopher and the period of 1745 to 1755 as decisive. Supplemented by a brief selection of political and philosophical excerpts.

———. *Jean-Jacques Rousseau: Ecrivain politique*. Grenoble: ACER, 1971. A complete and dense exposition of Rousseau's political ideas, set on a solid biographical base and accompanied by long citations. Emphasizes Geneva's political troubles and the importance accorded to the ideologically fluid period of 1728 to 1748.

Leigh, R.A., ed. *Rousseau after Two Hundred Years: Proceedings of the Cambridge Bicentennial Colloquium*. Cambridge, England: Cambridge University Press, 1982. Includes 14 essays by international scholars divided into two parts. The first, "Politics and Sociology," covers Rousseau's links with Kant, Hume, and Marx as well as his notions on language and equality. The second part covers a wide field including music and persuasive rhetorical devices. Certain individual essays are discussed in the "Articles" section.

Marejko, Jan. *Jean-Jacques Rousseau et la dérive totalitaire*. Lausanne: L'Age d'Homme, 1984. Collection Cheminements. Inspired by memories of May 1968, this psychological, philosophical, and theological meditation explores the connections between Rousseau and our contemporary experience of the gulag.

Mason, John Hope. *The Indispensable Rousseau*. New York: Quartet Books, 1979. A good selection of texts in English from most of Rousseau's works along with a biographical sketch and a short introduction to each selection.

May, Georges. *Rousseau par lui-même*. Paris: Seuil, 1969. Rpt. 1961. Ecrivains de toujours. Reedited and updated in 1994. This synthetic reading of the major texts of 1762 offers a coherent picture of Rousseau's character as well as his repeated artistic maneuvers.

Miller, James. *Rousseau: Dreamer of Democracy*. New Haven, Conn.: Yale Univer-
    sity Press, 1984. This analysis of Rousseau's writings on democracy and
    the ideal government argues that he created a new and modern concept
    of democracy and thus is rightfully considered a democrat.
Miller, Nancy. *The Heroine's Text*. New York: Columbia University Press, 1980.
    A chapter on *Julie* analyzes her ordeal as a daughter torn between her
    father and her lover, and later as a wife caught between her husband and
    her lover.
Noone, John B. *Rousseau's "Social Contract": A Conceptual Analysis*. Athens: Uni-
    versity of Georgia Press, 1980. With concrete language and practical
    examples, Noone fills in the gaps in Rousseau's social theory and offers a
    convincing rehabilitation of it. A sympathetic reading that considers
    Jean-Jacques seriously and pragmatically.
O'Dea, Michael. *Jean-Jacques Rousseau: Music, Illusion, and Desire*. London:
    Macmillan and St. Martin's Press, 1995. The opening analysis of
    Rousseau's writings on music leads to a larger consideration of the entire
    oeuvre. Interesting historical and biographical details (relations with
    Rameau), good comments on the role of accent and the affective power
    of the human voice in music.
O'Neil, John. *Seeing and Observing: Rousseau's Rhetoric of Perception*. Saratoga,
    Calif.: Anma Libri, 1985. Stanford French and Italian Studies, no. 41.
    Each of these two modes of perception has its positive and negative
    aspects. Stated baldly, seeing would be transparency, virtuous love, emo-
    tion, imagination, the self, and the inner world, whereas observing covers
    obstacle, sensuous love, reason, deception, others, and the outside.
Simon, Julia. *Mass Enlightenment: Critical Studies in Rousseau and Diderot*. Albany:
    State University of New York Press, 1995. Reads Rousseau through the
    concerns of the Frankfurt School about modern mass culture: reason as
    domination, public vs. private spheres, cultural production and commod-
    ification, the emergence of a capitalistic marketplace. Her discussion
    about Rousseau's prototolitarianism is deconstructionist in inspiration:
    "Individualism as a goal on a national scale easily translates into socially
    engineered conformism in the service of national security" (67).
Starobinski, Jean, Jean-Louis Lecercle, Henri Coulet, and Marc Eigeldinger.
    Jean-Jacques Rousseau: Quatre Etudes. Neuchâtel, Switzerland: Baconnière,
    1978. Starobinski discloses the psychological mechanism behind
    Rousseau's critique of society. Examining Sophie, Julie, and Maman,
    Lecercle suggests that they are different versions of woman's nature.
    Coulet investigates the nature of the pact between tutor and student,
    between the tutor and himself. Eigeldinger discusses Rousseau the prose
    poet and the *Rêveries* as an intimate journal.
Trachtenberg, Zev. *Making Citizens: Rousseau's Political Theory of Culture*. New
    York: Routledge, 1993. Argued as formal philosophy (i.e., mathematical
    formulations of "wants") and focusing on the *Social Contract,* this work

argues that "the cultural institutions [Rousseau] believes are needed to sustain society as it could be invalidate his explanations of how individuals can be free while they are obligated by the law—and thereby render that society illegitimate" (245).

Trousson, Raymond, and Frederic Eigeldinger, eds. *Dictionnaire de Jean-Jacques Rousseau*. Paris: H. Champion, 1996. A huge volume that contains dictionary style entries or short essays about people, events, places, literary and other artistic works having some connection with Rousseau.

Vance, Christie McDonald [Christie Vance McDonald]. "The Extravagant Shepherd: A Study of the Pastoral Vision in *La Nouvelle Héloïse*." In *Studies on Voltaire and the Eighteenth Century* 105 (1973). Rousseau uses the pastoral tradition even as he transforms it. The ideal of Clarens, an echo of the golden age and the natural state, contrasts with Paris and the corruption of modern cities. Against this background Rousseau sets his drama of love and passion, of natural man and the citizen, of religion and morality.

Williams, David. *Rousseau: Les Rêveries du Promeneur Solitaire*. London: Grant and Cutler, 1984. Critical Guides to French Texts, no. 35. Short and concise, this study guide focuses on the meanings of *rêverie*, the overall unifying structure of the book (e.g., interconnected themes of the self-portrait in the third, fourth, and sixth promenades), and nature. A good mix of close reading and larger speculations.

Wokler, Robert. *Rousseau*. New York: Oxford University Press, 1995. Past Masters. Wokler concentrates on Jean-Jacques as a "moral and political thinker," interweaving major and minor texts, explaining each in the light of the others.

Wokler, Robert, ed. *Rousseau and Liberty*. Manchester, England: Manchester University Press, 1995. A collection of essays by different hands that focuses on political questions and, of course, the *Social Contract*. The issue of freedom is examined from multiple perspectives.

Articles

Ages, Arnold. "Rousseau, Religion and the Odium Theologicum: The Testimony of the Correspondence." *Neohelicon* 20.2 (1993): 237–56. As seen in his letters, Rousseau's religious thought has three main aspects. Jean-Jacques distances himself from the philosophes, thinks dogma obscures true religion, and is indignant at his persecution by both Protestants and Catholics.

Arico, Santo. "The Arrangement of St.-Preux's First Letter to Julie in *La Nouvelle Héloise*." *Studies on Voltaire and the Eighteenth Century* 249 (1987): 295–301. Against Daniel Mornet, Arco argues that Jean-Jacques does in fact use a "traditional model of argumentative discourse" in this opening letter.

————. "The Arrangement of St.-Preux's First Letter in *La Nouvelle Héloïse.*" *Studies on Voltaire and the Eighteenth Century* 264 (1989): 1091–92. Shorter resumé of the previously cited article.

Attridge, Anna. "The Reception of *La Nouvelle Héloïse.*" *Studies on Voltaire and the Eighteenth Century* 120 (1974): 227–67. Examines the reactions, which ranged from harsh to rapturous, among the professional writers (such philosophes as Grimm and Voltaire, others like Fréron) and the general public.

Baker, Felicity. "La Route Contraire." In Simon Harvey et al., eds. *Reappraisals of Rousseau.* Totowa, N.J.: Barnes and Noble, 1980, 132–62. A subtle semantic analysis of words and phrases that articulate the fundamental paradox about forcing citizens to be free.

————. "Rousseau's Oath and Revolutionary Fraternity: 1789 and Today," *Romance Quarterly* 38 (August 1991): 273–87. Intending "to explore the emblematic force, for the political sensibility of today as for the fraternal impulse of 1789, of Rousseau's images of the individual's part in social and political change," this essay is a thoughtful antidote to those who see in Rousseau only incipient totalitarianism.

Birkett, Mary Ellen. "Gardening and Poetry: The Language of Love in *La Nouvelle Héloise* IV, 11." *Romance Notes* 26.2 (Winter 1985): 115–19. Julie expresses her unspoken emotions and her "uneasy alliance between nature and culture" through her Elysée, which is seen as a sort of poetic language.

Birn, Raymond. "Rousseau et ses editeurs." *Revue d'histoire moderne et contemporaine* 40 (January–February 1993): 120–36. A detailed discussion of the maneuvers and the finances behind the publication of *La Nouvelle Héloise* and the complete works.

Blanc, André. "Le Jardin de Julie." *Dix-Huitième Siècle* 14 (1982): 357–76. This Freudian reading of Clarens argues that Saint-Preux has eroticized the Elysée and transformed it into the forbidden body of Julie.

Bonhôte, Nicolas. "Tradition et modernité de l'autobiographie: *Les Confessions* de J-J Rousseau." *Romantisme* 17.56 (1987): 13–20. A sociological analysis of how Jean-Jacques used and transformed two literary traditions: the political memoir of aristocrats settling scores with the monarchy, and Protestant autobiography emphasizing grace, conversion, and the authorial "I."

Brady, Patrick. "Structural Affiliations of *La Nouvelle Héloïse.*" *L'Esprit Créateur* 9 (Fall 1969): 207–20. Relating dialogue structures, digressions, and themes to various period styles, Brady finds that digressiveness is more rococo, the rest of the novel closer to classicism and romanticism.

Braun, Theodore E.D. "Diderot, Rousseau, and Democracy; or Jacques and Julie." In John Stephen Martin, ed. *Transactions of the Northwest Society for Eighteenth-Century Studies* 18 (1989–1990; Calgary, 1991): 21–31. This comparison argues that Diderot is a more revolutionary writer, whereas

Rousseau remains committed "to the maintenance of the social and economic status quo" and is distrustful of the common people.

————. "La souveraineté populaire, la volonté génerale, et l'autocratie dans *Jacques le fataliste* et *La Nouvelle Héloise.*" *Diderot Studies* 25 (1993): 27–39. An expanded version of the preceding. Sees in the "false democracy" of Clarens a cynical, hypocritical, and authoritarian regime that belies all the ideals of the *Social Contract*.

Ceppa, Leonardo. "N'instruisez point l'enfant du villegois." *Belfagor* 45 (May 1990): 267–71. A rapid contrast of Saint-Preux's and Wolmar's pedagogical theories and how they explain Rousseau's thinking about his utopian Clarens. In Italian.

Cherpack, Clifton. "Narration and Meaning in Rousseau's *Emile.*" *French Forum* 13.1 (January 1988): 17–30. To answer his own question, "Is *Emile* then a self-subversive linguistic system to the point that consideration of its ideas requires adverting ones eyes from some or all of its narrative problems?" Cherpack links *Emile* with Pirandellian avant-garde fiction, orality, Bakhtin's dialogism, and utopia as a "boundary genre."

Coleman, Patrick. "Property and Personality in Rousseau's *Emile.*" *Romance Quarterly* 38.3 (August 1991): 301–8. Examines the contradictions between the economic considerations inherent in the notion of property and the psychological and cultural issues in possessing.

Conroy, Mark. "De Man on *The Social Contract:* Reading Rousseau's Fine Print." *Criticism* 31 (Winter 1989): 53–73. De Man's concern with ethicopolitical matters in Rousseau, which stems from his own project of subjugating language, is undermined by his own early Nazi writings.

Conroy, Peter. "Le Jardin polémique chez Rousseau." *Cahiers de l'Association Internationale des Etudes Françaises* 34 (May 1982): 91–105. Argues that Rousseau uses concepts and metaphors drawn from landscape design to articulate his critique of society.

————. "Rousseau's Organic State." *South Atlantic Bulletin* 44 (May 1979): 1–13. Examines how the organic metaphor of the human body underlies Rousseau's political discussion of how the state operates.

Coulet, Henri. "Le Corps et l'événement dans les six premiers livres des Confessions." In Roger Lathuillère, ed. *Langue, Littérature du XVII et du XVIII siècle*. Paris: Société d'Edition d'Enseignement Supérieur, 1990, 501–13. Compares Rousseau's theory of virtue with his own life experiences: vice is a means to virtue as Jean-Jacques balances responsibility between others, whom he always blames, and the *moi* he became.

Court, Raymond. "La Liberté et les libertés: Jean-Jacques Rousseau et la Révolution." *Etudes* 373 (July 1990): 27–40. A discussion of the *volonté générale* and of how Rousseau's thinking replicates the opposition between the *Déclaration des Droits de l'homme* and the Terror.

Crocker, Lester. "Droits individuels et corps social: Rousseau et quelques-uns de ses prédécesseurs." In Roger Lathuillère, ed. *Langue Literature du XVII et du XVIII Siècle.* Paris: SEDES, 1990, 487–99. Examines what Rousseau borrowed from Hobbes, Locke, and Burlamaqui on the notions of social body and of rights.

————. "Rousseau's Dilemma: Man or Citizen?" *Studies on Voltaire and the Eighteenth Century* 241 (1986): 271–84. Discusses the antagonism between the concepts of man (the individual) and the citizen (the group or community). Rousseau's favoring the latter would indicate a preference for authoritarian government over individual freedom and liberty.

————. "Rousseau's Two Discourses: The Philosopher as Rhetorician." In Robert Ginsberg, ed. *The Philosopher as Writer: The Eighteenth Century.* London: Associated University Presses, 1987, 15–47. A close reading reveals not only the rhetorical devices Rousseau uses so effectively but also the imprint that the authorial presence imposes on his readers.

Cusset, Catherine, "Cythère et l'Elysée: jardin et plaisir de Watteau à Rousseau." *Dalhousie French Studies* 29 (1994): 65–85. According to this comparison/contrast, Watteau paints an ironic image whose narrative inconsistency delays time while Rousseau's garden is discursive in nature, and therapeutically produces emotional changes in Julie and Saint-Preux.

DeJean, Joan. "*La Nouvelle Héloise,* or the Case for Pedagogical Deviation." *Yale French Studies* 63 (1982): 98–116. Teaching is a form of seduction, both for Saint-Preux and DeJean. Rousseau's tutors resemble Lévi-Strauss's bricoleur. An inevitable but unpredictable swerve mars all pedagogy, deflecting, for example, the plans at Clarens into madness.

Denman, Kamilla. "Recovering *Fraternité* in the Works of Rousseau: Jean-Jacques' Lost Brother." *Eighteenth-Century Studies* 29 (Winter 1995–1996): 191–210. A psychological reading of Rousseau's "projected political *fraternité* or repressed private *homosexualité.*" The object of Rousseau's sexual desires, this lost brother helps explain Julie's beating by her father, Jean-Jacques's antagonism to Grimm, and the identification of Rousseau more as Claire than as St.-Preux.

Ehrard, Jean. "Le Corps de Julie." In Raymond Trousson, ed. *Thèmes et Figures du Siècle de Lumières.* Geneva: Droz, 1980. Although Julie is never described precisely, she does achieve a real corporal presence through her activities, the reactions of others, and her own sexual appetite.

Ellrich, Robert J. "The Cultural Meaning of the Anti-Rousseau Tradition: A Hypothesis." *Romance Quarterly* 38 (August 1991): 309–18. Argues that the vehement opposition against Rousseau, both then and now, stems from his refusal to play the game by the rules. He thus becomes a danger who contests the very bases of society and culture.

Fabry, Anne Srabian de. "L'Architecture secrète de *La Nouvelle Héloise.*" *Australian Journal of French Studies* 19.1 (January–April 1982): 3–10. A résumé of her 1977 thesis and book, this essay points out several structural elements that make St.-Preux and not Julie the central character in the novel: the series of hearts he wins over; a binary rise (St.-Preux's canonization) and fall (Julie's degradation); the change in his status from the estate of Etange to Clarens.

Frayling, Christopher. "The Composition of *La Nouvelle Héloise.*" In Simon Harvey et al., eds. *Reappraisals of Rousseau.* Totowa, N.J.: Barnes and Noble, 1980. This dense discussion shows how the examination of rewrites and changes enriches our understanding of the text.

Fourny, Diane. "L'*Emile* et la question du livre." *Studies on Voltaire and the Eighteenth Century* 278 (1990): 309–19. Examines the mediation operated by the Book: at first forbidden because it replaces real life, the Book emulates Emile's socialization in the form of *Robinson Crusoe.*

Galle, Roland. "Sociopsychological Reflections on Rousseau's Autobiography." *New Literary History* 17 (Spring 1986): 555–71. After showing how some psychoanalytic interpretations are coherent, Galle argues that Rousseau's neuroses might be the enabling condition of his art and the fundamental reason for his success.

Galliani, R. "Rousseau, l'illumination de Vincennes, et la critique moderne." *Studies on Voltaire and the Eighteenth Century* 245 (1986): 403–47. Beginning with a minor inconsistency, the excessive heat in the autumn of 1749, Galliani argues that the illumination was really an invented incident, created in the crisis of 1762, rather than a real biographical event.

Gasbarrone, Lisa. "From the Part to the Whole: Nature and Machine in Rousseau's *Rêveries.*" *Studies on Voltaire and the Eighteenth Century* 267 (1989): 217–29. Argues that the machine and botany share a similar, constructive view of nature that contrasts with the more blurry and poetic vision of reverie.

Gerhardi, G. "Théories d'échange chez Rousseau et les physiocrates." *Studies on Voltaire and the Eighteenth Century* 263 (1989): 121–22. The interdependence, exchanges, and middlemen of physiocratic economics contrast with Rousseau's dream of solitary man, independent of others.

Gildin, Hilail. "The First Crisis of Modernity: Leo Strauss on the Thought of Rousseau." *Interpretation: A Journal of Political Philosophy* 20.2 (Winter 1993): 157–64. Explains why Strauss saw Rousseau as the author whose opposition to progress most fully articulated a major crisis in modern political and moral philosophy about natural rights.

Harari, Josue. "Therapeutic Pedagogy: Rousseau's *Emile.*" *Modern Language Notes* 97 (1982): 787–809. Deconstructs Rousseau's pedagogy by focusing on examples and anecdotes, not on theory. Pegagogy here is ruse, an effort to replace God, a phantom that desires its own impossibility.

Howells, R.J. "Désir et distance dans *La Nouvelle Héloise.*" *Studies on Voltaire and the Eighteenth Century* 230 (1985): 223–32. Repetitions, binary movements, and the notion of *écart* (separation, removal, and cutting off) are examined in this analysis of the dramatic structure of the novel.

———. "Deux histoires, un discours: *La Nouvelle Héloise* et le récit des amours d'Emile et Sophie dans l'*Emile.*" *Studies on Voltaire and the Eighteenth Cen-*

tury 249 (1987): 267–94. Investigates the close resemblances between these texts across five categories: their purpose or status as literature, story lines, narrative point of view, thematic structures, and a number of recurring leitmotifs.

————. "Rousseau and Voltaire: A Literary Comparison of Two *Professions de foi.*" *French Studies* 49 (October 1995): 397–409. A close comparison of two texts (Voltaire's is in the *Histoire de Jenni*) with emphasis more on their fictional frames and narrators than on their ideas. Despite personal animosities, Voltaire might have been influenced by Jean-Jacques.

Jackson, Susan Klem. "Redressing Passion: Sophie d'Houdetot and the Origins of *Julie ou la Nouvelle Héloise.*" *Studies on Eighteenth-Century Culture* 17 (1987): 271–87. Reads the *Confessions* and *Julie* simultaneously for their texts of repressed passion. Rousseau is both androgynous and hypermasculine as metaphors of (un)dressing and sewing uncover his hidden desire and deconstruct his textuality as sexuality.

Johnson, Guillemette. "The Divided Self in the *Nouvelle Héloise.*" *Studies on Voltaire and the Eighteenth Century* 278 (1990): 277–89. The virtuous unity at Clarens operates a series of substitutions and convulsions that provoke constant redefinitions of the self, such as Julie as Mme. de Wolmar.

Kamuf, Peggy. "Inside Julie's Closet." *Romanic Review* 69 (1978): 296–306. A series of substitutions (a portrait for Julie's body, Sophie for Julie) leads to a fetishism (Julie is more erotic fully clothed than undressed) that does not violate the laws and thus (Kamuf's pun) remains in the closet.

————. "Rousseau's Politics of Visibility." *Diacritics* 5 (1975): 51–56. Female modesty exists best when unnoticed. Unless they remain liminal and imperceptible, women in the state resemble actresses in the theater: a danger to male power and discourse.

Kelly, Christopher, and Roger D. Masters. "Rousseau on Reading 'Jean-Jacques': *The Dialogues.*" *Interpretation: A Journal of Political Philosophy* 17.2 (Winter 1989–1990): 238–53. A positive and sympathetic presentation of the *Dialogues,* situating them both in Rousseau's life and in his system of thought. Originally the introduction to the translation in the complete works published by the University Press of New England.

Krumm, Pascale. "Murs et matrice dans les *Confessions* de Rousseau." *Symposium* 44 (Winter 1990–1991): 252–63. Posits that Jean-Jacques sought out walls and circumscribed places like islands as peaceful refuges and that these "prisons" reflect his unconscious desire to return to the prenatal position and its security.

Kumbier, William. "Rousseau's *Lettre sur la musique française.*" *Stanford French Review* 6 (Fall–Winter 1982): 221–37. Following the lead of Derrida and de Man, Kumbier reads Rousseau's musical ideas through literary theory, applying concepts like presence and representation to melody and counterpoint.

Kusch, Manfred. "The Garden, the City, and Language in Rousseau's *La Nouvelle Héloïse*." *French Studies* 40.1 (January 1986): 45–54. Although both garden and city are based on closure, Rousseau differentiates them: the former represents stability and truth, the latter is unstable and mendacious, just like novels and narrative.

Labrosse, Claude. "Les lettres à Jean-Jacques Rousseau et l'invention de la littérature." *Textuel* 27 (February 1994): 13–29. Explores the exchange of letters between Rousseau and his readers, which constitutes "a kind of crypt of literary history" or "a window for observing the complexity of the literary process." The way readers like Marie-Anne Alissan de La Tour echo and relive Rousseau's texts gives us a new appreciation of what constitutes literature.

———. "Lecture et citations de *La Nouvelle Héloïse:* Réflexion sur la mise en pièces du texte." *Revue des Sciences Humaines* 196 (October–December 1984): 25–38. Theorizes how the *Nouvelle Héloïse* became "an archive of reading that is both instrumental and textual": citations are reprocessed and recycled through other sites of reading, such as private correspondences, journals, and books of excerpts.

MacArthur, Elizabeth. "Textual Gardens: Rousseau's Elysée and Girardin's Ermenonville." *Romance Quarterly* 38 (August 1991): 331–40. Examines the "two roles that language can play in influencing visitors' experience of a garden, and, by extension, viewers' interpretations of any visual art form."

Markovits, Francine. "Rousseau et l'éthique de Clarens: une économie des relations humaines." *Stanford French Review* 15.3 (1991): 323–48. Economics, philosophy, theology, and ethics are all part of this analysis of how Clarens affects social institutions, servants, and personal relations. Friendship, not liberty, is the ultimate ethical value at Clarens.

Mason, John Hope. "Reading Rousseau's First Discourse." *Studies on Voltaire and the Eighteenth Century* 249 (1987): 251–66. Reads the *Discourse* not just as philosophy but also as a biographical reaction to the experiences he was then living.

May, Gita. "Rousseau's 'Antifeminism' Reconsidered. In Samia Spenser, ed. *French Women and the Age of Enlightenment*. Bloomington: Indiana University Press, 1984, 309–17. Examines the paradox of modern feminists who condemn Rousseau and early feminists like Mme. de Stael, Mme. Roland, and George Sand who found in Rousseau a champion of their sex.

McDonald, Christie Vance. "Jean-Jacques Rousseau: The Biographfiend's False Friend." *Romanic Review* 66 (1975): 296–311. This review essay criticizes biographers who accept too close a connection between living a life and writing about it and also argues that a special sense of language (e.g., logocentrism and *écriture*) is essential when writing about Rousseau.

———. "The Model of Reading in Rousseau's *Dialogues*." *Modern Language Notes* 93 (1978): 723–32. Argues that Rousseau offers a model of reading that is immediately undermined by its own writing and concern with origins. Different from the dialogue that it nonetheless resembles, reading is a utopia of the word.

Moran, Francis. "Between Primates and Primitives: Natural Man as the Missing Link in Rousseau's Second *Discourse*." *Journal of the History of Ideas* 54.1 (January 1993): 37–58. Eighteenth-century travelers' reports and other discussions of the orangutan and primitive peoples influenced Rousseau's choice of the primitive and not the European as his norm for humanity.

Nilsson, Ann Marie. "Bakhtin on Rousseau." *Revue de Littérature Comparée* 68 (April–June 1994): 133–46. Examines the little Bakhtin did say and the enormous amount he did not say but could or ought to have said about time, love, and the bildungsroman in Rousseau, whose life has many parallels with Bakhtin's.

O'Dea, Michael. "The Dialogics of Desire in *La Nouvelle Héloïse*." *Eighteenth-Century Fiction* 7.1 (October 1994): 37–50. Analyzes the uniformity of tone in the novel and how all conflicts are muted. In fiction Julie's single voice and vision dominate, just as in music Jean-Jacques prefers a single melody to the complexities of harmonization and counterpoint.

————. "The Double Narrative of the Stolen Ribbon in Rousseau's Confessions." *Nottingham French Studies* 23.2 (October 1984): 1–8. Detects in the story of Marion a typical pattern: first Rousseau admits a fault, then he disculpates himself from any responsibility for it. This accuse/excuse reaction stems from his fear that readers will not understand him or his text correctly.

Oudart, Jean. "Comment dire? A propos de l'indicible dans les *Confessions* de J.-J. Rousseau." *Recherches et Travaux* 44 (1993): 135–45. To tell the whole truth he promised, Rousseau has recourse to techniques that allow him to speak the unspeakable, whether scatological or sexual: dirty talk, phony innocence, coded language, and wordless gestures.

Piau-Gillot, Colette. "La Misogynie de Rousseau." *Studies on Voltaire and the Eighteenth Century* 219 (1983): 169–82. A defense of Rousseau's attitudes about women, this essay distinguishes misogyny from our modern notions of antifeminism. Jean-Jacques's thought, similar to contemporary feminist ideas, is "a necessary corollary of his coherent system of thought."

Pezzillo, Lelia. "L'echec du *Contrat social:* A propos d'une critique récente de la théorie de Rousseau." *Dix-huitième Siècle* 26 (1994): 365–78. The impact of John Rawls, modern contractualism theory, and philosophical games like the "prisoner's dilemma" has regenerated our understanding of Rousseau's political theory.

Pomeau, René. "Le Paysage de *La Nouvelle Heloise:* L'Asile, l'espace." In Paul Hallberg, ed. *The Feeling for Nature and the Landscape of Man*. Gothenburg, Germany: Kungl. Vetenskaps-Vitterhets-Samhallet, 1980, 132–42.

Places reveal emotion and content. Men travel, whereas women are sedentary. Small, enclosed places are comforting and bourgeois (garden and chateau), whereas open spaces (mountains and lakes) are exhilarating but dangerous.

Ray, William. "Reading Women: Cultural Authority, Gender, and the Novel: The Case of Rousseau." *Eighteenth-Century Studies* 27.3 (Spring 1994): 321–47. Within the larger context of how the novel *genre* reiterates social anxieties about the female *gender,* Ray reads Rousseau's own cultural inscriptions. Whereas Julie provokes active responses from her readers, a passive Sophie only demonstrates an unawareness of the interpretive enterprise in which she is inscribed.

Reichler, Claude. "Comparaison n'est pas raison: Paul de Man lecteur de Rousseau." *Nouvelle Revue Française* 445 (February 1990): 58–68. An acute discussion of de Man's deconstruction of Rousseau with emphasis on both writers' concepts of language. De Man's misreadings and doctrinal bias constitute another sort of literary history.

Rétat, Pierre. "Le Temps des *Rêveries du promeneur solitaire.*" In Maxine Cutler, ed. *Voltaire, the Enlightenment and the Comic Mode.* New York: Peter Lang, 1990, 241–51. Discusses how Rousseau manipulates time (using verb tenses, temporal adverbs) to articulate both his imaginary happiness and his awareness of the plot against him.

Rex, Walter. "Sexual Metamorphoses on the Stage in Mid-Eighteenth-Century Paris: The Theatrical Background of Rousseau's *Narcisse.*" *Studies on Voltaire and the Eighteenth Century* 278 (1990): 265–76. Discusses three plays that use the theme of sex change before Jean-Jacques. The sexual metamorphosis in *Narcisse* might have a resonance in Rousseau's own change of identities.

———. "On the Background of Rousseau's First Discourse." *Studies in Eighteenth-Century Culture* 9 (1979): 131–50. Relates the ideological conflict of the *First Discourse* (initial praise turns to condemnation) to Rousseau's return to Genevan values after having given them up for Catholicism, Mme. de Warens, music, the opera, and Paris.

Ridehalgh, Anna. "Rousseau as God? The Ermenonville Pilgrimages in the Revolution." *Studies on Voltaire and the Eighteenth-Century* 278 (1990): 287–308. An overview of texts and behaviors (visits, festivals) that made Jean-Jacques a saint in public opinion. This deification appropriated the cult hero for different political ends as the Revolution changed direction.

Robinson, Philip. "Literature Versus Theory: Rousseau's Second Preface in *Julie.*" *French Studies* 44.4 (October 1990): 403–15. Argues that the dialogue preface is a humorous dramatization of the novel-as-imitation esthetic as well as a serious and authentic expression of the author's personal truth.

Rosenberg, Aubrey. "Food for Thought in Rousseau's *Emile.*" *Lumen. Travaux choisis de la Société canadienne d'étude du XVIIIe siécle* 14 (1995): 97–108.

Using a number of famous anecdotes, Rosenberg demonstrates how Jean-Jacques uses food as a motivational device to teach Emile and influence his behavior. Rosenberg also shows how Rousseau's practice differs from Skinner's behavior modification.

———. *"Julie ou La Nouvelle Héloise* Today." *University of Toronto Quarterly* 60 (Winter 1990–1991): 265–73. Asks why *Julie,* after its overwhelming initial success, has become largely forgotten by the reading public. Also discusses two recent novels that use it as a model and foil.

Rotureau, Christian. "Rousseau, fils coupable?" *Revue d'histoire littéraire de la France* 92.5 (September–October 1992): 801–18. Reverses the usual psychoanalytical interpretation of an early passage in the *Confessions.* The passage is more crafted fiction than fact and reveals a virile, powerful Jean-Jacques in contrast to his feminine and castrated father.

Runte, Roseann. "The Paradox of Virtue: Jean-Jacques Rousseau and *La Reine fantasque.*" *Studies in Eighteenth-Century Culture* 23 (1994): 47–54. This very minor parody of a fairy tale would offer an example of profligacy, the Queen Fantasque, to better offset the real models of virtue, Julie or Rousseau himself.

Saint-Amand, Pierre. "Rousseau contre la science." *Studies on Voltaire and the Eighteenth Century* 219 (1983): 159–67. Examines how Jean-Jacques transforms botany from science to emotion and passion. Botany offers a key to Rousseau's thinking about language and to his writing as "eternal objects of our felicity."

Scanlan, Timothy. "*La Nouvelle Héloise:* The Story of a Failure and the Success of a Story." *Modern Languages* 61.2 (1980): 71–80. Discusses why Clarens did not succeed as an imaginary experiment à la Zola or as an experience of transparency and interpersonal communication. The failure is part of Rousseau's masochism, just like Alceste's pleasure in losing.

———. "Secrets, Misunderstandings, Confessions, and the Triumph of Truth in Rousseau's *La Nouvelle Héloïse.*" *Orbis Litterarum* 47 (1992): 95–110. Problems of communication affect even these extraordinary characters who use language to keep secrets from each other despite the ideal of transparency. Paradoxically, fiction seems the most effective way to express truth.

———. "Perspectives on the 'Nuits d'Amour' in Rousseau's *La Nouvelle Héloïse.*" *AUMLA* 80 (November 1993): 93–99. Analyzes the physical lovemaking of Julie and Saint-Preux and how it relates to the rest of the novel.

Sclippa, Norbert. "La Nouvelle Héloise et l'aristocratie." *Studies on Voltaire and the Eighteenth Century* 284 (1991): 1–71. Explores how *Julie* connects to the sentiments and world vision of the aristocracy, which was experiencing an invigorating revival at this time. What began as a challenge to the social order ends in an acclamation of aristocratic tradition and the status quo.

————. "*La Nouvelle Héloise*, la noblesse et la bourgeoisie." *Studies on Voltaire and the Eighteenth Century* 265 (1989): 1617–19. Sclippa asserts that the novel confirmed the bourgeois way of life and ideals in its portrayal of aristocratic figures.

Sosso, Paola. "Rousseau tra San Paolo e la religione naturale." *Studi Francesi* 36.3 (September–December 1992): 525–30. A brief attempt to show points of convergence (i.e., conscience; the created world as proof of God) between Saint Paul and the "Profession of Faith."

Spaas, Lieve. "D'un Clarens à l'autre: Structures du désir sexuel dans *La Nouvelle Héloise*." *Studies on Voltaire and the Eighteenth Century* 284 (1991): 73–82. The family and estate of Etange bear many similarities to those of Wolmar even as they differ, most particularly in their bases of despotism and eroticism.

Stelzig, Eugene. "Rousseau's Reveries: Autobiography as Revision." *Auto/Biography Studies* 4.2 (Winter 1988): 97–106. Examines how Jean-Jacques "scripts" these revisions and redefinitions of his life in an attempt to retake "control of his public image."

Stewart, Philip. "Half-Title or Julie Beheaded." *The Romanic Review* 86 (January 1995): 31–44. A witty examination of the scholarship that has eliminated the name *Julie* from the title of Rousseau's novel and replaced it with *La Nouvelle Héloise*. Without both titles, the comparison and allusion in the latter lose most of their meaning.

Starobinski, Jean. "Les Descriptions de journées dans *La Nouvelle Héloise*." In Simon Harvey et al., eds. *Reappraisals of Rousseau*. Totowa, N.J.: Barnes and Noble, 1980, 46–62. A close reading of various days at Clarens, including ordinary tasks and activities as well as seasonal ones, explains Rousseau's romantic thought and his imaginative use of time.

————. "La Prosopopée de Fabricius." *Revue des Science Humaines* 161 (1976): 83–96. Analyzes the famous prosopopeia as a model of rhetorical and oratorical eloquence.

————. "Jean-Jacques Rousseau: Jours Uniques, Plaisirs Redoublés." In Trousson, ed. *Thèmes et Figures du Siècle de Lumières*. Geneva: Droz, 1980, 285–97. The space of a day is a privileged unit in Rousseau's memory and imagination. This bit of time allows him to place, find, and write his happiness within the larger sweep of time.

Still, Judith. "From the Philosophy of Man to the Fiction of Women: Rousseau's *Emile*." *Romance Studies* 18 (Summer 1991): 75–87. Discusses the shift in *Emile* from treatise to novel and emphasizes the distinctions between masculine and feminine concerns. Ends with a proposal for a new feminist reading of Jean-Jacques as both father and mother.

————. "The Disfigured Savage: Rousseau and de Man." *Nottingham French Studies* 24.1 (May 1985): 1–14. Uses de Man's own "invitation" to a "threefold act of production or, more accurately, re-enactment" in order to read de Man reading Derrida reading Rousseau. Concern with misreading, defacement, and dismemberment, as well as the illusion or nostalgia of presence, creates "the mania of interpretation [that] produces an excess of cognition" and little else.

Storme, Julie. " 'An exit so happy': The Deaths of Julie and Clarissa." *Canadian Review of Comparative Literature* 14.2 (June 1987): 191–210. Argues that Julie's death, like Clarissa's, is not a defeat but a victory for Julie's exceptional virtue in life. Since for Rousseau virtue is a continuous struggle, death is not the loss of happiness but rather the only means of preserving it.

Strong, Tracy. "Theatricality, Public Space, and Music in Rousseau." *Substance* 80 (Fall 1996): 110–27. Music and theater have political implications. Transparency in politics depends on the ears and voices (speech and song based on melody) that enable public festivals to become instances of perfect community.

Thomas, Paul. "Jean-Jacques Rousseau, Sexist?" *Feminist Studies* 17.2 (Summer 1991): 195–217. "The question is not *whether* [Rousseau] should be identified as a sexist. He should. The question is *how* and *why* we should set about so characterizing him." Women are deceptive, linked to appearance and reputation, whereas men are transparent.

Tonson, Stephen J. "The Father of Totalitarian Democracy: Jean-Jacques Rousseau." *Modern Age* 31.3–4 (Summer–Fall 1988): 243–51. This unsympathetic reading of the *Second Discourse* highlights its negative potentials. Restates that "Rousseau was the father of totalitarian democracy" and that he was "mad."

Trousson, Raymond. "Jean-Jacques Rousseau et 'les derniers des hommes.' " *Studi Francesi* 104 (May–August 1991): 249–59. A review of Rousseau's personal experiences as a lackey and servant leads to an analysis of this condition as alienating, resembling slavery, and unworthy of a true man or citizen. Clarens is the exception where servants have dignity.

————. "Le Rôle de Wolmar dans La Nouvelle Héloïse." In Trousson, ed. *Thèmes et Figures du Siècle de Lumières.* Geneva: Droz, 1980, 299–306. Invisible and nameless, placed in the shadows and seemingly cast in a minor role, Wolmar nonetheless has a critical effect on the action in the first half of the novel.

————. "Quinze années d'études rousseauistes." *Dix Huitième Siècle* 9 (1977): 343–86. Raymond Trousson, "Quinze annees d'etudes rousseauistes (II)." *Dix Huitième Siècle* 24 (1992):, 421–89. Two *états présents* or reviews of the critical literature on Rousseau from 1962 to 1992.

Undank, Jack. "A Fly on His Hand: Interpreting Rousseau's 'Useless' Sensations." *French Review* 62.2 (December 1988): 259–74. Moving eloquently through Condillac's sensationism and deconstructionist theory, Undank analyzes Rousseau's "oblique, uncentered style of perception." More than memory or nostalgia, these "useless" details produce a complex representation of a past bliss that the narrator cannot really recapture but that the reader can magically share.

Vampée, Janie. "Rousseau's *Emile ou de l'éducation:* A Resistance to Reading." *Yale French Studies* 77 (1990): 156–76. Sees *Emile* as performative and not cognitive. The reader is called upon to react. The reader's reading, like Emile's education, is not single or literal but multiple and figurative. Both must be constantly reenacted and not just observed.

Vartanian, Aram. "Derrida, Rousseau, and the Difference." *Studies on Eighteenth-Century Culture* 19 (1989): 129–51. Vartanian skillfully deconstructs Derrida's deconstruction of Rousseau's *supplément*, showing how and where the former misread the latter and produced his own philosophy rather than discovering Rousseau's.

Velguth, Madeleine. "Le Texte comme prétexte: Jacques Derrida lit les *Confessions* de Rousseau." *French Review* 58 (May 1985): 811–19. Rejecting the postmodern "deep disregard for the intentions of the author" (811), Velguth exposes how Derrida intentionally misread Rousseau and substituted his own "supplement," his own philosophy of nonpresence, his own pretext for Rousseau's text.

Villarverde, José. "Rousseau, un antiphilosophe au siècle des lumières, ou Rousseau contre le progrès scientifique." *Studies on Voltaire and the Eighteenth Century* 263 (1989): 475–79. A "modern" and a "son of the Enlightenment," Rousseau is nonetheless an antiphilosophe because, as a traditionalist and a conservative, he opposes change and innovation.

Wells, G.A. "Condillac, Rousseau, and Herder on the Origin of Language." *Studies on Voltaire and the Eighteenth Century* 230 (1985): 233–46. Gives the context for Rousseau's speculations on language. Also argues that eighteenth-century "dilettantes" were more perceptive than nineteenth-century professionals.

Wills, Peter. "Jean-Jacques Rousseau, Stowe, and the Jardin Anglais: Speculations on Visual Sources for *La Nouvelle Héloise*." *Studies on Voltaire and the Eighteenth Century* 90 (1972): 1791–98. A review of contemporary writings and engravings that Rousseau might have seen prior to creating his own "dream" landscape.

Wokler, Robert. "Perfectible Apes in Decadent Cultures: Rousseau's Anthropology Revisited." *Daedalus* 107 (1978): 107–34. Places Rousseau's "comprehensive anthropological theory" between Robert Ardrey and Lévi-Strauss, between physical evolution and social development, between the animal and the social. Language would be Rousseau's model for the development of society.

Woodward, Servanne. "Autobiographie et roman autobiographique: Rousseau et Marivaux." *Franzsisch Heute* 20.2 (June 1989): 129–35. According to this short list of differences, the novel is constructed and belongs to the past of writing, whereas autobiography keeps its secret, belongs to the present experience, and maintains the gap between the author and himself as a character.

Index

167

The Author

Peter V. Conroy Jr. is professor of French at the University of Illinois, Chicago, where he has taught since 1970 and served two terms as department chairman. In June 1990 Professor Conroy was awarded the *Prix d'Excellence* by the Chicago/Northern Illinois chapter of the AATF in recognition of his teaching and scholarship. In the spring of 1997 he was among the first to receive a Teaching Recognition Award that had just been instituted by the University of Illinois, Chicago.

In addition to 40 articles on a variety of eighteenth-century topics as well as such individual authors as Zola, Proust, and Camus, Conroy has written *Techniques of the Novel* (1972), a monograph on the novelist Crébillon *fils,* and *Intimate, Intrusive, and Triumphant: Readers in the "Liaisons dangereuses"* (1987), a study of Choderlos de Laclos. He translated François Dosse's *L'Histoire en miettes* for the University of Illinois Press (1994). He has published *Montesquieu Revisited* (1992) in the Twayne World Authors Series.

The Editor

David O'Connell is professor of French at Georgia State University. He received his Ph.D. in 1966 from Princeton University, where he was a National Woodrow Wilson Fellow, the Bergen Fellow in Romance Languages, and a National Woodrow Wilson Dissertation Fellow. He is the author of *The Teachings of Saint Louis: A Critical Text* (1972), *Les Propos de Saint Louis* (1974), *Louis-Ferdinand Céline* (1976), *The Instructions of Saint Louis: A Critical Text* (1979), and *Michel de Saint Pierre: A Catholic Novelist at the Crossroads* (1990). He has edited more than 60 books in the Twayne World Authors Series.

ISBN 0-8057-1616-5

90000